PRAISE FOR *THE UPSIDE*

"Over the many years I have spent in the business world, I have consistently noted that one of the common characteristics of successful companies and entrepreneurs alike is that they are exceptionally skilled in managing risk, both pure financial risk and long-term strategic risks. The publication of *The Upside* is very timely indeed . . . it will make you think differently about strategic risk. It will help you recognize—and act to take advantage of—the growth opportunities concealed behind the major threats your business will face in the next several years."

—DR. CLEMENS BÖRSIG,
Chairman of the Supervisory Board, Deutsche Bank AG,
formerly CFO/Chief Risk Officer, Deutsche Bank AG

ALSO BY ADRIAN SLYWOTZKY

Value Migration

The Profit Zone

Profit Patterns

How Digital Is Your Business?

The Art of Profitability

How to Grow When Markets Don't

THE

Upside

THE 7 STRATEGIES FOR TURNING BIG THREATS INTO GROWTH BREAKTHROUGHS

ADRIAN J. SLYWOTZKY

with

Karl Weber

CROWN
BUSINESS
NEW YORK

Published in the United States by Crown Business,
an imprint of the Crown Publishing Group,
a division of Random House, Inc., New York.
www.crownpublishing.com

Crown Business is a trademark and the Rising Sun colophon
is a registered trademark of Random House, Inc.

Library of Congress Cataloging-in-Publication Data
Slywotzky, Adrian J.
The Upside : the 7 strategies for turning big threats into growth breakthroughs /
Adrian J. Slywotzky.—1st ed.
Includes bibliographical references and index.
1. Strategy   2. Success in business.   3. Risk management.   4. Risk assessment.   I. Title.
HD61.S55 2007
658.15'5—dc22   2006101309

ISBN 978-0-307-35101-2

Printed in the United States of America

Design by Robert C. Olsson

10 9 8 7 6 5 4 3 2 1

First Edition

Dedicated to my parents,
Wolodymyra and Stefan Slywotzky,
who taught me how to think this way

CONTENTS

Contents

7
WHEN YOUR BUSINESS STOPS GROWING
Inventing New Forms of Demand

8
TREASURE ISLAND
Reversing Risks to Grow

REVERSING STRATEGIC RISK
The Upside Half-Day Workshop

THE UPSIDE

Introduction

From Risk to Opportunity

A N IMPORTANT historic site in south-central Pennsylvania provides a vivid look at how risk can be transformed into breakthrough opportunity. It's a hill called Little Round Top, and it happens to be the place where the nation we know as the United States may have come closest to ultimate extinction.

In the last days of June 1863, Confederate armies attained their deepest Northern penetration of the Civil War. They prepared to confront the Union forces near a Pennsylvania town called Gettysburg. If Robert E. Lee's armies could deliver a knockout blow, Northern morale, already shaky, might well collapse. Jefferson Davis, president of the Confederacy, had even prepared a proposal for peace talks to be delivered to Abraham Lincoln in the event of a Southern triumph at Gettysburg.

Late in the afternoon on July 2, 1863—the second day of fighting at Gettysburg—Confederate Lieutenant General James Longstreet began an attack intended to roll up the Union left flank. He moved his forces east in the direction of a sparsely defended hill known as Little Round Top. If the rebel army could overrun Little Round Top, it could sweep past the Union lines and threaten them from behind and above. The South could then cut off the Northern supply lines, gaining the victory Lee sought and perhaps winning the war outright.

Colonel Joshua Lawrence Chamberlain, commanding the 20th Maine, was ordered to hold the extreme left flank for the Army of the Potomac at all costs.

Chamberlain was an unlikely figure on whom to place the Union army's hopes of survival. He was a thirty-three-year-old teacher of religion, rhetoric, and languages at Maine's Bowdoin College whose knowledge of military tactics had come exclusively from his readings in the

1

Greek and Roman classics. Abhorring slavery and deeply committed to the Union cause, Chamberlain had left behind his wife and two small children to join the 20th Maine and had risen to the rank of colonel thanks to his instinctive leadership skills and the paucity of trained officers. Now he and his 385 men waited on the slope of Little Round Top for the Confederate assault.

The attack began around 4:00 p.m. Despite heavy losses, the 20th Maine stood their ground through five charges by the Confederate regiments. The exhausted Northern troops fell back as their numbers were thinned by Southern rifle fire, but after each assault they painfully retook the ground. "How men held on, each one knows—not I," Chamberlain later said.

As the South prepared for one final and decisive charge, Chamberlain looked around him. More than a third of his men were dead. The rest were out of ammunition, having exhausted their allotted sixty rounds. Another Confederate charge simply could not be repulsed. It was the moment of maximum risk for the 20th Maine, the Army of the Potomac, and perhaps the entire Union cause.

Realizing that to rely on defensive tactics one more time would be to accept inevitable defeat, Chamberlain made a bold decision. He ordered the men on his left flank, who had been drawn back, to fix bayonets and prepare to advance. As soon as they were in line with the rest of the regiment, the entire group of some 200 weary survivors charged, swinging forward into the Confederate forces like a gate being slammed shut. At the same time, the 2nd U.S. Sharpshooters, who had been placed by Chamberlain behind a stone wall 150 yards to the east, rose as one and fired a volley into the Southern ranks.

This unexpected two-pronged assault caught the exhausted Southerners off guard. Astonished at the blue tide swarming toward them, they turned and "ran like a herd of wild cattle."

Chamberlain's men took twice their own numbers in Confederate prisoners. The Confederate attempt to outflank the Union army had failed, and with it Lee's best hope to win a decisive battle on Northern soil. After another day of fighting, Lee's army retreated south on the afternoon of July 4. Never again would it be able to mount so massive an attack on the Union.

He saw the opportunity hidden in the moment of greatest danger.
Colonel Joshua Lawrence Chamberlain, whose bold risk-reversal strategy
saved the Union armies at Gettysburg.

Twenty months later, at Appomattox Court House in Virginia, Lee and his men were forced to surrender to the Union army led by Ulysses S. Grant. In recognition of Chamberlain's decisive leadership at Gettysburg, Grant gave a special role of honor at the ceremony to Chamberlain and the 20th Maine. As the defeated Southerners marched down the road to turn in their weapons and colors, Chamberlain, on his own initiative, ordered his men to stand at attention and carry arms as a sign of respect—a magnanimous gesture much admired by the war-weary soldiers on both sides.

Thirty years later, Joshua Chamberlain—by then the president of Bowdoin College and a four-time governor of the state of Maine—was awarded the Congressional Medal of Honor.

STRATEGIC RISK: KILLER OF BUSINESS MODELS

The lesson of Little Round Top is simple but vitally important: Your moment of maximum risk is also your moment of maximum opportunity.

The goal of this book is to show how you can recognize these moments of risk, anticipate them, and prepare yourself to transform them, making real the upside potential hidden within the downside risk.

Moments such as these are becoming more frequent and obvious in business. A perennial reality of business, risk is growing in intensity in the early years of the twenty-first century.

Your moment of maximum risk is also your moment of maximum opportunity.

There's a host of striking statistical evidence for the expansion of risk in recent years. Standard & Poors (S&P) rates more than 4,000 publicly traded companies each year. As Figure 1 shows, in the mid-1980s, over 30 percent of S&P stocks were rated A (high quality, low risk). By the mid-2000s, that figure had fallen to 14 percent. During the same period, C-rated stocks (low quality, high risk) had risen from 12 percent of the total to 30 percent—a tremendous criss-cross in less than two decades. The level of risk has been getting higher, and it has been rising across the board, affecting practically all the industry groups covered by S&P. The data are so clear that you may want to ask: What is happening to my company's risk level, and why?

FIGURE 1

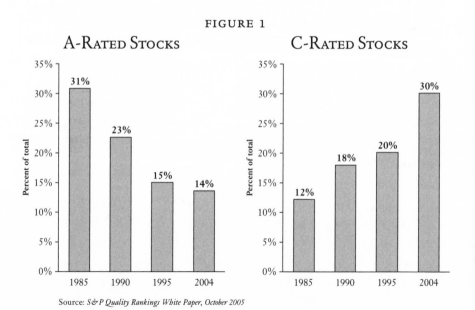

Source: *S&P Quality Rankings White Paper, October 2005*

Electrical utilities, an industry historically regarded as extraordinarily low-risk, provide a prototypical example. During the 1990s, the electric energy industry was rapidly deregulated. Consequently, as reported in a recent study by Jeremy C. Stein of Harvard and a team from National Economic Research Associates, the volatility of earnings (EBITDA) for the average electrical utility roughly *doubled* during the decade. Much of the increased risk in utilities was driven by regulatory changes. For other industry groups the causes are different, but the increase in risk level is pervasive.

Expansion of strategic risk has also led to an increasing number of market value collapses. From 1993 to 1998, 10 percent of Fortune 1000 companies lost 25 percent of their market value in one month. From 1998 to 2003, 10 percent dropped 55 percent in one month. And during the last twelve years, 170 of the Fortune 500 lost 50 percent or more of their value over a twelve-month period. Furthermore, it is now taking *longer* for companies that experience significant value declines to recover their lost value than it did just a decade ago.

The lesson: Strategic risk has become one of the greatest sources of lost value in the economy—perhaps *the* greatest. The implications for individual businesses are no less disturbing.

Companies that once owned seemingly invulnerable strategic positions have been reeling under assaults from quarters no one anticipated. You may sense that your company is likely to face its own Gettysburg moment somewhere, sometime soon.

This is why a growing number of business leaders are identifying strategic risk management as the crucial discipline for the first decade of the twenty-first century—one that managers at every level of the organization, from the factory floor and the departmental office to the executive suite, need to master and apply on a daily basis. One manager we know has gone so far as to say simply, "Strategy *is* risk management."

Unfortunately, the familiar ways of thinking about risk management won't help you cope with today's increased levels of risk.

Traditional risk management focuses on three categories of risk that are widely understood: *hazard risks* (fire, flood, earthquake), *financial risks* (bad loans, currency and interest rate swings), and *operating risks* (the computer system goes down, the supply chain gets interrupted, an employee steals). Most companies have risk managers who specialize in handling these kinds of risk. They work with insurance companies, finance and security experts, and other specialists to reduce risk levels and develop hedging strategies to minimize potential losses.

These kinds of risks are extremely important. But even more dangerous are the *strategic risks* your business faces. Strategic risk targets one or more of the crucial elements in the design of your business model. In some cases, it shatters the bond between you and your customers. In other cases, it undermines the unique value proposition that is the basis of your revenue stream. In still other cases, it siphons away the profits you depend on. And sometimes it destroys the strategic control that helps your company fend off competition. In the worst case, a major strategic risk can threaten all these pillars of your business.

Not all businesses face every form of strategic risk. But every business faces some. In fact, strategic risk comprises most of the total risk most companies face.

There are seven major kinds of strategic risk your business can prepare for. While your company no doubt faces other risks, such as regulatory or geopolitical risks, these seven cover the gamut of risks that threaten most companies' business designs.

1. Your big initiative fails. Think back to the last major project that you led or were part of (R&D project, new product launch, market expansion, acquisition, IT project). What were the odds of success at the outset? What is the true success rate of all your company's projects in the past five to ten years?

If you assess them honestly, the true odds of success at the outset of most major projects are less than 20 percent—which means the risk of failure is greater than 80 percent. Can those odds be changed? How? What specific moves have other companies made to radically alter the odds in their favor? Which of these moves can you use to dramatically change the odds on your next project, or even on your entire portfolio of projects?

2. Your customers leave you. Has your business ever been surprised by its customers—by sudden, unforeseen shifts in their preferences, priorities, and tastes? When this happens, the revenue base on which your company is built can erode very quickly. But there are companies that have found specific ways to beat customer risk. How have they learned to get inside the minds of their customers, anticipating surprises before they happen? What growth break-throughs did they create? Can you adopt their methods successfully?

3. Your industry reaches a fork in the road. When technology or business design shifts transform an industry, as many as 80 percent of incumbent firms fail to survive the transition. But a handful of companies have not only beaten transition risk but also turned it into an enormous growth opportunity—and a few have done it successfully more than once. What lessons do these survivors have to teach the rest of us?

4. A seemingly unbeatable competitor arrives. Your business may not yet have encountered a unique competitor, a Wal-Mart or a Microsoft, poised to dominate your market. When it does, is it possible to survive and thrive while other companies are being decimated? Who has done so, and how did they do it? How can their moves help you compete better even if you don't face an apparently unbeatable rival?

5. Your brand loses power. A great brand is supposed to be a fortress of value. Yet 40 percent of leading brands experienced significant value erosion in the past five years. In most cases, this erosion occurred because managers think about their brands too narrowly, overlooking the interplay between brand, product, and business design that determines the strength of the brand. How early can you detect brand risk? How can you reverse brand decline to create a new decade of growth? How can your investments across the entire business design help to strengthen—or undermine—the value of your brand?

6. Your industry becomes a no-profit zone. Many industries, from airlines and consumer electronics to groceries and cars, have found themselves suffering from increasing competition, growing customer power, and margin compression, until profits are driven practically to zero. What triggers the process? Can it happen to your business? Most important, what kinds of countermeasures can you launch to create new profit opportunities for your company, even if your industry has become a no-profit zone?

7. Your company stops growing. When sales growth hits a plateau, the impact is immediate and painful: the company share price suffers, new initiatives grind to a halt, and your best talent begins to leave the company. What can you do to defeat stagnation risk—without creating new risks in the process? How can you invent new forms of customer demand that can trigger new waves of growth, even in a seemingly mature industry?

Each of these categories of strategic risk is a potential killer of business designs. Just as a category four hurricane can uproot a forest or level a neighborhood, when one of these risks strikes, it can ruin a piece of the business design that you've painstakingly built your company around. And all tend to be overlooked or underestimated by managers who assume that their company's strategy (along with the dangers that threaten it) is the concern of a select few senior executives, or that major risk events such as the ones they read about in the newspaper only happen to the other guy.

Both assumptions are wrong. Strategic risk management belongs on the agenda of *every* manager. And any company that remains in business long enough is certain to be struck by one or more strategic risk events—often, as is increasingly common, by several at once.

Of course, there's no way to eliminate strategic risk altogether. But understanding and anticipating it, shaping it, and implementing the specific countermeasures that have proven to be effective can enable a company to dramatically improve its odds for surviving and even thriving in today's risk-rich environment—and to discover the upside potential concealed behind the frightening mask of downside risk.

The first two jobs of strategic risk management are to sidestep the unnecessary blows and to mitigate the blows you can't avoid. You can avoid the biggest hits to your company's value through a strategic risk management system that uses the principles and techniques described in the rest of this book. Remember Warren Buffett's first rule: *Preserve your capital.* And also his second rule: *See the first rule.*

Doing this well also solves half the growth problem that most companies face: You can build on a strong base, rather than spending time and treasure to rebuild to the stock price you had five years ago.

ANTICIPATION:
RECOGNIZING THE FOCAL POINT OF RISK

The ability to react brilliantly when confronted by a potentially fatal risk is extremely valuable. Even more valuable is the ability to *anticipate* risk and develop an attack plan to deflect and transform it in advance.

Perhaps no one exemplifies this skill better than the coach of American football's New England Patriots, three-time Super Bowl winner Bill Belichick.

> *The risk you face is inversely proportional to the relevant preparation you do.*

Coach Belichick's method of preparing his team for a game is all about downsides—about anticipating risks. One week before the game, Belichick and his coaches meet to ask: What will our opponents do to us? On what kind of long passes will they try to connect? What holes in our defensive line will they try to exploit? How will their punt-return unit try to break a big one and get more favorable field position at the start of a drive? What will their defense do to put pressure on our quarterback and force a costly turnover?

Belichick and his staff conjure up one horror story (risk) after another. And then they ask: Is it possible to reverse every one of those? More often than not, they do. Belichick's teams use their detailed knowledge of the opposition's habits to turn defense into offense. As described by Bruce Laird, a defensive back who was coached by Belichick years ago:

> The better you came to know [your opponent's game plan] and master it, then the more it all became instinct. That meant we were not back on our heels, letting the offense have the initiative, but we were attacking, and we felt we knew what they were going to do. That's one of the reasons we got better as the season went along; we started 1–4, and then won eight in a row.

And that's why competing against Belichick is so frustrating: He has played out more games in his head than any other coach or team.

Perhaps Belichick's greatest triumph was the Patriots' upset win in the 2001 Super Bowl over the St. Louis Rams. By some measures, the Patriots had no business being in the Super Bowl that year. They were led by a rookie quarterback who'd been pressed into service when the star quarterback was injured early in the season. They'd given up more first downs, more rushing yards, and more passing yards to their opponents than they'd achieved.

By contrast, the Rams featured quarterback Kurt Warner, who'd passed for 4,353 yards and 41 touchdowns with just 13 interceptions. Led by Warner, the team had averaged 9.2 yards per pass, "almost as if they didn't need a second down," in Belichick's words. Even more important, they boasted one of the greatest offensive backs in football history, Marshall Faulk, then just twenty-eight years old, at the height of his abilities, coming off an unprecedented four straight years averaging over 2,000 rushing and receiving yards from scrimmage. With a tremendous combination of size, quickness, and running speed, Faulk routinely turned 5-yard pass receptions into 20-yard gains. This was an awesome team, and few observers gave the Patriots much of a chance.

But they had a secret weapon: Coach Bill Belichick and his remarkable methods for anticipating threats and then reversing them. Unlike most other coaches, Belichick didn't believe that game preparation should focus just on finding the opposition's weaknesses. Instead, it should focus on identifying the opponent's strengths and then figuring out how to take them away. Accordingly, Belichick spent the week before the Super Bowl teaching his defensive squad to focus its efforts on stopping Marshall Faulk. As described by journalist David Halberstam, who worked closely with Belichick on the extraordinary book *The Education of a Coach,* "The game plan was to key in on him [Faulk] and wear him down on every play. They were going to hit him every time he had the ball, and hit him every time he didn't have the ball."

To reinforce the single-minded concentration on Faulk as the focal point of risk, Belichick spent the week of scrimmages before the Super Bowl standing behind his defenders, shouting at them, "Where is he? Where is he?" Only when he overheard members of the defensive squad yelling, "Where is he? Where is he?" to one another as they walked into a team meeting was Belichick satisfied that he'd fully transferred his obsession with Faulk to the men who would have to counter him.

In the end, Marshall Faulk gained a mere 76 yards. New England kept the explosive Rams offense in check, the game remained close throughout, and in the final seconds, Adam Vinatieri kicked a field goal to give the Patriots a 20–17 win. It was the first and most amazing of their three Super Bowl championships.

Belichick's approach and track record illustrate a crucial aspect of the risk challenge. In virtually every situation that is rich in risk, it's possible to anticipate the major sources of risk and to take many specific steps that will improve the odds that you will win. (The notion of improving the odds applies as well in personal situations, such as education or career. For an example, see Notes, pages 242–243.)

PROTECTING YOUR BUSINESS DESIGN

The most dramatic and exciting examples of risk reversal pertain to the big threats that can destroy your business. But being smart about risk is not just about historic turning points such as Little Round Top or a Super Bowl. It's also about the many small but vital adjustments you can make to your business design every day, adjustments that can make it more durable, more flexible, and less vulnerable to risk.

There's an entire repertoire of de-risking moves that smart companies have developed over the years. They include reducing fixed costs, engineering faster response times, capturing early warning information that others don't have, developing and testing numerous product design options, generating continuous, multi-angle customer data, and many other tactics. In *The Upside*, we'll explore the whole repertoire and see how risk-smart companies have used them to turn negative risk energy into a huge positive. Expanding your repertoire of specific moves can help to design an extremely risk-resilient business.

In 1916, after several years of lobbying, American architect Frank Lloyd Wright won the commission to design the Imperial Hotel in Tokyo. Wright was delighted to win, but he was acutely aware of the many tough challenges he faced.

The single greatest challenge for the project was the frequency of earthquakes in Japan and the fires they started. Wright responded to this

Master of risk.
Where a rival architect might have been content to design a conventional structure,
Wright faced the reality of future risk and devoted extra time, effort,
and creativity to producing a building that would withstand that risk.

challenge by creating a unique design for the building. For resiliency, he used cantilevered slabs of reinforced concrete that rose from a specially designed, flexible foundation. To make the structure fireproof, Wright used only masonry materials, reinforced concrete and brick. To make the building lighter and lower its center of gravity, the brickwork in the lower part of the structure was filled with reinforced rods, while the upper bricks were hollow. To further reduce the overall weight, the roof was made of lightweight copper instead of traditional heavy tile.

The Imperial Hotel was scheduled to open on September 1, 1923. That day, Tokyo experienced one of the worst earthquakes in its history. All around the Imperial Hotel, buildings collapsed. The entire area was reduced to rubble. The only building left standing, virtually unharmed, was the Imperial Hotel. It became a refuge for Tokyo citizens and travelers left homeless by the disaster, and the hotel's place in Japanese lore and architectural history was secure.

Designed to survive the inevitable.
In the aftermath of the massive September 1, 1923, earthquake in Tokyo
the new Imperial Hotel was still standing unharmed, thanks to the risk-reduction
design strategies of its architect, Frank Lloyd Wright.

Like the Imperial Hotel, your business faces the risk of a difficult-to-predict but inevitable calamity—"earthquakes" that remake the business landscape, such as the big seven we described a few pages back. Are there proven techniques for reducing your business's vulnerability to strategic risks, and the volume and price fluctuations that they create?

Consider Toyota, which is generally regarded as the world's best-managed automobile manufacturer. Toyota's enormous financial and marketplace success—and its ability to thrive even as its industry and the worldwide economy undergo repeated shifts and shocks—stem not merely from the company's well-earned reputation for producing fine vehicles. They also derive from a series of smart business design decisions that, in combination, have made the company more durable, flexible, and risk-proof.

Toyota has made several difficult de-risking choices: it took steps to dramatically lower its fixed costs, thereby reducing the financial risk posed by a recession or a sales slowdown; it reduced cycle time in both manufacturing processes and new product development, enabling the company to respond more quickly to change; it developed a uniquely flexible manufacturing system that permits production of several vehicle models on a single assembly line; it created a broad portfolio of vehicle models, reducing the risk of losses from a decline in popularity of any single style; and it enhanced and strengthened the Toyota brand, including developing and maintaining the highest service and product quality standards in the industry.

Is this merely plain old good management? Not at all. It involves conscious choices made very differently by different competitors. Detroit automakers, for instance, evolved a system with high fixed costs and very low variable cost. That was a bet on steadily rising volumes, and the bet proved wrong. The important point is that, given the essential nature of the industry, it was a much higher risk position.

You can design your business for durability, flexibility, and lower risk.

As a result of Toyota's choices, its business design is architecturally sound. When we compare it, point by point, with that of a major U.S. competitor, Ford, we see why Toyota is prepared to survive the strategic shocks and shifts that are constantly occurring in the auto industry.

FIGURE 2

COMPARATIVE RISK PROFILES: FORD VS. TOYOTA

	FORD	TOYOTA
FIXED COSTS	High	Low
CYCLE TIME	Long	Short
MANUFACTURING FLEXIBILITY	Low	High
SINGLE-PRODUCT DEPENDENCE	High	Low
BRAND MOMENTUM	Downward spiral	Upward spiral

Managers who want to reduce their risks can learn from companies such as Toyota and its counterparts in other industries: Coach, Tsutaya, Samsung, Target, Procter & Gamble, and others discussed throughout the book. The de-risking methods developed by these companies can help you to design a more flexible and resilient business, and to be better prepared to transform major risk events into huge upside opportunities.

TRANSFORMING RISK INTO OPPORTUNITY

What prevents most businesses from practicing this kind of strategic risk management? The necessity of learning a new way of thinking.

The conventional wisdom is that risk and reward go together—that to get great upside results, you need to accept big downside risks. Risk, in this view, is simply a painful but inescapable fact of life.

Except that risk and reward are *not* always inextricably linked. It's possible to reduce the risks you face at the same time as you improve the returns you enjoy. In fact, it's not only possible but essential.

The leaders of today's most successful companies aren't risk *takers*, they're risk *shapers.* They think day and night about the risks they face and are continually working to develop and implement strategies to reduce them and transform them into breakthrough growth opportunities. That is why Toyota, Coach, Tsutaya, and the other great risk shapers are both *more profitable* and *less risky* than their industry rivals.

Initially, this counterintuitive view sounds too good to be true. But it has a precedent from the business world of the early 1980s. The conventional wisdom then was that you could have high quality *or* low cost, but not both. There was a sense of resignation about the products we bought, from high-ticket items such as cars to mundane products including blenders and TVs: "If we want better quality, we're going to have to pay a lot more. That's just the way it is."

And it was true—until Japanese makers of cars and electronics destroyed the conventional wisdom. They did so by developing a new way of thinking based on using specific questions and innovative analytic techniques for tackling quality problems.

Suddenly it became clear that high quality and low cost could be achieved simultaneously if you thought differently and changed your processes. In time, ideas and tools such as Total Quality Management, Continuous Improvement, and Six Sigma spread through companies and entire industries. Today, levels of quality and cost control once considered impossible are required just to survive in the marketplace.

THE UPSIDE OF RISK REVERSED IS OFTEN TEN TIMES GREATER THAN THE DOWNSIDE

The quality-and-cost conundrum was the big business problem a quarter of a century ago. Today, the problem is strategic risk. Those who are among the first to practice the new approach to risk will enjoy a huge advantage.

You might ask, how huge? The evidence suggests that a smart approach to risk management can multiply long-term company value by a factor of ten times or greater. Making the right choice at a crucial decision point can improve your future prospects dramatically. The graph that illustrates the difference might look like this:

FIGURE 3

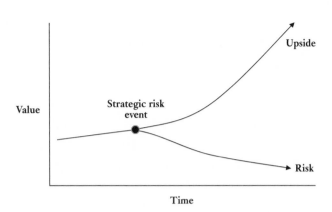

If this seems impossible, consider a few case examples.

When Toyota launched its Prius hybrid car project, it took on a risk of one to two billion dollars—the amount it stood to lose if the Prius never got off the ground. By making the right risk-reduction moves, Toyota turned the risky Prius project into a major success, with an upside in the neighborhood of $15 to $25 billion—a tenfold improvement.

Target and Samsung achieved comparable results. Almost a decade ago, both companies were at a similar crossroads. In discount retailing, Target faced a seemingly unbeatable competitor, Wal-Mart; in consumer electronics, Samsung was burdened with a low-end brand image, a reputation for poor quality, and no history of innovation. Left unmanaged, these risks would have led to a steady decline in value for each company, amounting, over time, to a loss of perhaps $5 billion in market cap. Instead, both companies took aggressive steps to reverse the risks they faced. As a result, both not only fended off the threat of value decline but actually increased their value by amounts in the $40 to $50 billion range—another tenfold increase.

Coach, the maker of fashion leather goods and accessories, did better. Facing a radical shift in customer preferences, it moved quickly to reverse that risk and get ahead of the curve of customer change. In the process, it transformed a potential $500 million loss in value into a company value increase of roughly $10 billion—a twentyfold increase.

Finally, consider the iPod. When Apple began developing this new product, it invested less than $100 million in the process. If the iPod had been a complete failure, the company would have lost that amount—not an enormous sum, but a meaningful loss for a company the size of Apple. Instead, Apple's use of techniques to manage and reverse project risk transformed that potential loss into a new business that has increased Apple's value by tens of billions of dollars.

How did they do it? We'll tell the stories of all five companies, and others like them, in the chapters that follow.

You may never find yourself, as Joshua Chamberlain did, at a pivot point where your company's history swings between utter defeat and incredible triumph. But every day, the organizations you help to run and the people who rely on you face many risks that carry enormous potential on both the upside and the downside. This book is about recognizing those potentialities and knowing what to do about them—about preparing to be a risk shaper in your own sphere of influence, creating upside value that is several times greater than the downside.

CHAPTER ONE

Changing the Odds

Why 90% Right Often = 0:
How to Improve the Odds on
Your Most Important Project

G ROWING YOUR BUSINESS depends on new projects—creating
new products, entering new markets, finding new customers, and
acquiring new operations. Likewise, improving your business depends
on major new projects, such as upgrading your IT system, simplifying
your manufacturing processes, and streamlining your supply chain. But
at the moment of launching any project, there's a problem that most of
us don't come to grips with: the inherent, all-too-human tendency to be
overly optimistic about the odds of success.

What are the odds that the new venture your company is about to
launch will produce a marketable product within the next eighteen
months? What are the chances the merger your company is about to con-
clude will create rather than destroy shareholder value? Out of twenty
new products now in development in your lab, how many will be on the
market two years from now? And of those, how many will be profitable?

Even approaching such questions in a spirit of objectivity is very tough
for most people. As researchers Daniel Kahneman and Dan Lovallo explain in their article "Delusions of Success," "We chronically overestimate, to a dramatic degree, the odds of project success." We look at a
project with a 5 percent chance of success and we think the odds are 30
percent; we look at a 10 percent chance and we think that it's 50 percent.

It's natural for businesspeople to look on the bright side when estimating their chances for success. Optimism generates energy. Those who
are chronically pessimistic attract few followers and accomplish very little. But optimism has an Achilles' heel: It causes you to overestimate the
true odds at the outset. Take a minute and think about the true odds in
most common business scenarios. A close look at the data suggests that

19

the failure rate for many types of projects is in the range of 60–80 percent. (See Figure 1-1 for typical failure rates for specific project types.)

FIGURE 1-1

TYPICAL FAILURE RATES
FOR SPECIFIC PROJECT TYPES

Hollywood movie	60%
Company merger or acquisition	60%
Information technology project	70%
New food product	78%
Venture capital investment	80%
New pharmaceutical product	Over 90%

In truth, every project you undertake is a kind of suspense story. How and when and where will it go wrong? What unexpected obstacles will arise to derail it? There are many, many ways a project can fail. They range from undercommunication among team members to conducting too few experiments and considering too few options when designing the new product or the new business; from relying on a flawed technology to using a technology that works but costs too much or takes too long to develop; from failing to anticipate a competitor's preemptive move to inaccurately forecasting consumer demand; and from overlooking the need to retool your marketing infrastructure to support a new product to ignoring the time bombs planted by internal politics that will blow up any chance of successful implementation.

> *When you overestimate the odds, you will underestimate the investment needed to win.*

This list of traps and pitfalls is far from complete—you can probably extend it dramatically based on your own experience. Consider all the ways that a project can fail and you may find yourself wondering how it is that any projects succeed.

Of course, many projects do succeed. Some IT programs work phenomenally well; some new products become enormous hits. But too often, excessive optimism impedes project success by underestimating the investment and the sense of urgency needed to drive the crucial de-risking moves. The people in marketing are consulted only twice rather than ten times about the details of the CRM project; the new product reaches the market six months too late, with a vital feature or distribution channel overlooked and omitted. Time, energy, and treasure are wasted, and the expected growth breakthrough never happens.

The first step in changing this picture is carefully estimating the true odds—overcoming the natural human tendency to be overly optimistic with a bracing dose of realism and data. The purpose is not to demoralize the effort. It's to give you a clear, accurate sense of what's really needed to make your project succeed—how much investment is needed (usually twice as much as you were planning), how many smart moves you have to make, how many contingency plans you need to prepare, and how smart a business model you need to design.

Projects live in a tough, probabilistic world. Even if you do everything right, the odds can turn against you. And if you misread the odds and underinvest, you can guarantee that the project will fail. There are so many ways to underinvest—not just financially but also in terms of time, energy, emotion, resilience, options considered, conversations held, experiments conducted, simulations run, market trials conducted, tires kicked, and doors slammed. Making matters worse is the fact that for many types of business initiative, success is an all-or-nothing matter. Unless *all* the elements required for success are in place (the right technology, the right value proposition, the right customer set, and so on), the project can fail—completely. This little-recognized reality of project risk can be described by the simple formula "90% right often = 0."

Thankfully, there are proven techniques for changing these odds for the better. The fastest way to learn about them is by studying the companies that pioneered them. For example, the Japanese automaker Toyota created several of the most powerful of these techniques while developing the Prius—a blockbuster product whose odds of success were less than 5 percent when Toyota embarked on its development in the fall of 1993.

21

Toyota Changes the Odds on the Prius

Step inside the minds of the leaders of Toyota in the early 1990s. The company was riding high, enjoying growing market share and unrivaled profitability. Any manager in this situation might have been tempted to be complacent or even arrogant.

But Toyota's executives responded to success differently: They were extremely worried. They'd seen how complacency had weakened many other successful companies, including the great American automakers. They feared that, despite their current success, a feeling of product maturity was setting in. Hungry, cost-conscious, hyperefficient competitors such as Korea's Hyundai were emerging, eager to do to Toyota what Toyota had done to Detroit's Big Three.

The interior monologue of Toyota's leaders at this inflection point might have sounded like this:

We've created great breakthroughs in quality, pricing, and fuel efficiency. These have made us the world's fastest-growing and most profitable car company. But what about tomorrow? What is the next great breakthrough in our industry? How can we ensure that we will create the breakthrough, rather than be victimized by it? What must we do to anticipate the risks that success will bring and transform them into opportunities before they blindside us?

You might call this "competing in advance," a strategy for preempting risk by outthinking it, much as chess master Garry Kasparov plans his fifth move partly to fend off the forking attack his opponent might launch with his seventh move. Competing in advance may not be a formula for personal serenity, but it's a powerful tool for success if you are trying to protect your company from its biggest risks.

In an effort to make sure that Toyota would remain in the forefront of the auto industry, the company decided to mount an all-out effort to create the first great car of the twenty-first century, almost a decade before that century would arrive. In 1993, a team of ten Toyota board members met to imagine the qualities that a breakthrough car (which they code-named the G21) for the coming century should have. They envisioned a car that was comfortable, safe, pleasant to drive, appealing to female motorists, low-polluting and environmentally friendly, and highly fuel-efficient—sound ideas, but amorphous. An engineer named Takeshi Uchiyamada was assigned to convert them into a concrete proposal.

Uchiyamada, a specialist in techniques for eliminating noise and vibration, wasn't an obvious choice for the role. He had never headed a new-vehicle development team. But from 1991 to 1993, he'd led a task force that reviewed Toyota's R&D process from head to toe. This turned out to be crucial preparation for the G21 challenge. It exposed him to many parts of the company and deepened his understanding of the disparate technologies that Toyota had developed. He had become an expert in the inner workings of the company, its many strengths and its less-obvious weaknesses.

He had also learned where the company's most talented engineers were. Now he recruited ten outstanding engineers representing all of the key technologies that would go into the G21: the body, the chassis, the engine, the drive system, production technology, and so on. All were in their early thirties, old enough to have experience but young enough to be flexible.

They worked for months to give a concrete form to the G21 concept. They then brought their proposed car to the company's executive vice president of R&D, Akihiro Wada. Uchiyamada explained that his team hoped to create a small sedan that delivered 47.5 miles per gallon, about 50 percent better fuel efficiency than the Corolla, a comparable current car. At the time, it must have seemed to Uchiyamada an impressive proposal. He probably presented it with no little satisfaction, even a bit of quiet pride— which would have made the reception he received doubly shocking.

Wada listened politely, then replied, "Fifty percent better is not enough. Our competitors would quickly overtake us. Please double it."

Uchiyamada was taken aback by Wada's challenge. "At that moment I felt he demanded too much," is how he later put it in his understated manner. This was the first in a series of blows that would have shattered the psyches of some less-resilient managers.

Shaken but determined, Uchiyamada returned to the drawing board. He realized that the higher performance bar meant that he would have to rethink his assumptions about the G21. Tinkering with existing technology wouldn't suffice. It would require a major leap to an unproven system that existed only as a blue-sky concept Toyota had been studying—the hybrid engine. Even today, Uchiyamada shakes his head when he thinks about the nature of the challenge: "There were no models, no comparisons, no benchmarks. Everything had to be created from scratch, with no guarantee that any of it would work."

What's more, Toyota wasn't the only company considering the hybrid engine. Everyone in the car business had heard rumors about hybrid experiments at Honda and Ford. How far had they advanced? When would they announce a breakthrough? No one knew, but the existence of competing projects must have sharpened the anxiety Uchiyamada felt when he realized he'd have to commit to a hybrid model. It wouldn't be enough to create a successful new design; he also had to do it faster than the competition.

Given the realities, the G21 project was a long shot. Takehisa Yaegashi, who joined the Prius effort as project leader, put it this way: "We didn't think it was impossible, but the odds were very low. Perhaps 5 percent; perhaps even less."

One in twenty. Would you bet a billion dollars on those odds? That would be a very tough call. But the people at Toyota didn't merely put their chips down and spin the roulette wheel. They made a series of moves to change the odds.

The first step in de-risking your project is to recognize the true odds of success; the second is to change them.

Recognizing the complexity of the technical problems the company faced, Uchiyamada needed to find new ways to surface problems and solve them quickly. He started by creating a new system designed to facilitate communication and joint problem solving among his team members.

The system started with a dedicated physical space. They called it *obeya*, the big room. It was equipped with personal computers and two computer-aided design workstations. Team members were asked to assemble in this room daily to work together on the G21 project—the first time this had been done at Toyota.

Uchiyamada also created a virtual space, an electronic mailing list compiled to encourage team members to quickly and broadly disseminate key issues and problems as they arose. Over time, this list grew to include three hundred people.

Of course, e-mail wasn't a new technology at Toyota, but the way it was used on the G21 project was new to this relatively hierarchical, formal company. Here's how Ikujiro Nonaka, a professor of strategy at Hitotsubashi University, described the process in his article on knowledge creation at Toyota:

> "Equal access to information" was one of Uchiyamada's action guidelines for the G21 project. . . . In an ordinary product development project at Toyota, when an employee found a problem he reported it to his boss. And if the problem couldn't be solved, it would be reported to the chief engineer, who would notify other engineers who could be affected by the problem. This was a time-consuming process. In the Prius project, by contrast, the engineers could post an e-mail to the mailing list immediately after discovering a problem. Anyone who read the e-mail and had a solution could immediately post the necessary information.

The visual metaphor for this kind of communication is not a pyramid or even a network but rather a sphere, as in the old definition of God attributed to the fifteenth-century mystic Nicholas of Cusa, a sphere "whose circumference is nowhere and whose center is everywhere." Everyone on the mailing list stands equally close to the center of the action, and everyone is capable of *being* the center at a particular moment in time—able to draw energy from everyone else in the group to solve today's most pressing problem.

By replacing the hierarchical, command-and-control communications model with the innovative equal-access system, Toyota sent a clear message: The best minds in the company should focus on any and every problem related to the G21.

At the time, no one could know for sure how effective the new system would prove to be. In retrospect, we can see that the intense focus probably raised the odds of success for the project from the 5 percent range to perhaps 10% . (As the story continues, we can watch as the scoreboard keeps changing.)

Uchiyamada also spent a great deal of time anticipating problems that, upon a bit of reflection, were entirely predictable. He introduced other innovations designed to preempt them. For example, when a new vehicle is ready to go on line, Toyota usually sends resident engineers (REs) to work at the manufacturing plants so that they'll be available to handle any problems that arise during the early months of production. For the G21 project, they assigned *reverse* REs from the manufacturing plants to take part in the design development process. The point was to identify possible manufacturing glitches *before* the car was ready for the assembly line and eliminate them in the blueprint stage. Another odds-raising move. **15%**

Uchiyamada's redesign of the product development process was methodical, conscious, and deliberate. On the first page of the notebook he carried everywhere and cited constantly in conversations, he wrote down the process guidelines as he discovered them. In retrospect, they read like a cross between an engineering manual and a collection of Zen sayings: "The technology should be evaluated by everyone, regardless of his specialty." "One should think of what is best for the product, instead of representing one's own department's interest." "When discussing technologies, one should not care about one's age or rank."

A central strategy according to Uchiyamada: To achieve the seemingly impossible, under intense time pressure, with no historical points of comparison for guidance, demands fast, continual learning. In turn, this requires drawing on the knowledge, experience, and insights of everyone in the company, and often outside the company as well.

Tackling risk reduction in this spirit often meant drastically increasing the demands on the team—for example, considering some eighty different types of hybrid engines early in the life of the project. (Imagine for a moment investigating eighty prototypes of *your* next product.)

Grueling, yes. But the logic was simple: If the team could find the one true standout option for the engine, they would change the odds of success by a couple of percentage points. **17%**

On closer inspection, many of the eighty engine concepts turned out to be impractical for one reason or another. The hybrid team quickly narrowed the options to twenty. They purchased specialized, ready-made computer simulation software with which to run most of their performance tests. Unfortunately, it didn't meet the unprecedented demands of the brand-new hybrid technology. (It was the kind of unwanted surprise that the team faced dozens of times in the process.) So Toyota's engineers set out to rework the software extensively before it could be used.

This was a huge job in itself, as if a biologist studying a new array of specimens had to design and build a new kind of microscope before he could even begin the work.

Once the new software was ready, the rounds of synthetic testing could begin. The G21 team narrowed twenty system-design possibilities down to eight, then four, then had an intense bake-off among the final four. Uchiyamada recalled: "This last stage was the toughest. We were able to find the most fuel efficient engine, but we didn't know which of the four would be lowest-cost. We ultimately chose the one that was the most efficient and the simplest of the four. We were hoping that *relative* simplicity would translate into lowest cost."

The survivor of all these brutal comparisons was an extraordinary engine—efficient and relatively simple in design. Now the team had to do the same thing for the suspension, the styling, and other parts of the car.

The strategy was one of *creating excess options*, in order to find the single most powerful answer. It was even applied to the car's overall styling. Toyota maintains seven separate styling studios around the world, each normally working on a different vehicle category—small cars, trucks, minivans, and so on. But for the high-stakes G21, soon dubbed the Prius, all seven studios were asked to submit designs, which were judged by a panel of fifty Toyota people of various ages. 20%

In *The Wisdom of Crowds*, author James Surowiecki describes the process by which, in the early phase of any new technology, the market weeds out dozens of different products to settle on a dominant design. His point is that you don't need a creative genius to identify the best design for a new product; the combined reactions of thousands of ordinary people can be just as smart. Toyota moved that market mechanism and its competitive magic in-house. It created multiple options that competed against each other internally, capturing the "wisdom of the crowd" for the project's benefit.

In retrospect, it looks brilliant, and it was. But it was also forced by necessity. Remember, the hybrid project was unprecedented, with no guidelines or historical comparisons. The intense time pressure meant that, for the first time in its history, Toyota had to make a go/no-go decision on a new car model without having a working prototype. Under the circumstances, the mind-boggling, almost compulsive excess-options process was the only practical way of ensuring that the right engineering options were chosen, because there were no safety nets, no time for fixes, no margin for error.

As the hybrid development continued, Toyota faced another critical juncture: Could it solve the battery problem? The Prius required the creation of a new battery that would be just one-tenth the size of existing batteries for electric vehicles and far more impervious to heat and cold. This one challenge could have sunk the entire venture. When early versions of the battery were installed, an engineer had to accompany Toyota executives during road tests and monitor the battery from the backseat with a laptop to keep it from bursting into flames. Needless to say, this was not considered a satisfactory safety system.

Toyota dislikes relying on external expertise. As a company spokesman puts it, "It's not in Toyota's DNA to outsource a key technology. We want to have the knowledge and the experience in-house." In this case, there was no viable option. Toyota met with other companies to explain the battery problems and eventually decided to partner with Matsushita Electric to design and produce the battery, and then later to sell it to other automakers. This step helped reduce financial risk by providing another revenue stream to help pay for the Prius development process. (Subsequently, other licensing deals for various hybrid technologies helped even more.) And since the battery was built by a Matsushita-Toyota joint venture, Toyota did not lose control of a key technology. **25%**

Another key technological breakthrough lay in recognizing that powerful electronic devices for managing the flow of electricity between the battery and the electric motor were crucial to making the car both quiet and powerful. The hybrid car would need more controls and transition management than a conventional internal combustion engine, including new computer chips to make it work. Toyota spent time with chip specialists to assemble the right electronic pieces for the massive, three-dimensional hybrid puzzle. But the advanced chips needed were not readily available, even from outside sources.

The solution was for Toyota to build its own factory north of Nagoya, Japan, where it fabricates self-designed power controller chips. Sometimes changing the odds means changing your business design—in this case, by expanding the scope of the company's activities. Toyota had to hire a team of semiconductor engineers, then educate them about the car business and specifically the new hybrid technology. It was costly and time-consuming, but raised the odds a little further. **30%**

Every one of the moves made by Uchiyamada and his team (the battery partnership, the chip manufacturing plant, and the excess-options strategy) kept notching up the odds. Uchiyamada himself compares the process to the one NASA used in response to President John F. Kennedy's historic 1961 challenge: "before this decade is out, to land a man on the Moon and return him safely to Earth." Like NASA, Toyota mapped out the new technologies needed, developed a timetable for each, and then set to work on the whole array of projects simultaneously, cross-referencing and cross-fertilizing among teams as needed.

We asked Uchiyamada how he managed to keep the morale of his Prius team from cracking through all these challenges. He responded, "I've found that morale is always high among engineers when they know they have a chance to be the first in the world to solve an important problem." The fact that Toyota's management was also clearing a path for success ahead of the engineers didn't hurt.

In August 1995 (just a couple of years into the project), the hybrid team had a big meeting with the company's top management to discuss scheduling. Uchiyamada announced that they could get into production in late 1998 or 1999. "Wrong answer," said the new company president, Hiroshi Okuda. "We need to have a car on the market before the end of 1997."

Imagine the reaction of the team members to this latest shock. Uchiyamada described his consternation in his unique style: "I have to admit that we were against the decision. Our team believed it was too demanding. Even Mr. Wada was initially against it."

Hindsight always minimizes past difficulties once they've been conquered, but Uchiyamada still remembers vividly what the Prius team was up against. Asked when it became clear to him that the Prius was really going to work, he answered, "June 1997"—which was the deadline, six months before the scheduled start of production, for locking in the car's final specifications. This was a down-to-the-wire process, with no wiggle room for failure.

In the end, the first Prius rolled off the assembly line in October 1997—two months *ahead* of Okuda's impossible target date.

Now notice a hidden advantage of Toyota's excess-options strategy:

having agonized over the crucial initial design choices, the Toyota engineers *knew* that they had the "bones" of the Prius right. Thus, they had no hesitation about putting the pedal to the metal in the subsequent development phases, knowing that all of their efforts were being channeled into the one best possible design platform and that they would not be wasting time on second thoughts or reexamining earlier decisions.

Pedal-to-the-metal timing was another odds-raising move. When a project is completed faster, you get everybody's undivided attention. Furthermore, the risk of "economic entropy" is greatly reduced. There's less time for unexpected events to intervene—new competitors, technological changes, economic upheavals, shifts in customer needs or tastes—that could make your new project obsolete before it is launched. 35%

UCHIYAMADA and his team had solved dozens of impossible problems, but one remaining issue constantly preyed on his mind: Could Toyota manufacture this unusual machine at anything resembling a reasonable cost?

Just as creating the magic of fuel efficiency had consumed 1994 and 1995, creating the magic of manufacturability consumed 1996 and 1997. A new set of characters entered the battle—the people who knew how to make large metal objects at very high volumes and very low cost.

One key issue was to figure out how to build this magical machine on an existing platform. That one move could raise the odds by 5 percent or more, because Toyota wouldn't have to build a new factory and could save twelve months and $500 million. It also would have experienced crews who knew how to run the system.

By 1996, with so many impossible problems solved, confidence was building in the team. Confidence was there on the surface, but beneath the surface, running through the whole process, lay an intense undercurrent of fear: "If we can't get it on an existing platform..." After all, even if the Prius drove like a dream and sipped gas rather than guzzling it, if it cost $6,000 more than a comparable sedan, virtually no one except a few well-heeled customers would buy it.

You can often predict the success of a project by observing how much fear there is on the set, or in the lab, or in the prototype plants. The number of "this'll-never-work" moments. The sobering realization that if the company doesn't solve this one problem, the whole project can just collapse.

The hybrid team did solve the manufacturing problem. It took months to figure out how, but they did put it on an existing platform and produced it for less than a fortune. **40%**

THE FIRST PRIUS was sold in Japan in the fourth quarter of 1997 and was followed by about a thousand more. Internationally, the launch did not garner significant attention.

The Internet was starting to soar, claiming much of the world's attention. The other deafening sound came from Detroit, as the newly popular SUVs and light trucks were ringing the cash registers with profits of as much as $10,000 per unit.

After an incredible, painstaking, filled-with-all-nighters journey, the Prius team had produced a car whose odds of success were—what?

Certainly not 100 percent. There was $1 billion in development expense that had to be paid back. They would need to sell at least 300,000 to 400,000 cars to do that.

Chris Steele-Perkins/Magnum Photos

Turning project risk into industry breakthrough.
Project leader Takeshi Uchiyamada with the Prius.

31

Certainly not 80 percent. Even if customers wanted the car, Toyota wasn't their only choice. Honda was coming out with a hybrid. And who knew how many more carmakers would jump in next year and the year after.

It's early 1998. You're the Prius project manager. The odds in 1993 had been 3 to 5 percent. What were the odds in the first quarter of 1998?

TOYOTA'S MOVES TO CHANGE THE ODDS

As we pause at this critical juncture in the story of the Prius, think about the moves Toyota made to raise the odds on the Prius project.

- Set the goal higher (50 percent fuel efficiency improvement is not enough).
- Get young, flexible-minded engineers.
- Set up an *obeya* (the big room where everyone meets).
- Set up the e-mail sphere.
- Move up the deadline (pedal-to-the-metal timing).
- Test eighty different engines.
- Test twenty different transmissions.
- Draw on seven different styling options.
- Work on the battery technology with Matsushita.
- Own the specialized chip-making technology.
- Dedicate two-thirds of the company's prototyping capacity.
- Use an existing platform.

How many of these types of moves can you adapt for your next big project?

APPLE AND THE iPOD

Steve Jobs of Apple is a technological visionary. But a visionary perspective, even supported by immense charm and salesmanship, isn't enough for commercially successful innovation. You also need a subtle system for translating visionary ideas into products people want, concrete applications they will buy, and business designs they will support. It is Jobs's unique ability to put all these elements together that has made him today's most interesting high-tech project manager.

Ironically, the creation of the iPod emerged from a *missing* feature in Apple's successful iMac computer—the lack of a CD burner. During 2000, Jobs had been so focused on the iMac's new operating system that (as he has since admitted) he didn't see, or didn't stop long enough to concentrate on, the meaning of a digitally based trend that was exploding all around him, namely, the CD-ripping, file-downloading, and peer-to-peer-sharing transformation of the music business into a user-controlled, digitally based activity. It's ironic given the fact that Jobs, like most plugged-in kids who came of age in the 1960s and 1970s, was a pop music nut. But by 2000 the pop music scene had drifted off Jobs's radar—so much so that he didn't think to include a CD burner when designing the iMac, an omission that looked worse and worse as the months went by and the digital music revolution gathered force.

Eventually, something clicked. Jobs ordered the iMac hardware designers to incorporate CD burners as standard equipment in all future iMacs. But he also started asking an intriguing set of questions. Apple's specialty had always been taking activities that other computers make possible and making them dramatically easier, more intuitive, more creative, more fun. How could Apple do that with music? Most important, how could it be done in a way to create the big new business that Apple needed as a follow-up to the success of the iMac?

If this was to work, the product would have to be brilliant, embodying all of the stylistic flair and ease of use for which Jobs-inspired designs had long been noted. But the business design would have to be equally brilliant, finding ways to capture value that some of the biggest and smartest companies in the world had somehow overlooked. And it would all have to be done fast, since Jobs, creative as he is, knew that the high-tech world boasts many other creative thinkers whose footsteps he could hear close behind. (Toyota was competing in advance against Hyundai. Jobs was competing in advance against the likes of Sony and Samsung and Panasonic.)

If Apple was going to create a profitable system for making digital on-line music easy and fun, the first step would be to create jukebox software for storing, managing, sorting, and editing music files. Apple's programmers were more than up to the challenge. But Jobs was in a hurry. Could he buy the expertise Apple needed rather than creating it from scratch?

As it happened, he could. Jeff Robbin, a recently departed employee of Apple, was working on a jukebox product named SoundJam. It wasn't ready for market, but Robbin had left behind a good reputation at Apple. So Jobs bought Robbin's company and asked him to transform SoundJam into a program with Apple-level stylishness and ease of use. Within four months, Robbin had a prototype of something the company decided to call iTunes.

It was a building block. Jobs, trying to think two steps ahead, was already planning the other blocks he'd need to make his vision work.

Like every teenager of the 1970s, Steve Jobs remembered the Walkman. It had made high-quality audio stylishly, comfortably portable, instantly rendering the old transistor radio obsolete and selling over 300 million units for Sony. Why not create a Walkman for the 2000s—a portable music player that could hold and transport all your digital music? And do it as only Apple could, with sophisticated style and ease of use.

The iPod effort began in April 2001.

Out of the starting gate, the odds for the iPod were no better than, say, 10%. Too low? Travel back in time to 2001. Apple wasn't really the right company; Sony was, or Panasonic, or Samsung. The cost of creating the device was going to be high. As for the network software to sell and manage the music (the iTunes project that had started this endeavor), the music industry was developing competing alternatives called Press-play and MusicNet. And the market for paid music downloads didn't necessarily exist and might *never* exist; after all, the consumer had an alternative called Napster that offered a fairly attractive price—free.

The project had just one obvious thing going for it: Apple was a cool company, and iPod was potentially a very cool product.

Jobs set about changing the odds. The first step was setting an outrageous schedule, much as Toyota had done with the Prius. Normal, reasonable development time for this kind of consumer-electronics project might be a year and a half, maybe a little more. Jobs decided that the project would have to be done in nine months.

Why drive your people to extremes by setting a ridiculous deadline? There were two factors, one external and one internal. The external factor: The iPod was not an obscure concept (everybody else remembered the Walkman and the Discman too). At least four global companies, including Sony, could make and market one. If just one of them showed up in the market ahead of you, they could seize the advantage. But the bigger reason for Jobs's ultra-rapid schedule was internal. One of the most precious commodities in the world is undivided attention. Set a reasonable eighteen-month timetable, and it's hard to get people's undivided attention. Set a nine-month timetable, and everybody gets very focused.

It had worked at Toyota, and now it worked at Apple. People talked to each other all the time. They tested different angles and ideas. It was the same excess-options strategy that Toyota had used: Overinvest in the right projects and let others languish. As the reject pile grows larger, so do the chances of finding the right solution—and raising the project's odds of success.

Undivided attention also attracted energy and participation. With the crazy schedule focusing everybody's mind, the iPod grew from a handful of people (Jobs and a couple of others) to a dozen, to a couple of dozen, to fifty, which is a lot of people at a company the size of Apple.

What followed was a pretty big conversation. Jobs doesn't believe in serial development (step A, handoff to step B, handoff to step C, etc.). Jobs prefers parallelism, or rather synchrony, with everyone talking to each other all the time—chip people to software people to design people to marketing people to manufacturing people.

Over in Nagoya, Toyota had done the same thing a few years earlier, when it created the *obeya*, the big room where all the players—engine people, transmission people, battery people, styling people, electronics people—could talk to each other, as well as its "spherical" e-mail network to promote equal access to information. In Cupertino, it looked a little different ("endless meetings everywhere"), but it worked in the same way ("playing together, every step of the way").

Now, playing together is not paradise. Independently thinking people have been known to disagree, often and with intensity. There has to be a referee (Steve volunteered), a timekeeper (Steve as well), and a lead debater (Steve again). The psychic cost of running such a conversation far exceeds the dollars poured into the project. And it is far more powerful in raising the odds. In fact, the big dollars without the big psychic cost of the conversation will fail, guaranteed. But when you combine the financial investment with the emotional investment, you improve the odds of project success enormously. Most project managers in the world do spend the dollars. But they don't drive the conversation with the energy, intensity, and intelligence of Steve Jobs. The high rate of project failure should be no surprise.

Apple kept looking for ways to improve the odds. The team cast a wide net in searching for the right software and components, they refused to cut financial corners, they focused intensively on the user design, and they made deals with partners to secure a time advantage over potential rivals.

Apple soon learned that Toshiba was working on a tiny, 1.8-inch disk drive that could hold thousands of songs—exactly what the iPod needed, but so expensive that other companies had balked. Jobs said, "Go for it," and Apple cut an exclusive deal for the drives, in the process adding a few points to the still-daunting odds of success, maybe to 15% .

Next, Apple discovered that a little company called PortalPlayer had created technology that could serve as the guts of the iPod. Apple licensed the technology and shaved a couple more months off the schedule. 18%

Meanwhile, Apple's engineers spent their time on the things they knew best—how to design an intuitive user interface and a beautiful package that would delight customers. Their motto: Think big, but simplify. Apple understood the technical challenges and the likely consumer demand well enough to know what the iPod needed to do and how to make it not just attractive but irresistible. Jeff Robbin recalls:

I remember sitting with Steve and some other people night after night from nine until one, working out the user interface for the first iPod. It evolved by trial and error into something a little simpler every day. We knew we had reached the end when we looked at each other and said, "Well, of course. Why would we want to do it any other way?"

The iPod's sleek design and simple-to-use interface further increased the odds. **25%**

The outpouring of favorable publicity that resulted when the iPod was launched in October 2001 also helped. It provided unpaid advertising worth more than all the thirty-second TV spots in the world. **30%**

Even with software and hardware that worked and a beautiful product design, the iPod was still far from a guaranteed success. The market was still untested, the device was expensive, and rival companies with far more experience in the consumer electronics business were on Apple's

"Why would we want to do it any other way?"
The elegant design of the original iPod.

heels. And the online music business on which the iPod was based was in chaos, with the free-download sites being sued for piracy by the record companies and the record companies squabbling with one another over control of their music libraries. There was still plenty of reason to believe that the iPod could end up alongside the Apple Newton in the annals of project risk.

If the starting-gate odds in 2000 were 10 percent, how high were they at the end of 2001?

For Steve Jobs and his team, it was all just beginning.

Apple's Moves to Change the Odds

Take a moment to reflect on the story of the iPod so far. What moves did Apple make to change the odds? Here are a few to consider:

- Work fast to preempt the competition.
- Capture your people's undivided attention.
- Have everybody talking to everybody.
- Buy or license technology rather than making it from scratch.
- Focus on the one thing you do best (interface design).
- Design and redesign until perfection feels inevitable.
- Make the first release so cool that the world has to notice.

How many of these types of moves can you use in your next new-product launch?

Prius, Act II:
It's All About the Business Design

The creation of a technologically sound car did not eliminate the risk in Toyota's launch of the Prius. After all, previous efforts to market environmentally sound, efficient vehicles (such as all-electric cars) had failed due to lackluster customer response, doubts about any new technology, and drivers' fondness for their powerful, familiar internal-combustion machines. How could Toyota reduce the risk involved in trying to create a market for this new kind of car?

One way was by casing the competitive arena into which it would be launching the Prius. The value proposition offered by the new hybrid car would be its eco-friendly energy formula. But the new technology would mean that the car would cost $3,000 to $5,000 more than a comparable standard-engine car. So Toyota's marketing avoided direct price comparisons. The customer selection would have to be relatively affluent, environmentally concerned drivers rather than the traditional economy-minded buyers of cars such as the Corolla or the Camry.

The combination of odds-raising project moves practiced by Toyota transformed the Prius initiative from a dubious long shot into a project with a fighting chance of success. By 1997, when the first Prius was ready to be launched in Japan, the odds had been improved from less than 5 percent to perhaps 40%. Pretty good, but the company wasn't yet finished with its odds-shifting initiatives. If the Prius was to be the global success and industry breakthrough Toyota sought, the firm would need to make quite a few more clever moves.

One way Toyota further improved the odds in its favor is the *stepping-stone technique*. This involves organizing a series of two or more new-project efforts, the second and third building on learning gleaned from the earlier tries. You've encountered the stepping-stone technique if you've ever bought an early version of Microsoft software. Microsoft's version 1.0 of any product represents an initial probe into the market. Version 2.0 gets much better. By version 3.0, Microsoft is hard to beat.

Imagine a game of baseball in which the batter is out after just one strike. Not many runs would be scored. But baseball offers the hitter three strikes—three chances to succeed. That's Microsoft's strategy. With each swing, as the company's knowledge base increases, the probability of success grows—from perhaps 20 percent for version 1.0 to 40 percent for version 2.0 to 70 percent or better for version 3.0. Those are terrific odds in a one-in-ten world.

Toyota used a similar approach. The 1997 Prius was decent but no barn burner. (Takehisa Yaegashi admits, "We really didn't have enough time to finesse the styling and driving performance of the first-generation Prius to make it attractive enough for most car buyers.") And when Toyota's American executives studied it (and brought back a few sample cars to California's Orange County for test drives by potential buyers), the reaction was strongly negative. A story in *Fortune* magazine recalls, "Some drivers didn't like the feel of the brakes; others complained that the interior looked cheap, that the arm rest was too low, that the rear seats didn't fold down . . . a baby stroller wouldn't fit in the trunk."

Wisely, Toyota executives initially decided *not* to launch this version of the Prius in the important U.S. market. Instead, they sold it only in Japan, where the defects that American buyers complained about seemed far less consequential. (After considerable debugging, Prius 1.0 was sold in the U.S. in 2000.) And what Toyota got right with Prius 1.0—fuel efficiency nearly double that of comparable sedans—was so good that the car captured a foothold in the marketplace, making Prius 2.0 possible.

The second-generation Prius, launched in 2003, offered even better mileage, more room, improved styling, and vastly better handling. The cost of some of the hybrid equipment was also reduced by some 70 percent. Word of mouth was overwhelmingly positive, and in most of the United States the waiting list for a new Prius was several months long. Suddenly the odds for success were in the range of 50%.

Getting the product right was one crucial element in the Prius success story. Without a great car, Toyota would have had nothing. But the car wasn't enough. (Remember, 90 percent right often = 0.) The little-known magic ingredient in beating project risk is the *business design* that the company uses to surround and support the new product. Great moves to improve the product can raise the odds from 5 percent to 50 percent. Great design of the business can carry you the rest of the way (see Figure 1-2).

That's also the secret behind most project failures. Companies spend 98 percent of their energy on making the product work and getting the customer to buy it. There's no energy left over to wrestle with the ugly but vital question, "What's the right way to design the *business* behind this car, or game, or music player, or in-vehicle safety system?"

FIGURE 1-2

Comparing Hybrid Business Designs: Honda vs. Toyota

DESIGN ELEMENTS	HONDA	TOYOTA
CUSTOMER SELECTION	Moderate income	High income
UNIQUE VALUE PROPOSITION	Energy efficiency	Energy efficiency, driving experience, style, electronics
PROFIT MODEL	Lower-margin cars	Higher-margin cars
STRATEGIC CONTROL	Patents	Patents, chip manufacturing capabilities, lower-cost position, "green" and "high-tech" brand

Let's compare the business designs of the two companies selling hybrid cars, point by point.

Customer selection. Honda aims to sell its Civic and Accord hybrids to the same moderate-income families that buy the traditional gas-powered models. Yet both are priced at around $3,000 over their conventional counterparts, an enormous differential for moderate-income customers. (And neither one boasts gas mileage as high as that of the Prius, meaning that savings on gas will take longer to earn back the hybrid price premium.) By contrast, Toyota started by promoting its Prius to higher-income car buyers who care about the environment and enjoy the prestige of owning one of the world's most advanced consumer products. Now that sales volume has pushed the price premium of the Prius (versus a comparable Camry) to just over $1,000, Toyota has the best of both worlds—a car with a prestige image that is surprisingly affordable.

Unique value proposition. Both Honda and Toyota promote their hybrids on the basis of fuel efficiency. But the Toyota car can also claim a series of other unique elements, including more up-to-date styling, advanced electronics, and especially a distinctive driving experience that features great handling. Another win for Toyota.

41

Profit model. Because of its moderate-income market base, Honda is forced to accept low margins. Toyota, on the other hand, enjoys much higher margins, especially on its Lexus and Highlander SUV hybrids, which are based on the Prius hybrid technology.

Strategic control. Both companies own patents on specific aspects of hybrid technology. But as we've seen, Toyota also controls its own chip manufacturing capabilities; has created other unique processes for vehicle design, development, and manufacturing; and has also built a more fully developed and widely recognized "green" and "high-tech" brand—all of which provide additional advantages over its Japanese rival.

Not surprisingly, Toyota owns an enormous business advantage over Honda in the hybrid marketplace. According to figures compiled in November 2005, Toyota is selling at a rate of about 105,000 Priuses annually (along with over 40,000 hybrid Lexus and Highlander models), with a goal of selling 1 million hybrid vehicles a year by 2010. Honda's hybrid sales of all models total less than 50,000. And it takes an average of eight days for Toyota to move a Prius off the dealer lot, versus five to eight *weeks* for Honda to move a hybrid Civic or Accord.

> *Winning companies devote as much energy to designing a great business model as they do to designing a great product.*

Is Toyota selling a better car? Yes. And when the better car is backed by a better-designed business model that multiplies the product advantages, the result is a set of interlocking strengths that are hard for a competitor to match, let alone beat. Combine a great car with a great business design, and the odds for success reach 90% .

Anyone can get lucky once. Was the Prius project just plain lucky? If its success was random—if Toyota succeeded with a series of idiosyncratic moves that others can't imitate—there may be little we can learn. But if it's systematic, the result of a conscious strategy developed by Toyota managers in response to a genuine understanding of the true risks and how to deal with them, then maybe we can profit from studying the Toyota playbooks.

Toyota's history demonstrates that there's more than randomness at work. The company has already done more than most to de-risk its business. It has worked to reduce fixed costs and to reduce inventory. It has driven down cycle times on everything from manufacturing to development. It has created flexible factories, where five to seven different vehicles roll off the same assembly line. Now it has turned its focus on the "untameable" dragon of project risk, and has applied and invented a whole array of moves to turn a 5 percent probability of success into 80 percent or more.

From 1955 to 1980, Toyota worked at becoming the best manufacturer in the business. From 1980 to today, it has worked on becoming the best product developer. Not one but a series of great new car models show its progress. The Lexus, the Hilux, the Prius, the Scion, the Highlander hybrid, the Lexus hybrid . . . the record tells us the company is learning how to tame the project risk dragon, and creating a system for raising the odds on the most important projects in its pipeline. (For an update on how recent developments have affected the fortunes of the Prius, see Notes, page 245.)

Toyota's Further Moves to Raise the Odds

Here's a list of the best de-risking moves from the second phase of the Prius story:

- Initially, launch in Japan only (leaving room for improvement).
- Plan for model 2.0 (electronics, panel, more room).
- Launch in United States after debugging (stepping-stone technique).
- Create a distinctive look for model 2.0 (traveling ad).
- License out hybrid technology (to Ford and Nissan, offer to GM and all others).
- Design the business model as carefully and shrewdly as the car.

iPod, Act II

It's the end of 2001. The iPod has been launched to rave reviews for its beautiful all-white design, easy-to-use interface, relatively big (5 GB) memory capacity, and unique wheel control. It has also drawn skeptical derision for its high price at $399. As the jokesters said, iPod "stands for

Idiots Price Our Devices." At the same time, Apple releases its iTunes software—but it's simply a library application for storing music, useful but not terribly innovative or exciting.

With his healthy ego, messianic zeal, and history of success, Steve Jobs makes a delightful target for critics and naysayers, and they settle back in hopes of watching his latest crazy gamble go up in flames.

But it sells. Within weeks, the iPod overtakes the few competing music players (such as a now-forgotten machine called the Nomad Jukebox) to become the leading device of its kind.

Still, Jobs and Apple recognize that they're only one-third of the way to success. They don't allow version 1.0 of the iPod device or the broader Apple music business to stand on its own for long. Innovations follow quickly. (It's the same stepping-stone concept that Toyota used, swiftly replacing a good first-generation Prius with a very good second-generation Prius.)

In March 2002, Apple announces a 10 GB iPod priced at $499. In July, the second-generation iPod appeared with up to 20 GB of memory, a fancy "touch wheel" rather than the original mechanical wheel, and most important, the ability to work with either Mac- or Windows-based software.

Suddenly Apple is reaching out to the PC world, the vast bulk of computer users. Steve knows that he is playing in a new arena now—the world of consumer electronics, where gold and platinum records and blockbuster movies have a universal, not just niche, appeal. Everyone wants an iPod, and Apple wants everyone to own one. Sales surge. The odds of ultimate success move up to 50%.

As the iPod gets upgraded, so does iTunes. By mid-2002, playlist management capabilities have been added to the iTunes software, making it easy for users to assemble their own music collections according to artist, genre, theme, mood, and so on. Behind the scenes, Apple has begun working on a prototype version of iTunes that will facilitate legal music downloading (potentially replacing the legally shaky piracy services such as Napster).

By April 2003, Apple has introduced the ultra-thin, third-generation iPod, which will include memory options up to 40 GB. Raves from early users, celebrity endorsements, fabulous free publicity, and a few hip television commercials combine to help make the iPod a must-have style accessory as well as a gadget for techno-geeks and music mavens.

AP Images/Tony Cenicola/The *New York Times*/Redux

The real upside is often far greater than we imagine.
The expanding universe of iPod products and accessories—
a business with annual revenues greater than $10 billion.

In the same month comes the biggest breakthrough of all: the launch of the iTunes Music Store, an online music downloading Web site run by Apple, built into iTunes software, and offering songs by all four of the major record labels—EMI, Sony BMG, Universal, and Warner Brothers. The interface is easy to use, the content is broad, and the pricing is user-friendly—a flat and affordable 99 cents per track. Apple hopes that iTunes will sell a million songs in the first year.

It sells a million songs in the first week.

What does it all mean for Apple? After several years of having been relegated to a niche computing space, Apple has reentered the public consciousness as an innovator and a powerful force in business and technology. Since the introduction of the iPod and iTunes Music Store, Apple's stock has risen steadily, with the iPod as the primary driver of Apple's revenue growth. The iPod has gone from generating just 2.5 percent of Apple's revenue in 2002 to 33 percent in 2005. As a result, the compound annual growth rate for Apple's total revenue was 34 percent between 2002 and 2005.

It shows what can happen when you bet the company on a great project, and then keep changing the odds until you win the bet.

Apple's Further Moves to Raise the Odds

- Follow version 1.0 with improved versions—fast (stepping-stone technique).
- Reach out to broader markets (Windows).
- Capitalize on brilliant design with celebrity-driven publicity.
- Build a customer-serving infrastructure (iTunes Music Store) to support and enhance the great product (iPod).
- Keep adding capabilities to fuel growing customer demand.
- Design the business model as carefully as you design the product. (For more detail on the iPod business model, see Chapter 6.)

Mars Pathfinder
Changing the Odds on a Shoestring

As a real-world project manager, you may well say, "I can see how the odds can be raised on a single project. But in my company, we don't have the luxury of focusing on one project at a time. We've typically got dozens or even hundreds of projects under way. A lot of them start small. But they all have potential, and we hope a few will blossom into the blockbusters of tomorrow. How can I raise the odds of success when I have to juggle scores of balls at once—and when the resources I have at my disposal are severely limited?"

In this situation, the challenges are even greater. But perhaps there is a way they can be overcome. Consider the example of a project developed within a large government bureaucracy, within strict budgetary constraints, that still managed to change the odds of success.

The Mars Pathfinder, a small spacecraft carrying a little six-wheeled roving computer named Sojourner, landed safely on Mars on July 4, 1997. Designed and built for NASA at the Jet Propulsion Lab (JPL) in Pasadena, California, the remote-controlled Sojourner traversed the Martian surface, taking photos, analyzing soil and rock samples, and measuring weather conditions. Intended to operate for a week, Sojourner outlasted expectations by a factor of twelve, sending back data until September 27, 1997. In all, Pathfinder conducted fifteen chemical analyses, collected more than 17,000 photographic images, made 8.5 million measurements of atmosphere pressure, temperature, and wind speed, and transmitted 2.3 billion bits of information, providing unique and invaluable insights into the geological history of Mars.

This success was achieved despite the facts that Pathfinder used a series of new and untried technologies, was developed under intense time pressure, and cost less than $265 million—one-fifth the cost of each Viking mission. There were several unique elements of the Pathfinder project that altered its odds. They included:

Time compression. The Viking probe was created over eight years; the Pathfinder team was given less than four. To make this possible, NASA scheduled aggressive concurrent engineering and test phases.

Mixed organizational systems. Most engineers at JPL, including those who worked on Pathfinder, take part in several projects simultaneously. It's a good way to keep people busy and productive, but it also scatters attention and extends schedules. JPL assigned a full-time cognizant engineer to supervise each Pathfinder subsystem, living and breathing that assignment and taking final responsibility for its success. The broader insights of the cognizant engineers served to organize and control the work of the hundreds of part-time contributors and repeatedly saved the project from schedule slippage and errors.

Single-string design. Most spacecraft are built with duplicate components for reliability. Pathfinder was designed with just one component for each job. This raised one type of risk, as the craft would survive only as long as its weakest component. But it also made the Pathfinder and Sojourner smaller, lighter, and cheaper. This design strategy caused the engineers to focus intensely on reliability. Throughout development, the team members obsessed over making each part as bug-free as possible, knowing such details could make or break the entire mission.

Brutal prioritization. Like many R&D projects, NASA programs are prone to "mission creep"—a gradual expansion of objectives that makes projects ever more costly, complicated, unwieldy, and prone to fail. Short on time and money, the Pathfinder team was ruthless about resisting mission creep, restricting their scientific and engineering goals to what they knew was possible within the established constraints, and when necessary cutting back on the most ambitious objectives to save the project as a whole. For example, they deliberately used an obsolete chip in the computer brain of the rover, making it "dumber" and "slower" to save precious watts of energy while retaining enough intelligence for the basic requirements.

Breaking with organizational tradition. The time and money pressures of the Pathfinder project forced managers to violate institutional norms. For example, it's standard operating procedure at JPL to design custom components for every new spacecraft and either build them in-house or contract them out. This means that even simple elements usually cost millions. For Pathfinder, selected components, such as the Motorola radio that connected the Sojourner rover to the landing craft, were bought off the shelf. The break with tradition saved huge amounts of time and money. The radios ended up being so cheap that JPL bought thirty different models, then tested them rigorously to pick the best unit, saving millions of dollars in the process.

Raising the odds for your own resource-constrained projects is possible if your organization makes a real commitment to bringing the project in on time and under budget, and is willing to let conventional systems get busted in the process.

REUTERS/Landov

Simple, cheap, and incredibly effective.
Built on a shoestring budget and on an accelerated schedule,
the Mars Sojourner roving explorer outperformed expectations by a factor of twelve.

(For more perspectives on the challenges of managing a complex portfolio of projects, see "Changing the Odds for a Portfolio: MGM and Merck," in Notes, page 246.)

DE-RISK YOUR BUSINESS

A careful study of project histories can provide valuable lessons for what to do and what to avoid. When considering the full array of new projects, (whether new product, M&A, IT, or new business) history offers an almost endless array of examples of project success and failure. (See Figure 1-3 for some of the most notable.)

FIGURE 1-3

HISTORICAL PROJECT FAILURES AND SUCCESSES

ICONIC FAILURES	TOTAL-EFFORT SUCCESSES	SHOESTRING TRIUMPHS
Edsel (1950s)	Boeing 707 (1950s)	Ford Mustang (1964)
Betamax (1970s)	IBM 360 (1964)	Nucor (1966)
Lisa (1980s)	Apollo program (1960s)	MS-DOS (1980s)
Challenger (1980s)	Sony Walkman (1979)	eBay (1995)
Newton (1990s)	Ford Taurus (1986)	Pathfinder (1996)
Boston's Big Dig (1990s)	PlayStation (1994)	Google (1998)
Webvan (1990s)	*Titanic* (1997)	*The Blair Witch Project* (1999)
AOL/Time Warner (2001)	iPod (2001)	YouTube (2005)

There are several questions that can help managers begin applying the lessons in this chapter to their own world of project risk.

1. How many projects do we have in our system? How much are they really consuming (in terms of cash, management hours, attention units, opportunity cost), and how much are they slowing down our most important projects?

2. What is our single most important project? What are its true odds of success?

3. What are twenty things we can do to improve the odds of success of our most important project? How much will the odds increase if we do them all?

Answering the "true odds" question is tough. Here's a simple device to get started. Think about your single most important project and profile it by placing check marks in the appropriate places on the lines below:

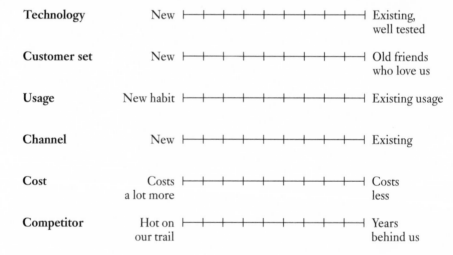

Technology	New	Existing, well tested
Customer set	New	Old friends who love us
Usage	New habit	Existing usage
Channel	New	Existing
Cost	Costs a lot more	Costs less
Competitor	Hot on our trail	Years behind us

If all your check marks are on the right-hand side of the chart, your odds might be as high as 20 percent. If they're all on the left, the odds may be 5 to 6 percent.

The Prius profile, for example, looked like this at the start of the project:

Technology	✓
Customer set	✓
Usage	✓
Channel	✓
Cost	✓
Competitor	✓

The technology was new, as were the customers. The usage was similar, the channel was similar, but the cost was dramatically higher, and the Honda was coming out with hybrids not far behind Toyota. Result: nowhere near 20 percent odds of success, but maybe 5 percent. That's climbing Mt. Everest, not a gentle hike in the Berkshires. But Toyota made it happen, and invented techniques and methods that we might be able to adapt and apply as well.

CHAPTER TWO

Why Do Customers Surprise Us?

Reducing Customer Risk Through Knowing, Not Guessing, What They Want

HAVE YOU EVER been blindsided by changes in your customers? Have you ever felt that half or more of your marketing dollars are wasted? Were the surprises and the waste really unavoidable?

Perhaps the most insidious strategic risk we face is decimation of our customer base by shifts in behavior, preferences, and demographics. These shifts may happen gradually or literally overnight. Either way, they can destroy our business design.

Customers are people—unpredictable, irrational, emotional, curious, and highly prone to change. Customers can't keep still. They resegment themselves from product buyers to value buyers to price buyers and then back again. Their priorities change from quality to price to solutions to style to brand. They get richer. They get poorer. They get excited by and attracted to different styles, different offerings, different ways to buy. They get better informed. They get more demanding. They decide to shop at different places; they start buying shirts through catalogs, jewelry from a TV network, vacations online. They want bigger cars. Then smaller. Then really bigger. Then really fuel-efficient. They pledge allegiance to product brands. Then store brands. Then no brands. They want carbohydrates, then they don't.

Every time customer priorities shift, your business design is at risk. Your value proposition gets a little fuzzier, a little out of focus. You lose a little business from a few customers; they decide to peel away once in a while and buy a couple of items from another supplier. Then you start losing customers altogether. (That's a little more worrisome. But at least you've still got your old reliables.) Then you start losing your most profitable customers, the 20 percent that generate more than 80 percent of the income. A trickle of tiny changes turns into a torrent of departures. And a 1 percent loss of revenue turns into a 6 percent loss of profit.

Customer risk is the most subtle and perhaps the most widespread risk of all. It's also the most unnecessary.

THE GENIUS OF KNOWING 5 PERCENT MORE

How can you take action to prevent customer risk? You can't force people to buy from you. As Yogi Berra once said, "If the people don't want to come to the ballpark, nobody's going to stop them."

No, you can't "stop them," but you can reduce the risk of losing customers by reducing the *uncertainty* that creates the risk in the first place. After all, that's what risk is about—not knowing what's going to happen, what your customers are thinking, what they want, what they will do, what they will respond to. If you could know those things, you could react appropriately with the kinds of pricing, marketing, and service offerings that would motivate them to stay.

This is why the best countermeasure for defeating customer risk is creating and applying *continuous proprietary information* about your customers. It's answering the question: What do we know about customers that others don't? And then using that knowledge to make and keep profitable customers for life.

> *Risk is just a very expensive substitute for information.*

The first step is to develop a healthy fear of ignorance, followed by steps to move your organization from guessing to knowing—shifting the frontier that separates what you know from what you don't know, and thereby reducing the area in which betting (and therefore risk) are unavoidable. Even a 5 percent shift in that frontier can translate into millions of dollars in revenues and profits. Risk shapers save money and improve their odds of success by creating and then using information others don't have to build unbreakable bonds with their customers.

KNOWLEDGE INTENSITY

Proprietary information is a critical component of customer risk insurance, but not always the whole story. For the best players, proprietary information is the cornerstone of a system with several key components. These include:

- Persistently *asking the toughest and most probing questions* about customers, their needs and interests, and the ways in which the company's business processes can serve those customers better. Always asking: "What am I afraid to find out? And how can I find it out today?"
- Having *models or algorithms* that convert the flow of proprietary information into an "aha!" that the company can act on, especially *pricing systems* that align customer preferences and the company's economics so as to maximize the flow of value to customers along with profits to the company.
- Having programs that *organize the most important elements in the customer relationship* (such as customized product offerings, reward programs, and service interventions) so that satisfactory transactions evolve, little by little, into strong, lasting, low-beta, and highly profitable relationships.
- A *customer-centered culture*, inculcated and reinforced through training and incentives, that gives employees the skills and enthusiasm they need to keep doing the right things for the customer and the business.
- A *culture of experimentation*, in which it's customary to test product offers, prices, terms, and other conditions with an open mind, relishing counterintuitive results and "failed" experiments just as much as obvious successes.

The ultimate outcome of building a business around proprietary customer information is the creation of *knowledge intensity*—a way of doing business by which the myriad unknowns that characterize every company have been systematically tracked, quantified, studied, analyzed, and codified so as to reduce uncertainty, enhance predictability, and enable managers to make more accurate decisions than ever before.

How often? All of the time? Nowhere near that often. But increasing the frequency of right actions from, say, 50 percent to 60 percent makes an enormous difference in the success of any business. Even a 1 percent increase can make a big difference. "Getting and working the numbers" is hard, but those who've done it know it pays off.

Knowledge intensity companies create and apply ten to twenty times as much information as their rivals do. And they are always looking for more.

At Coach, the maker of luxury bags and accessories, managers have figured out how to develop and apply customer insights that enable them to track and profit from even the most unpredictable shifts and twists of the fashion business. At the Japanese media giant Tsutaya, the staff have learned to sense how the tastes of their customers are evolving even before the customers themselves do.

Let's look at how these firms are reshaping the risks they face.

OUTDANCING CUSTOMER RISKS IN THE LUXURY FASHION MARKET: COACH

Lew Frankfort has a dream. In fact, it's a dream he's had over and over again for the past few years.

In this dream, he imagines himself at home, but not the actual house he and his wife inhabit in an upscale New Jersey suburb, nor their week-end house by the beach in New York's fashionable Hamptons. Instead, it's an imaginary house teetering on the slopes of a tree-covered hill that overlooks the slums of the Bronx. In the dream, those slums are far darker, more run-down, and more dangerous than in real life. One false step, and the house is apt to go sliding down into the depths . . . taking Lew with it.

Frankfort doesn't have anything against the Bronx. He grew up there, son of a New York City cop and a stay-at-home mother, and he attended Hunter College, a local branch of the famed City University of New York (then tuition-free), which has educated generations of working-class kids from New York's immigrant communities.

But today, as one of the most successful executives in the world, he has a fancier lifestyle. And his company, Coach, Inc., is one of the most profitable and fastest-growing businesses in the United States. No wonder that when Frankfort imagines the possibility of somehow losing it all, he gets nervous. His style as CEO is shaped in part by those early mornings when he wakes up from that nightmare of living on the brink of the abyss. "He's scared of failure, and he will tell you that," says his twenty-five-year-old son, Sam.

THE WORLD OF FASHION is characterized by significant customer risk. It is a world of fads and frenzies, driven by whims beyond reason. The only certainty in fashion is erratic change, the inexorable fact that whatever color or fabric or style is hot today will be colder than cold by this time next year.

What's more, the precise timing of the changes is key to success in the fashion industry. The curve that represents the life cycle of most fashion hits looks like this:

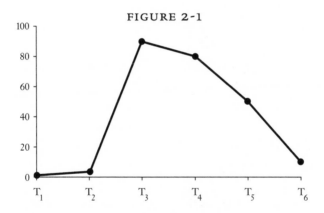

FIGURE 2-1

Between points T_2 and T_3, the style takes off. That is where a fortune can be made. It makes information about the style virtually priceless at point T_2, but ubiquitous and therefore practically valueless at point T_3.

It's a rare company that can traverse this minefield successfully on a consistent basis. Even more rare is the long-established company that can update a set of classic styles and make them as hip and forward-looking as next month's *Vogue*—and stay ahead of the trends, year after year, without alienating its traditional customers.

Coach is such a company. Long famous for its classic women's handbags, Coach has become a $2.5 billion fashion leader in its segments, trailing only Gucci and Louis Vuitton in the $13 billion global market for high-end leather goods and accessories. This happened thanks to the knowledge-based strategy devised by CEO Frankfort and team—a strategy that has enabled Coach to capture and retain one of the largest and most desirable niches in the fashion accessories business, keeping up with and even anticipating the constant shifts in customer tastes.

Coach was launched in 1941 in a loft in New York's SoHo district by a leather craftsman named Miles Cahn, who loved the way old baseball gloves became softer, more supple, and more burnished the longer they were used. Cahn gave Coach bags the same softness, durability, and classic styling as an old outfielder's mitt, creating ladies' purses designed in elegantly understated black or brown and featuring simple brass turn-locks and little other decoration. The bags were expensive but so well made that they were considered an excellent value, and starting in the 1970s, Coach even offered free refurbishing for worn or damaged bags no matter how long they'd been owned.

For many women lawyers, financiers, and executives in the 1970s and 1980s, a classy Coach bag was an essential accessory to the well-tailored suit, the pastel blouse, and the silk scarf or necktie—a way of telling the world, "I've arrived."

Coach had a comfortable niche in a traditional market. Conventional wisdom in the fashion business said that American women could be counted on to buy two bags per year, an everyday bag and one for special occasions. (According to statistical studies, the precise figure, as of 1988, was 1.9.) Coach had its share of that spending. But ironically, the durability and classic styling of Coach products actually worked against the company's long-term prospects. Coach bags lasted so long that women rarely needed to replace them. And while they never represented the acme of current fashion, they also never looked dated, again reducing the need to buy new.

So Coach rolled along through the decades, an icon of good taste but far from an exciting business to own. But in the mid-1990s, the landscape of Coach's marketplace began to change in ways that upset the company's equilibrium.

The change was driven in part by changes in women's lifestyles. The initial feminist push into the workplace was giving way to a world in which women had leadership roles in more industries. As the pressure on women to prove they "belonged" diminished, women's business attire became less formulaic, less mimicking of men's suits, and more overtly feminine. Hard-sided leather briefcases and discreet, subtly styled handbags such as those made by Coach were no longer required. Instead, handbags became fashion accessories, ways to update a look and feel stylish without buying a new wardrobe.

Furthermore, as women's lifestyles became more complicated, the types of bags women carried began to multiply. In addition to handbags and briefcases, there were tote bags, backpacks, weekend bags, duffel bags, clutches, diaper bags, and specialized bags for carrying gym gear and groceries and laptop computers. Women wanted bags in a range of sizes and shapes for activities ranging from an evening out on the town or an afternoon at the kids' soccer game to a Saturday at the mall or a weekend at the beach. By the early years of the new century, American women were buying 3.5 bags per year.

As the market grew in the 1990s, Coach was determined to get its fair share of the growth. In the mid-1990s, that wasn't happening. As women and their needs evolved, Coach stuck to its classic styles, shapes, and colors, and gradually become less relevant to changing customer tastes.

It's the classic version of customer risk: The customer evolves, the company doesn't. It's an invitation to disaster.

Lew Frankfort had gone to work for Coach in 1979. When Sara Lee bought Coach in 1985, it made Frankfort president, and then chairman and CEO in 1995. Frankfort had already introduced major changes at Coach. He'd created a multichannel distribution system for the company, including freestanding Coach stores and a catalog business. He had also begun building a powerful database of customer information, based on a continuous stream of data and a multi-angled vision of customer behavior. This data base would play a crucial role in Coach's risk turnaround.

In 1996, the year after Frankfort became CEO, he hired Reed Krakoff, a young designer at Tommy Hilfiger, to bring a new fashion sense to Coach. The two men quickly developed a strong rapport—to this day, Frankfort likes to talk about how they finish each other's sentences. They also quickly faced a moment of maximum risk.

Lew Frankfort and Reed Krakoff have transformed Coach from a classic brand into a hot young fashion house.

In 1996, Coach's continuous customer tracking system was sending some disturbing signals to Frankfort, Krakoff, and the Coach team. The company's sales growth rate in Japan dropped abruptly, from more than 30 percent down to single digits. This was one of those critical Little Round Top moments where the speed and effectiveness of response make all the difference.

"Fortunately, our continuous tracking and our multiple views of the customer provided us with a way to attack this problem," Frankfort says. "We did a deep dive into our information to get at the root causes of this sudden shift. In particular, we focused on our data on 'new customers' and 'lapsed customers.' We found out why new customers were down, and as to lapsed customers, we found out exactly why they left and what competitors they had moved to."

It was clear that the Coach model had to evolve quickly. Frankfort and Krakoff had to find a way to refresh the product line, make it more relevant to modern women, and give the company a new, more fashion-forward image—while still maintaining the company's enviable reputation for high quality. It also had to avoid alienating the loyal customers who knew and loved the "old" Coach.

Krakoff and Frankfort tackled the problem in stages. They started coming out with small changes, then quickly went on to make bigger moves. In 1998, they came out with the Neo handbag, a new version of a classic Coach design that was lighter, slimmer, and outfitted with more interior pockets. Customers liked it.

The company went on to introduce its second lightweight mixed materials line, Mercer, just a year later. But Hamptons, introduced in 2000, was a real turning point for the brand, not only because of its fabrication—canvas twill with contrasting leather trim—but because it was the company's first true lifestyle collection. Coach was able to present the brand from head to toe, including products from hats and outerwear to handbags and accessories.

The company's next major innovation was the Signature collection, a new line of bags scheduled for introduction early in 2001. Further departing from Coach's traditional all-leather styling, the Signature bags

*The traditional Coach store, like the Coach product line,
exuded understated, classic elegance.*

were made of leather and fabric emblazoned with the letter *C*. The colors were conservative (gray, brown, khaki, and black) and the design was traditional, but for the new Coach it would represent a coming-out party.

Although Coach had tested the move exhaustively, the nagging question remained: How well would Coach loyalists respond to the new look? The company leaders about to make the fateful go/no-go decision must have been nervous, but they pulled the trigger. And the bags were a huge success, confirming that customers were willing to buy a new look from Coach. Krakoff and Frankfort had permission to push their experiments a little further.

They followed the Signature line with new products in innovative sizes and shapes. One major breakthrough was the "wristlet," a zippered rectangular bag just 4 by 6 inches. This new product grew out of Coach's research into how women were using their purses. (Management's constant curiosity about and scrutiny of the customer are probably the most powerful weapons in Frankfort's arsenal.)

Coach noticed that sales of cosmetic cases were rising steadily—faster than they thought made sense. They began asking about it. What were women doing with all those cosmetic cases? The women they interviewed told them that they wanted a small bag (that could fit inside their larger handbags) in which the most vital items could be kept—a lipstick, a credit card, keys, a driver's license, and a cell phone. This system made necessities immediately accessible and eliminated the scrounging through the dark recesses of overloaded handbags. The cosmetic cases worked all right for this role, but women were ready for a purpose-designed accessory. Krakoff listened hard, went to his drawing table, and within a few months the wristlet was born. Introduced in 2001, the accessory was an immediate hit. During its first ten months, it morphed into twenty-five varieties and generated over $4 million in sales. Today, Coach sells over $40 million worth of wristlets in thirty different styles.

In the years since these first successes, more new Coach products have been created in an expanding range of styles, shapes, colors, and materials. Suddenly, pink and yellow and bright blue and green are all Coach colors—not just the browns and blacks and tans of old. Coach stores sell not just bags and wallets and luggage but also gloves, shoes, scarves, sunglasses, even jewelry and watches. In spring 2003, Coach launched the Hamptons Weekend collection, a line of traveling bags made of durable, water-resistant synthetics and displayed in the stores stuffed with beach towels and flip-flops to symbolize the new, more casual Coach style. A more recent innovation is the Madison collection, a line of satin or jewel-bedecked bags that go from day into night. Launched in December 2004, it soon represented 5 percent of store sales.

In nature, evolution often operates by spinning out a startling array of variations to find out which ones will work. Under Lew Frankfort, Coach has been using variation as a discovery tool. Some of its new products may fade after a few months on the shelves. But Coach will have learned which products its customer base responds to. Those designs will become the stars of the company's next-generation product lineup and the inspiration for still more new ideas in the next round of variation, experimentation, and winnowing.

Like the Coach product line, the Coach retail stores have been redesigned to send an inviting message to a new generation of customers.

Coach stores have changed as well. Dark, clubby wood paneling has given way to bright, high-ceilinged stores with wide-open front doors and sample bags displayed on open shelves rather than in glass cases, so that customers feel invited to handle and admire the products.

To help him guide and collaborate with Krakoff, Frankfort has steeped himself in the language of design. His office on 34th Street in New York's fashion district is filled with art books, prints by the likes of Giacometti and Calder, and classic Coach designs from the 1960s. He views his job as a series of creative challenges—to keep Coach exciting as customers change and demand new things.

But the reshaping of Coach is not all about sheer artistry or brilliant, intuitive design choices that come out of Krakoff's soul (with strong support from Frankfort). Frankfort is above all a numbers guy, and he runs Coach accordingly.

Coach occupies the fastest-growing niche in the fashion accessories business—the "affordable luxury" level, priced higher than mass-market products but below premium brands such as Louis Vuitton, Prada, and Gucci. (A typical Coach bag might cost $300, less than half the cost of a high-end competitor's bag.) Cost-conscious customers appreciate Coach's combination of an accessible price point with high quality and a fashion-forward look. It's a new focus for Coach and a promising one that actually enables the company to mitigate its risk level by diversifying its product platform and broadening its customer base. It involves a richer product collection, more frequent introductions, and managing a higher level of complexity.

Here is where Frankfort's passion for numbers comes in. For a risk shaper such as Frankfort, it's not enough to guess what will work for Coach's unique target market. Frankfort and his team have to *know*. Hence he works hard to transmit this passion for numbers to everyone around him.

Coach's top thirty managers are greeted at the office each morning by a voice-mail message reciting sales figures from the day before. (During peak holiday sales periods, the updates come three times a day.) You had better learn the numbers and figure out what they mean before Lew calls. Mike Tucci, Coach's president of North American stores, puts it this way: "You need to make the numbers dance to stay invited to the party."

Coach's data base doesn't include only sales figures; those are simply outcomes. It also includes a steady stream of customer input measurements, as the company constantly looks for the *drivers* of consumer choice. Knowing the surface of the market and how it's shifting is important, but knowing the currents beneath the surface matters even more. Today, Coach spends over $5 million per year on marketplace testing of new products, using many lenses to read the market, including more than 60,000 one-on-one customer interviews, telephone surveys that reach 500 customers at a clip, numerous market experiments, competitive analyses, prototype studies, and in-store product tests. Coach's customer data base has grown to include over 9.7 million households. Frankfort himself visits Coach stores and department stores a few times each week, eager to supplement the bird's-eye view provided by survey data with ground-level impressions straight from the mouths of customers.

Coach constantly looks at its customer base from many different angles, studying metrics such as customer satisfaction, competitive rating, positive buying intent (cross-checked against actual buying behavior), new customers, lapsed customers, price response, response to new varieties of product, and response to variations at the micro level (demand for crimson versus vermilion or blue versus aquamarine). The combination of all these partial views helps Coach construct an incredibly precise moving picture of the customer.

Based on advance reactions to proposed products, Coach frequently alters designs and expands plans for styles that prove surprisingly appealing. (Recently, a new product tested wildly popular relative to baseline numbers. Production plans were doubled.) Frankfort is especially fond of what he calls quick-and-dirty research—last-minute, small-scale surveys that provide on-the-spot confirmation of a strategy or highlight the need to make a change.

In some cases, the results drop directly to the bottom line. One prelaunch survey disclosed that the new Hamptons Flap Satchel could command a price of $328, a full $30 more than the amount that company insiders had predicted would be the limit of customer spending on the item. Tags and signs were quickly reprinted, and sales proved brisk.

Importantly, Reed Krakoff, the artistic side of the partnership, is no self-important prima donna. He buys into Frankfort's customer-centered, data-driven approach to decision-making. "When something doesn't sell," Krakoff says, "I never say, 'Well, people didn't understand it.' If people don't understand it, it doesn't belong in the store." This humility is totally out of step with the big-ego syndrome found at some designer-driven companies.

Coach's in-depth knowledge lets it tailor merchandise presentation to fit the customer demographics at particular store locations. For example, in conservative midwestern towns, the most trendy products might be kept toward the back of the store, while the same items might be front and center in New York, Miami, or Los Angeles. Factory outlet stores carry popular older styles, which are also featured in periodic "old favorites" promotions at department stores.

Coach also uses its knowledge of customer habits to guide its product introduction strategies. For example, research shows that the best Coach customers visit the store every four to five weeks. This dictates the rhythm at which Coach rolls out its own products and floor set changes.

One of the keys to effective use of proprietary information is *data frequency*—having continuous data through constant probes into the marketplace, as opposed to sporadic or periodic snapshots of the moving market, from which the size and direction of customer shifts can only be inferred.

Coach understands these principles of data frequency. Constant communication with customers helps the company turn sharply when market attitudes shift. When preppy styles came back into fashion in spring 2004, Coach had anticipated the trend and was ready with pink-and-green bags and accessories. When Coach management noticed that the new Ergo bag had sold out just a few days after its launch in Japan (where the company's most fashion-forward items first appear), they quickly ramped up production, having recognized sooner than most companies would have that they had a hit on their hands.

Sporadic data = high risk. Continuous data = low risk.

Another fresh insight came in February 2002, when Frankfort noticed a spike in same-store sales growth during a weekly review of the numbers. "What's going on here?" he asked. He requested a more detailed study. Frankfort's instinct is always to follow the data back upstream, so as to find the moment of origin—the key change in customer behavior or attitudes that is driving the perceived shift.

In this case, research revealed that Latina customers were increasing their Coach purchases. Inside a week, Frankfort had ordered an acceleration of plans for a new store in south Florida (one of the country's biggest Latina markets), and Coach began running Spanish-language ads for the first time. Sales to Latin women began to grow even faster.

Coach has taken the greatest risk in its business—customer shifts—reversed it, and created a growth breakthrough. As a result of its direct, continuous, and unfiltered customer connections, Coach has steadily grown in sales, margins, and market share since 1999, significantly outperforming its rivals Gucci and LVMH and steadily gaining on them in terms of worldwide popularity. Since 2001, Coach's sales have grown by an annual rate of 23 percent, while earnings have grown by an annual rate of 40 percent. In just two years (2003–2005), Coach's market share has increased from 18 percent to 23 percent.

Shareholder value has followed suit. In 2000–2001, Sara Lee, in a two-step transaction, spun off Coach as a freestanding company. Since then, Coach's stock has risen twentyfold. By contrast, the stock of LVMH, Louis Vuitton's parent company, increased by 9.6 percent over the same period, while Gucci's has declined by 6 percent.

Coach is also encouraged by growth in particular markets that are key to its long-term success. Take Japan, which represents about one-fifth of Coach's worldwide market. Coach sales there have quadrupled, from under $100 million in 2001 to over $400 million in 2006, and in 2003 the company grabbed the number two spot in that country's market for imported accessories (trailing only Louis Vuitton).

The key has been catering to Japan's youthful, hip market. The average Coach customer in Japan is in her early thirties, several years younger than in the United States. Success among the young in Japan is seen as a bellwether for further growth among trend followers throughout the world. Sure enough, sales to the eighteen-to-twenty-four-year-old market segment now account for about 20 percent of Coach's U.S. sales, up from just 5 percent in 1996. "Our brand now has enough breadth of personality to serve multiple consumers well," Frankfort reports. "At our San Juan store, I once saw four generations shopping together: a teenage girl, her mother, her grandmother, and her great-grandmother. They all had Coach bags. Another time, I visited our store in Woodfield, near Chicago, and I saw a woman clad in mink, dressed to the nines, and a woman UPS driver, both picking items from our product line."

The new Coach demographic is a key element in the company's re-shaped risk profile: "Our current business model is much less risky than before because we have a broader price spectrum, a broader range of items, and goods appropriate for a broader list of occasions—day and night, summer and fall, work and formal events." Now, no matter how customers' needs, tastes, and lifestyles may shift, Coach is ready to shift with them.

But the shift in style wouldn't be working for Coach if it hadn't been accompanied by a thoughtful realignment of the entire business design. To see how the pieces fit together, consider Figure 2-2, which compares the business designs of two types of makers and marketers of luxury fashion accessories, the designer-driven model (such as Gucci or LVMH) and the information-driven model used by Coach.

FIGURE 2-2
Comparing Luxury Fashion Accessory Business Designs: Designer-Driven vs. Coach

DESIGN ELEMENTS	DESIGNER-DRIVEN	INFORMATION-DRIVEN (COACH)
CUSTOMER SELECTION	Top income	Middle to top income
UNIQUE VALUE PROPOSITION	Fashion, brand prestige	Hitting the target of customer needs, monthly refresh of product line
PROFIT MODEL	Enormous margins	Frequency, growing suite of products, share of customer wallet
STRATEGIC CONTROL	Brand	Information and brand

As it evolved its business design, Coach significantly de-risked its business. It cut fixed costs by careful outsourcing; it cut development cycle time by 30 percent; it reduced inventory levels to one-third the level of its rivals. It has developed a broader spectrum of products, purchase occasions, and price points; it can shadow the constant shifts in the market, contracting and expanding product lines as needed.

Most important of all, however, it created a continuous, multi-angled, highly accurate flow of customer information. This flow allows it to see threats early, to craft the right products in response, and to adjust production volumes with extraordinary accuracy.

Coach will no doubt face many new risks in the future. It has designed a business that will help it see those risks sooner, react faster, and craft a response that is uncannily accurate relative to what customers want and will pay for.

Of course, in any business, staying close to the customer is never a one-time-only deal. Customer risk, in other words, never goes away. It just changes shape and specifics. The best you can hope for is to outdance it for a season, which wins you the opportunity to do it all over again.

To his credit, Frankfort has been cautious about expanding too far too fast. He reports turning down numerous licensing deals as well as offers to buy other brands. But the possibility of a miscue when a company is growing quickly is always present.

So despite the success, there are still plenty of risks to keep Frankfort tossing and turning at night. But based on what he has achieved so far, we can include him on the short list of business leaders who are building the world's most knowledge-intensive companies.

COACH'S DE-RISKING MOVES

How many of Coach's de-risking moves could be adapted to your business?

- Create continuous customer information.
- Use multiple customer touchpoints to improve demand forecasting.
- Monitor early warning signals of customer change through detailed sales data.

- Reduce fixed costs (moving from 75 percent insourced in the mid-90s to 100 percent outsourced in 2002).
- Shorten new-product cycle time (releases every four to five weeks, up from twice a year).
- Learn through multiple new-product variations (twelve to twenty-eight per release, up from two to three).
- Shorten concept-to-shelf lead time (eleven months, improved from fifteen months).

TOUCHING CUSTOMERS AGAIN AND AGAIN: TSUTAYA

Like fashion, the media business is whipsawed by constant, difficult-to-predict customer change. In today's world, the flood of new media products—thousands of new movies, television programs, music CDs, books, magazines, video games—is mind-boggling. These products can be broken down into hundreds of categories, large and small, each with a complex, overlapping, constantly changing array of customers and potential customers. There are massive mainstream hits to be deployed and, one hopes, ridden to blockbuster profits—the *King Kong*s and *Da Vinci Code*s and Morning Musumes of the world (the last being a popular Japanese singing group). But there are also countless niche products, each potentially profitable and cumulatively important for generating store and Internet traffic and steadily increasing sales—Italian opera CDs, world music by bands from South Africa to Pakistan, DVDs of independent movies, books on architecture and flower arranging and Swedish cooking and dozens of other categories.

The challenge to media distributors is daunting. Any single store, no matter how large, can only order and carry about 10 percent of the new videos and CDs available at a given time. So picking the *right* 10 percent is crucial to a retailer's success. Pick wrong a few times—by failing to anticipate that a particular hip-hop singer is on the verge of a breakthrough with mainstream audiences and that you'd better stock six times the quantity of his next CD—and you'll find yourself turning away disappointed customers. Keep it up and your store becomes the place neighborhood kids describe as having "nothing" even as your shelves groan with brand-new unsold merchandise.

How could any retailer, no matter how savvy, possibly know what kinds of music and movies and games and books will be demanded next week by millions of customers in thousands of demographic and cultural and geographic and aesthetic subcategories? It's impossible. The only way to know is to stop trying to figure it out and instead let the customers tell you themselves. Which is what Tsutaya does.

Tsutaya might be described as Japan's Blockbuster, Amazon, and Barnes & Noble rolled into one—the nation's premier distributor of entertainment and information, which sounds fairly impressive. But company president Muneaki Masuda doesn't describe it in such mundane terms. Instead, he says his aspiration is to create "the world's number one *planning* company," and he calls the Tsutaya stores "just a platform" for the pursuit of that goal. What on earth does he mean? Delve deeply enough into the Tsutaya story and you begin to understand.

Tsutaya started in 1983 with a single video-rental store. It became Masuda's platform in 1985, when he bought the store and placed it under the umbrella of a new company, which he called Culture Convenience Club Co., Ltd. (CCC). But Masuda's vision for the business didn't take shape fully until an epiphany he experienced while watching the credits rolling at the end of the 1987 Kevin Costner/Brian De Palma film *The Untouchables*. Buried in those credits—but flashing in bold letters for Masuda—was the line "Men's suits by Giorgio Armani." Masuda had earlier been a fashion-industry executive, and in the 1980s, he says, Armani was "like a god" for him. The link between the Italian designer and fashion arbiter and a popular gangster flick launched a series of fruitful ruminations for Masuda.

Movies, he realized, had a crucial role to play in modern life. In a Japan that (like much of the developed world) was awash with material goods, mere products were no longer a source of meaning or satisfaction for most people. Now they wanted something more: freedom, choice, individual expression, all culminating in that vague yet powerful totality we call *lifestyle*. And where would a person go to learn about lifestyles and perhaps to pick one out for himself or herself? The movies, of course, where the stars, sets, costumes, cars, music, and images combine to create worlds of varying styles—compelling, seductive, unique. Or if not the movies, then the worlds of television or music or magazines or books— all repositories of culture where the richness and variety of contemporary

On the trail of the customer.
Muneaki Masuda, the former fashion-industry executive,
turned a video-store chain into Japan's most deeply knowledgeable
marketer of consumer goods and services.

life find their fullest expression and are made available for anyone to enjoy and emulate.

CCC, then, could be more than just a video store. It could be a wide-
ranging cultural source, its popularity driven by its understanding of
customers and of the deep longing for style embodied in their movie
rentals and other media choices.

It was a grandiose vision, but one that needed to be rooted in business
practicalities. Masuda set about building CCC in workmanlike fashion.
Over the following decade, the Tsutaya chain expanded rapidly, mainly
through franchising. In keeping with what he envisioned as the company's broad cultural mandate, Masuda also introduced and expanded
new product lines in the stores—music CDs, books, magazines, and
video games. Tsutaya, he decided, would be a "multi-package" store offering all kinds of media products. It would also be a "multi-use" store,
where products could be bought, rented, or sold (used CDs and videos
are part of Tsutaya's inventory). At the time, there was no other chain of
media stores offering such a breadth of products and services in Japan.

In those early years, Tsutaya's risk story was simple: The company,
which had started on a shoestring, had to generate enough cash to stay
afloat, while avoiding entanglement in price wars with older, larger com-

petitive chains. Masuda employed a simple technique to stay under the competitive radar: He launched new stores under a variety of names, thereby disguising their connection with CCC. Only after the chain had grown to the survivable size of around 300 stores did he consolidate them all under the Tsutaya banner.

In the late 1990s, as Masuda continued to explore the implications of his cultural vision, he made a misstep. He decided to extend his company's scope up the value chain to include the production and broadcasting of video content. In 1996, CCC invested in digital satellite broadcaster DirecTV, and Masuda became president of Japan's DirecTV subsidiary.

The investment never worked. DirecTV struggled with stiff competition for the Japanese market from other satellite companies, and Masuda disagreed over strategy with other corporate shareholders. By 1999, Masuda had left DirecTV, and CCC sold its holdings in the company.

Many other executives, in Japan or anywhere, would have withdrawn into private life and licked their wounds. Masuda could also have simply retrenched, resuming his efforts to expand the store chain and drastically scaling back his ambitions. Instead, he turned the setback into a springboard for opportunity.

During his three years of struggle to make the satellite TV venture profitable, a newer technology for distributing cultural content had emerged—the Internet. For a time, like many other businesspeople, Masuda watched the Internet cautiously, uncertain whether its appeal would be broad and truly lasting.

Then, in the autumn of 1998, another risk moment occurred, and another epiphany struck. This time, it came through a periodic survey of Tsutaya customers. When the responses to a routine question about what new services customers would like to have available were tallied, Masuda and his team were stunned to find that fully 48 percent had asked for Internet-based options—the ability to scan Tsutaya inventory and order products online, for example.

The customers were sending a clear signal: The Internet mattered to them. That meant it mattered to Masuda. And when the DirecTV deal collapsed, he quickly turned his attention to take advantage of the new medium. Masuda redeployed his twenty team members who had worked on DirecTV to create a new venture called Tsutaya Online (TOL).

It would be an Internet-based organization designed to expand the business potential of the Tsutaya store chain through the power of digital data.

TOL was launched in July 1999, and it ushered in a new phase of development for the Japanese culture giant. Masuda would use the combined power of proprietary information and the Internet to combat the single greatest risk his now-large media company faced: customer risk due to the volatility of tastes in movies, music, and books.

By 1999, the Tsutaya store chain already had a large customer base. As with America's Blockbuster, customers needed a membership card to rent videos at Tsutaya, and the membership scheme had given CCC access to a rich trove of information about individuals' buying habits and tastes. Beginning in the late 1980s, the company had been among the first to invest in technology for managing and mining customer data, beginning with a point-of-sale system to allow headquarters to track inventory and sales patterns across the entire chain. (Masuda had read a book on computing, learned that information costs would plummet over time, and said, "We've just got to do this.") Each time a customer buys a product from Tsutaya, the purchase is recorded and transmitted to a company-wide database for analysis by the marketing division: Who is buying? Where is she buying? When is she buying? What is she buying? And (by extrapolation) what will she probably buy next?

Initially, Tsutaya used its customer data much as other sophisticated retailers do—to improve its demand forecasting, which allowed the stores to increase sales in specific product categories and to reduce the levels of unsold inventory. The creation of TOL—Masuda's second business platform, after the Tsutaya store chain—turned the company's already rich database into a source of new and deeper connections with customers.

It started simply enough, with a Web site that could keep consumers posted on the latest entertainment news while serving as a convenient communications channel between CCC and the members of the Tsutaya store chain. Over time, it has dramatically expanded in usefulness and reach, going mobile by becoming part of the cell phone–based DoCoMo network (i-mode), wildly popular among Japan's young "thumb generation"—millions of kids who go nowhere without portable access to their friends and their favorite Web sites, including TOL. Today, there are over 10 million registered TOL members, of whom 40 percent use i-mode as their chief link to CCC.

Here are some of the ways CCC uses TOL to bring greater "culture convenience" to its customers—even as they create greater efficiencies and a more powerful flow of proprietary information for CCC:

• *Online shopping, product reservations, and checking availability of products at Tsutaya stores.* When you hear about a hot new record or movie, you can ping TOL on your PC or phone and have your local Tsutaya store hold a copy for you. The system increases store traffic, boosts customer loyalty, and saves in-store personnel time and energy. It also provides Tsutaya with a nationwide early warning network that alerts the company whenever a groundswell of interest in a particular artist or product is building, making out-of-stock sales losses virtually obsolete.

• *Mail-magas—e-mail magazines sent by Tsutaya to mobile phones or PCs.* There are dozens of different *mail-magas,* each focused on a particular artist or movie, music, or video game category. Visit TOL, sign up to become a Tsutaya member, and pick the *mail-magas* you want to receive. TOL sends out 100 million of them every month. The result is a constant stream of new-product information to avid fans and customers—and a steady flow of data to Tsutaya about which culture categories are growing, shrinking, and changing over time.

• *Keitai coupons, sent regularly to i-mode cell phone users.* If you're a Tsutaya member, you'll get these electronic coupons on a regular basis, providing you with a discount on movies, music, or books that fit your interests. No physical coupon to print out or lose—just show your i-mode cell phone screen to the clerk behind the Tsutaya counter and claim your discount. About 100,000 people use the coupons at Tsutaya stores every month. They like the savings. What's in it for the company? A powerful inoculation against customer risk. Tsutaya finds its coupon users shop 22 percent more frequently and spend 7 percent more than customers without coupons.

• *Tsutaya Online recommendations.* TOL combines online and offline data to offer specific video, music, and book recommendations based on a customer's past purchases. Thanks to an extensive series of marketing experiments, including one that analyzed comments from

1,500 Tsutaya members to identify forty-seven unique movie factors, TOL is more precise than other attempts at creating media recommendation engines. It can differentiate, for example, between customers who like grisly war movies and those who prefer less gory battle scenes. These recommendations are so accurate that they now drive over 60 percent of TOL's sales.

TOL is a great tool, but much of its power lies in the interaction between CCC's online and offline platforms. It's one of the relatively rare instances when the promised synergies of click-and-mortar retailing have actually been realized. Tsutaya collects information about its customers both online and offline, giving it an unusual 360-degree perspective on the market.

Even more unusual, parent company CCC actually *uses* the flood of data thus generated to inform its business decisions, to plan for everything from purchases to store-specific-merchandise assortment to special promotions. Far more typical is for company executives to let such information accumulate for want of a strategic sense of its importance and a practical knowledge of how to deploy it. It's a paradox: Media companies are data-rich but application-poor. Muneaki Masuda is one of the few executives in the worlds of video, music, and other forms of entertainment and information to recognize how crucial this approach could be for the media business, and how to actually make it work.

From 5 Percent More to 1,000 Percent More

Tsutaya's system continues to evolve. It started by being responsive to consumer preferences, getting far beyond the trap of "average customer" thinking to analyze customer *variation*—what does this specific customer value? The result was to reduce the company's customer risk by enabling greater precision both in customer selection and in the value proposition being offered.

With increasing sophistication, the system now provides proactive services that make CCC an even more valuable cultural resource for customers. Favor a certain pop band or singer? Tsutaya knows, because you picked a free subscription to her *mail-maga* and bought her last two CDs with coupons it sent you. Now it will alert you by phone or e-mail to let you know when her latest album will arrive in the store, will keep a copy on hand for you, will notify you about her upcoming concert tour, and will even buy tickets at your request.

People with a serious concern about a nation's culture sometimes get very nervous about the growing power of massive distribution companies such as Tsutaya. One might assume that Tsutaya's system would tend to favor established stars, major record labels, and a few hits, tending to homogenize the media world and, in practice, narrow the scope of consumer choice. (That's actually a pretty good description of how the old music business model worked.)

Precisely the opposite is true. Tsutaya continually scans its database in search of under-the-radar products with the potential to reach larger audiences. It frequently selects such products from the back shelves and promotes them via coupons, *mail-magas*, and store placements. And with Tsutaya having gradually built a reputation as Japan's hippest outlet for movies and music, fans take the recommendations seriously. Little-known movies that quickly vanished from theaters, obscure indie pop groups on unknown labels, and cult music albums with a small but ardent fan base have all found new life at Tsutaya, and some have even broken through to mainstream status as a result.

Being able to manage a vast database of detail about customer variation allows Tsutaya to give artists a second chance at finding an audience, something traditional media systems have been notoriously bad at doing. Of course, the same capability further reduces Tsutaya's risk profile, decreasing the company's dependence on a few mega-hits and increasing its profitability from the "long tail" of thousands of media products that each have small but enthusiastic followings and whose sales, cumulatively, are as significant as those of the superstars.

TOL is the most powerful customer-facing technology deployed by CCC. But the company also uses technology behind the scenes to help its franchised stores grow. The company's advanced systems include:

• Area Marketing System (AMS), a company-wide database system that enables management analysis of sales activity in each market area.

• Proxy Ordering System, a centralized system that allows Tsutaya headquarters to analyze daily and hourly merchandise trends in each store and place merchandise orders on behalf of franchisees.

• Tsutaya Navi, a knowledge-sharing system that allows headquarters to send information to stores and allows stores to upload management solutions on topics such as increasing sales, ordering appropriately, reducing costs, and reducing investment. Thus, Tsutaya Navi allows headquarters and stores to bidirectionally share the knowledge for success.

The use of such technologies to plug customers into Tsutaya's enormous reservoir of merchandise and help them find their way to the cultural products they love offers a real service in today's hypersaturated media world.

Tsutaya's knowledge-intensity efforts started modestly, by learning more about its customers a little at a time. But as the number and sophistication of Tsutaya's tools for gathering and using data have grown, so has the company's relative advantage. Today, by comparison to other media companies, Tsutaya's active knowledge base about customer interests and preferences is ten to twenty times as great. A 5 percent edge over what your competitors know is extremely valuable. But a 1,000 percent edge is almost literally priceless.

Customers are responding to Masuda's customer-centric vision. Here's how one journalist describes the scene at a flagship Tsutaya store:

One recent evening in Tokyo's futuristic Shibuya neighborhood, Tsutaya's six-story store was humming, literally. . . . Packed with a mobile phone rental outlet (now discontinued), a Starbucks coffee shop, rows of listening booths and boxes of electronics, the showcase store combines the messy feel of a fraternity house with the high-tech buzz of the classic 1982 film *Blade Runner*. Young Japanese with variously dyed hair and camouflage pants crowd each other in the aisles as the latest pop music blares from hidden speakers.

But travel a few miles east to a different Tokyo neighborhood—the upscale Roppongi, long famed for its discos, clubs, bars, and restaurants crowded with tourists and foreigners but also home to a series of fashionable new high-rise apartment buildings where celebrities, bankers, and business executives live—and you experience a very different Tsutaya style.

The Roppongi Tsutaya Tokyo is sleek, colorful, and fashion-oriented. The first thing you see is a series of tables piled high with alluring Japanese and Western fashion magazines. Nearby shelves gleam with rows of lavishly illustrated books on art, architecture, design, travel, cooking, cars, and other lifestyle topics. Upstairs, where movies and music live, there are listening stations mostly occupied by languid teenagers sampling the latest American or J-pop (Japanese pop) CDs. But there's also a wall decorated with covers from vintage 1950s vinyl jazz albums (not for sale) and a case laden with artfully themed cross-media product displays: books on the films of Alfred Hitchcock or Steve McQueen, for example, alongside expensive boxed sets of the movies themselves and CD compilations of the soundtrack music. These are upscale goods for the sophisticated denizens of Roppongi, where the average customer age ranges up as high as thirty-five (compared to the usual Tsutaya range of twenty to thirty).

What every Tsutaya store has in common, however, is an intense focus on the customer. Chat with a manager and you learn that store employees are hired less on the basis of product knowledge and more on the basis of "client orientation," and that staff compete to master the names, faces, and product tastes of as many regular patrons as possible. Store hours? At the Roppongi store, they run from 7:00 a.m. to 4:00 a.m.—though the manager admits that the Tsutaya store "in the countryside" where he formerly worked was open only until 1:00 a.m.

The Tsutaya stores mirror the personality of the company's president. Masuda is a retail enthusiast. He loves to talk about the spirit of the Tsutaya stores and is constantly looking for new ways to make them feel even more exciting, captivating, and invigorating. Here's how he explained the quest to us:

> Japan today is an affluent country. Our basic needs have long been satisfied. We are saturated with goods and information. Now we want more from life. Even a seller of soft drinks understands this. You need liquid to stay alive. But you don't sell bottled water by telling people, "Drink or die!" You offer them something that tastes good. It's the same

Offering customers "something that tastes good."
Tsutaya's glittering Roppongi store, designed to cater to the specific interests
of an upscale audience attuned to fashion, art, architecture, music, and design.

with our stores—they must "taste good" to make the customers want to come back. For example, that's why we have Starbucks in the stores—because when you see a celebrity sipping coffee at a corner table, it makes you feel good about being at Tsutaya.

Today, the 18 million Japanese who carry the blue-and-yellow Tsutaya membership card are served by over 1,200 stores. Masuda plans to expand the chain to 3,000 locations—not an arbitrary goal but one calculated using sophisticated demographic and geographic analysis as the number needed to put a Tsutaya store within ten minutes of every man, woman, and child in Japan. Simultaneously, the entire chain is being shifted toward next-generation Tsutaya stores: bigger, more diversified, located in prime retail areas, and focused on lifestyle products and services as well as traditional media products "so as not to be caught up in price competition," according to Masuda. (Like the leaders of Toyota, Masuda is competing in advance.)

But Masuda's lifestyle vision—and his strategy of serving customers better through proprietary information—reaches beyond the Tsutaya stores and even beyond the Internet and cell phone connections enabled by TOL. The next phase of growth for CCC includes a growing network of connections with other companies through the power of that blue-and-yellow T-card. This is Masuda's third platform (after stores and Tsutaya Online), and it has the potential to be the most powerful and revolutionary of all.

Having studied the shopping habits of its customer base and identified areas of greatest cross-marketing potential, Tsutaya started by creating service partnerships with the Lawson, Inc., convenience store chain and Eneos, Nippon Oil Corp.'s nationwide string of auto fill-up stations. Soon the string of alliances expanded: a men's clothing chain, restaurant chains, a sporting goods store, a hotel chain, an airline—two dozen in all (so far) with more than 25,000 retail locations. The Tsutaya membership card lets users enjoy discounts and earn rewards by shopping at all these places. Buy a rice ball at Lawson's, fill up your car at an Eneos gas station, or stay overnight at a Tokyu Hotel, and you accumulate Tsutaya points. Later those points can be converted into more discounts, coupons usable at alliance retailers, or special gifts from Tsutaya.

The customers love it. (One retailer's survey found that customers used two main criteria in deciding where to shop: The first was convenient location; the second was availability of T-points.) The T-card alliance system encourages more return visits (and more risk reduction) for CCC. It also produces meaningful savings and benefits for customers. "This is not about 'capturing' customers," Masuda insists. "What customer wants to be 'captured'? It's about giving customers one membership card to replace a dozen cards from a dozen different retailers, and make their lives easier and more convenient."

CCC is now developing the T-card platform as a new source of growth. In 1988, it set up a subsidiary to handle one phase of this business, a licensing operation to help alliance partners market to Tsutaya members. For example, it might arrange for a free gift for Tsutaya customers—a sample bottle of perfume, say—from a marketing partner. The gift promotes the partner's business at the same time as it further enhances the value of the T-card for customers.

In July 2005, Tsutaya followed up by launching a new ad agency named CCC Communications (a co-venture with Web site producer IMJ Corp.) to create online advertising informed by CCC's wealth of consumer behavior data. In some cases, CCC knows more about its marketing partners' customers than they do. For example, consider the Gusto fast-food chain, a T-card alliance member. By analyzing data on how and when the T-card is used for purchases, CCC can analyze Gusto's sales by store, by menu item, by demographic category, by geography, even by hour of the day. Is CCC in a position to become, in effect, the restaurant chain's marketing department? Masuda only smiles and says, "Someday, perhaps."

With all three business platforms in place, and as the web of customer linkages and the power of the company's database has grown, CCC has prospered. Between 2001 and 2006, average annual revenue per customer rose from $49 to $106. Today, Tsutaya has 1,273 stores throughout Japan, and is number one in movie rentals and music sales and number three in computer games and books (and rapidly gaining on the leaders). One Japanese adult in five (and almost 40 percent of those in their twenties) carries a Tsutaya membership card. The TOL Web site has 8.7 million members and is the most popular destination on the i-mode Internet, with over 50 million page views per month. In 2006, company revenues will be $1.9 billion, generating $120 million in profits and a $2.3 billion market capitalization.

Deep knowledge about customer tastes and behaviors turns the risk of shifting customer priorities into a major growth opportunity.

Muneaki Masuda and CCC have done a remarkable job of capitalizing on cultural trends of the past decade. There's no doubt that Masuda is personally attuned to the interests and desires of Japanese consumers. But it's not a matter of being clairvoyant. As Masuda says, "I could not predict today's social conditions ten years ago. All I did, perhaps, was to run along each age."

Since most companies fail to "run along each age" and instead lag behind, that modest achievement has been enough to catapult Tsutaya to the top of its industry, at least for a while. No one's risk story ever really ends. Today, Tsutaya's cultural portal business is at yet another crossroads. The new inflection point is the sudden rise of digital distribution to a position of dominance in the media industry. Radio podcasts, movie and TV downloads, and digital book distribution are poised to make the same breakthroughs digital music made three years ago. Where will this leave CCC?

The Tsutaya retail stores will continue to play a significant role in CCC's business. Young people have always liked getting together someplace colorful and loud, and as Masuda himself says, "I can meet you at the Tsutaya store—I can't meet you online."

As for the digital spaces where most media buying will take place in the future, Tsutaya is as well positioned as any company to occupy them. TOL and all its subsidiary technologies—*mail-magas*, *keitai* coupons, and the rest—give Tsutaya a huge head start in finding, understanding, and serving media customers, at least in Japan.

Just as Coach expanded its offer, Tsutaya de-risked its business by expanding its offer to cover a broader spectrum of its customers' needs. As their preferences changed, Tsutaya could move with them.

And as with Coach, the key actor in Tsutaya's de-risking is continuous, proprietary information flow. Information flow helps avoid excess inventories and stockouts, delivers the right mix to every store in the system, and gives early signals of shifts in customers' tastes, allowing Tsutaya to shift with them or even slightly ahead of them.

Other major risks come from a different direction. Ask Masuda about the future risks his company faces, and he comes up with a surprising answer: "The main risks we face are internal." CCC's future growth, Masuda worries, may be limited by two factors. One is technological: Can the complex IT systems that have fueled much of CCC's success continue to expand and adapt to an ever more complex array of needs and partner relationships, all while protecting the privacy rights of customers? "If we lose control of our customer information, we are in big trouble," Masuda says. It's an issue he and his team are working on continually.

The second factor is people. Masuda likes to complain, with a laugh, "I have a great vision for this company. The trouble is that no one else here understands it!" He is joking—but not really. CCC is built on a unique, customer-centric idea focused on cultural and lifestyle aspirations and given tangible form in an array of swiftly changing, continually analyzed data about consumer behaviors, which provide the company and its marketing partners with new methods of creating value for customers. It's a powerful concept, but conveying it clearly to a growing list of Tsutaya store franchisees is a huge challenge. Raising a generation of leaders who will be prepared to implement the vision through future growth, including possible overseas expansion, is an even bigger challenge. "Our people must understand our vision—not just intellectually, but internally as well," Masuda says.

So like the leaders of Toyota, Masuda isn't taking any victory laps. "We've come a long way," he says. "But we have much, much more to do."

Tsutaya's De-Risking Moves

How many of the de-risking moves employed by Tsutaya could be adopted by your business? Here's a list of some of the most powerful moves to consider.

- Collect and use continuous customer information from many sources (loyalty partner firms, online and offline sales, Internet contacts, etc.).
- Multiply customer touchpoints through the T-card bonus point system.
- Create targeted customer offerings (recommendation engine, coupons, *mail-magas*, etc.) through deep data dives.
- Broaden the portfolio of product offerings to reduce risk from a sales downturn.
- Optimize product mix and balance by store by analyzing local customer data.
- Reduce inventory costs and lead times through hourly trend analysis and automated product ordering.

Companies like Coach and Tsutaya have achieved extraordinary levels of knowledge intensity, gathering and using proprietary information at a rate dramatically higher than their conventional rivals (see Figure 2-3).

FIGURE 2-3
10X PROPRIETARY INFORMATION

	CONVENTIONAL MODEL	KNOWLEDGE INTENSITY MODEL
FREQUENCY	Annual or less	Monthly or more
NUMBER OF INTERVIEWS/YEAR	4,000–6,000	40,000–60,000
LEVEL OF RESOLUTION	National/aggregate	National/aggregate Regional Local Individual Purchase occasion
EXPERIMENTS	Few	1000s

KNOWLEDGE INTENSITY IN THE B2B ARENA

Coach and Tsutaya have shown that proprietary information can reverse customer risk in the business-to-consumer (B2C) world. Is it possible to do the same in the business-to-business (B2B) world?

In 1985, Johnson Controls (JCI) participated in the auto industry strictly as a maker of frames for car seats, a foam-cutting operation based on low-cost labor that enjoyed scant opportunities for long-term profit growth. JCI supplied only one-quarter of the value of a car seat, and it was disadvantaged in the bidding process for contracts because it dealt with purchasing agents after the specifications had been set. It operated in the lower right-hand corner of the customer's decision-making map (see Figure 2-4). It had little insight into its customers' future plans, and could be undercut at any time by a competitor willing to produce the identical part for a few dollars less.

FIGURE 2-4
CUSTOMER'S DECISION-MAKING MAP

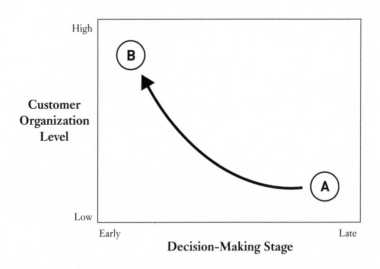

Over the past two decades, JCI developed broad auto-parts assembly, integration, and R&D skills that few of its competitors share. How? Through intensive study of its automaker customers, and using the proprietary knowledge it develops to create uniquely valuable new-product and service offerings. JCI has invested to learn, in extraordinary detail, its customers' internal activity chain, and how those activities tie to the income statement and balance sheet. It has learned where the cost problems are and where capital is needlessly tied up. And it has learned the politics of its customers' decision-making process.

JCI's customer teams operate at customers' facilities to see firsthand the customers' key problems and concerns. JCI also conducts frequent, small-scale experiments to learn what innovations will work for those customers. It does so in a way that strictly limits the costs and the risks of each experiment. At JCI, you'll hear that it's absolutely okay to fail, so long as "you fail fast and you fail cheap." Doing a constant series of these experiments enables JCI to know things about its customers' key issues that others don't.

JCI now designs and assembles not just seats but entire vehicle cockpits. It also conducts more consumer research on interiors than any automaker. JCI's Comfort Lab analyzes what drivers and passengers really want from auto interiors and then translates those insights into new features, such as a TV-VCR unit to be built into the overhead panel of cars or minivans. JCI supplies automakers with millions of these units a year.

Thanks to its application of knowledge intensity, the company owns a bigger share of a bigger market than ever before. From previously providing about $450 worth of content for each car, it now creates more than $1,300. Moreover, JCI's point of contact with customers is no longer just the purchasing department but rather the entire design and engineering team. It has moved from its initial position of "late/low" to the "high/early" position (Figure 2-3, point B) in the customer's decision-making process. It gets an early view of each customer's long-term product plans, and it can see what's coming two to three years down the road. And because of its expertise and its unique information, it can help to shape those plans for the benefit of both parties.

JCI has significantly de-risked its business through knowledge intensity by creating proprietary information on consumer preferences and automaker economics, and by becoming embedded early in the customer's planning process for each new or redesigned car model. In that way, JCI does not have to guess; it *knows* what its customers' future requirements will be.

In the pharmaceuticals industry of the early 1990s, Cardinal Health was a leader in the rapidly growing but low-margin distribution business. In contrast to other distributors, though, Cardinal invested aggressively to learn about its customers' economics, and about new ways to help improve customers' processes and to increase their profitability. Today, Cardinal Health has used its proprietary information to expand its field of operations into a wide range of related services, including automated, patient-specific drug distribution systems; customized, procedure-specific surgical supply packages; and drug formulation, manufacturing, and packaging services for pharmaceutical makers.

In addition to learning the specifics of its customers' economics, Cardinal has thrived by studying its customers' risk profiles and developing products and services to help mitigate those risks. For example,

Cardinal's Pyxis drug distribution technology significantly reduces medication error rates in hospitals, sharply reducing exposure to lawsuits and liability for patient injuries.

Furthermore, Cardinal looks downstream to understand end-user needs. Just as JCI uses its Comfort Lab to analyze consumer preferences, Cardinal runs a packaging technology center that develops proprietary information on packaging usage and value to customers. And Cardinal's cross-functional teams operate on site at hospitals, pharmacies, and other customer locations, getting valuable information on the process and economic realities of the customer's world.

Just as JCI works "high/early" with engineers and business decision makers, Cardinal has earned its way into the high/early position on its customers' decision map. It now works with senior-level executives to define the initiatives that will most improve customers' financial performance.

As JCI and Cardinal illustrate, B2B companies can create continuous, proprietary customer information in several ways: (1) invest the time and effort to know the customer's world—the internal activity chain, the income statement, the balance sheet, and the politics of the customer's decision-making process; (2) have teams operate at the customer's facility; (3) perform constant, small-scale, low-risk in-market experiments to see what's really valued and how much it's worth; (4) create unique information about the customer's customer (as JCI does with its Comfort Labs, and Cardinal does with its studies of patients' needs); and (5) create "high/early" customer relationships. Becoming a vital part of the customer's decision process is the best way to anticipate the customer's priorities and help shape the future for the benefit of both parties.

DE-RISK YOUR BUSINESS

A few questions you can use to apply this chapter to your own situation:

1. How does our company's system for gathering, tracking, and using continuous customer information compare to the systems in place at Coach, Tsutaya, JCI, and Cardinal Health?

2. How many in-market experiments did we do in the last twelve months? What did we learn from those experiments? How much marketing waste was avoided as a result?

3. If we did generate a significant amount of proprietary information, how did we use it to build a better business model? How did we use it to change the following:

- Customer selection
- Unique value proposition
- Scope
- Profit model
- Strategic control

If we didn't change any of these elements of our business model, how could we and should we have changed them?

4. How would we rate our system for creating and using proprietary information? (Check the appropriate point on each of the following scales.)

CUSTOMER INFORMATION FLOW

	1	5	10	
Sporadic	├─┼─┼─┼─┼─┼─┼─┼─┼─┤			Continuous
Mostly survey	├─┼─┼─┼─┼─┼─┼─┼─┼─┤			Mostly experiment
Generalized	├─┼─┼─┼─┼─┼─┼─┼─┼─┤			Individualized
Somewhat connected to organization	├─┼─┼─┼─┼─┼─┼─┼─┼─┤			Completely connected (training, metrics, compensation)

For Coach, Tsutaya, JCI, and Cardinal, most of the check marks are on the right-hand side. It took them five years to get there. But they experienced better profit and lower risk at each step along the way, simply by watching (closely and continuously) what customers did and asking them (repeatedly and in many ways) what they wanted.

CHAPTER THREE

The Fork in the Road

Transition Risk and the Secret of Double-Betting

CUSTOMER RISK is often slow, even imperceptible. Transition risk is more like the Big Bang—a sudden, violent shift that can wipe away most or all of the value of your business.

In business, transitions usually take one of two forms: the emergence of a new technology that renders old technologies (and the companies built upon them) obsolete, or the creation of a new business model capable of radically outcompeting existing models in the same space. When either kind of transition occurs, the business landscape is quickly and dramatically altered, and companies that are unprepared are likely to be devastated.

Every time a major transition from one technology or business design to another occurs, slow-footed or blindsided companies pay the price. Yet it's all so unnecessary. It's not as if such shifts are unprecedented or unpredictable. In recent decades, there have been several dozen major technology or business design shifts (see the list in Figure 3-1). They provide enough stories, statistics, and lessons to enable companies to know the odds of failure, to be better informed about what's likely to happen in their industries, and to be better prepared to capitalize on it.

Transitions, by their nature, are unexpected. Yet, paradoxically, they've occurred so often in history (including business history) that no business leader should ever really be completely surprised to encounter one. Being prepared for a transition, and knowing how to turn it from threat to growth, ought to be part of the strategic arsenal of every executive, because experience shows that you'll live to see one.

FIGURE 3-1

Some Major Transitions
of the Past Fifty Years

FROM	TO
Cable excavators	Hydraulic excavators
Calculating machines	Mainframe computers
Mainframe computers	Minicomputers
Minicomputers	PCs
14-inch disk drives	8-inch disk drives
PC software	Internet software
8-inch disk drives	5.25-inch disk drives
Analog phones	Digital phones
Analog cameras	Digital cameras
5.25-inch disk drives	3.5-inch disk drives
Storage hardware	Storage software
Integrated steel mills	Mini mills
Hub-and-spoke airlines	Point-to-point airlines
Independent bookstores	Chain bookstores
Chain bookstores	Online book retailing
Independent video stores	Chain video stores
Chain video stores	Online video subscriptions
Auto insurance agents	Direct insurance selling
Grocery coffee	Café chains
Conventional gas-fueled cars	Hybrid vehicles

SYNTHETIC HISTORY

One of the problems we have with understanding transition risk is that when we look at the past, we see *one* history. Because we know what happened and have assimilated those events into our view of the world, that real-life history appears inevitable: "How could it have happened any other way?"

It's very easy and very tempting to produce after-the-fact rationalizations for events that startled us when they happened. Listen to political pundits the day *after* a close election. Every single one has a clear, logical, iron-clad explanation of why candidate A edged out candidate B—including all the pundits who were absolutely certain a day earlier that candidate B was sure to win. In the same fashion, when the Dow Jones falls, the analysts have no trouble explaining the factors that made the drop inevitable—weakened earnings expectations, uncertainty overseas, a sluggish housing market. Given the exact same data and a *rising* Dow, the same experts will offer an equally plausible set of explanations for that result—rising productivity, consumer confidence, lower interest rates.

We look backward, see one historical path, and quickly learn to view it as obvious and inevitable. In the same way, when we look ahead, we see one future history. We call it our "base forecast," or the "most likely case," or the "default scenario." While some part of our mind knows that there is always uncertainty about the future, another part quickly gets comfortable assuming that the one future we consider most likely is, somehow, real and even inevitable. That one assumption leads to lazy, careless *non-thinking* about the future.

To remedy this blind spot in our thinking, we need to change how we view both the past and the future.

When we look at the past, we need to see a number of dominant alternative histories that could easily have occurred: The Greeks lost the Battle of Salamis to the Persians, ensuring Asian dominance of western Europe. Joshua Chamberlain's men were routed on Little Round Top, Lee's army took control of the state of Pennsylvania, and the South won its independence. The levees in New Orleans were expanded and strengthened before Katrina hit.

Or in business: The medieval European laws against compound interest were never revoked. The Model T was invented and marketed by an enterprising Russian. IBM decided not to get into the computer business. Xerox successfully commercialized the mouse and the graphical user interface. Apple opened up the Apple operating system to everybody.

What would have happened? How would our world be different today? Which fortunes would never have been created? Which fortunes would have been multiplied beyond imagining?

For a comparison, consider chess, the ultimate game of strategy. In midgame, a great chess master such as Garry Kasparov surveys the board and sees a dozen possible synthetic future histories playing out. Identifying the one future history he wants to make real, Kasparov works backwards through the story to identify the single best move he can make right now—the one with the best options and the best odds, and the first step on the particular pathway Kasparov wants to create.

Of course, Kasparov *must* make a move—it's required by the rules of chess. In real life, we don't have to. We can postpone our decision, letting time pass and letting a little more history turn from synthetic to real before we decide. But waiting is a narcotic: pleasurable, habit-forming, and ultimately fatal.

Synthetic History as a Tool for Managing Risk

Habitually thinking about the world in terms of multi-branched possibilities (what Argentine author Jorge Luis Borges called "the garden of forking paths") is a different way of viewing life, one that is incredibly humbling, because it acknowledges the vital role of chance in the history that produced us. As we'll see, it can also be amazingly profitable, because seeing many possible futures is a first step toward choosing among them and then working to make real the future you prefer.

Here is an example from synthetic history—the story of the downfall of Microsoft in the 1990s. If you don't remember when that happened, your memory isn't playing tricks on you. The story that follows blends events that actually happened with others that *could* have happened if one or two key people had made slightly different choices at crucial branching points in history. Just as there have been many possible pasts, there are many possible futures—and the one you'll experience tomorrow depends on the choices you make today.

In May 1994, three middle managers at Microsoft, then a dominant force in the world of computer software, were recruiting at Cornell. Windows 95 was being prepared for a major launch, and most customers and analysts anticipated a launch even more successful than Windows 3.0 in 1990 (the one that helped to destroy all those PC software companies). Everybody in technology wanted to work for Microsoft.

But something else happened at Cornell. The Microsoft managers got to see how the students lived, computed, and communicated. To their astonishment and horror, everything was online—course schedules, course catalogs, student chat rooms, and rock concert schedules.

The software that made it possible to access and browse and use all this easily available information wasn't Windows. It was an obscure program called Mosaic from an equally obscure company called Mosaic Communications Corporation (later to be renamed Netscape).

For the Microsoft managers, life was about the desktop and the Microsoft programs that controlled it. For the students at Cornell, life was about the Web site and the Mosaic program that accessed it. Windows could be on the verge of becoming irrelevant. A perfect trip spoiled.

When they got back to Redmond, one of the three managers, a technology assistant named Steven Sinofsky tried to get his bosses to listen to their sobering, even terrifying story. No one responded. Microsoft's strategy, as Bill Gates had said a hundred times, was Windows. Gates had the whole organization focused on it. There weren't any attention units left over for anything else.

In a last-ditch effort, Sinofsky sent an e-mail with the subject line "Cornell is wired" to Gates and the other technical staff at Microsoft. In the most urgent terms, it raised the alarm about the importance of the Internet.

Imagine Sinofsky's surprise when Gates himself showed up at the door of his office just minutes after receiving the e-mail. Surprise turned to shock and dismay when Gates delivered a sarcastic tongue-lashing. "What do I have to do to get you people to focus?" Gates demanded. "It's about Windows, and about doing whatever it takes to get it right. Which is not 50 percent of our attention and not even 90 percent but 120 percent. Understand? That leaves less than zero for us to waste on a bunch of kids at some college in upstate New York and some dinky software company that'll either go under or get inhaled in the next eighteen months." Gates paused. "Am I getting through, Mr. Sinofsky?"

"Loud and clear," Sinofsky managed to reply. Gates turned on his heel and left.

That was the beginning of the end of the Microsoft empire. As everyone knows, within three years, Netscape and a host of other Web-based companies had grown to dominate the now Internet-driven computing world. When Microsoft belatedly tried to get in on the action with its 2001 launch of a powerful Windows browser, it was a classic case of too little, too late. Microsoft shares, which had split five times between 1987 and 1994, never split again. Today the company is worth one-quarter of its total value on that fateful day in May 1994 when Steven Sinofsky first saw that other future—a future that Microsoft refused to see.

DOUBLE-BETTING AND THE LESSONS OF HISTORY

Even great companies can be damaged or destroyed by an unforeseen, unprepared-for transition. But the greatest companies—including, in this instance, Microsoft—have antennae out to detect when turbulence is coming, and they cultivate a mind-set capable of rapid, often violent changes of direction. They also pursue strategies that maximize their chances of surviving even when their industries are torn apart by extreme change. This mastery of risk shaping is a difficult skill to acquire, but it can be the most important strategic insurance a company can buy.

In the real world, everything we described in our synthetic history of Microsoft actually happened, right up to the moment when Steve Sinofsky wrote his "Cornell is wired" e-mail and hit the send button.

That's an important point. When you use synthetic history to track your company's alternative pasts and possible futures, getting the facts right is crucial. What were the real forks in the road? What were the genuine options at the time? What were the most probable competitor responses? What unresolved uncertainties could have changed the landscape? What indicators could have been tracked to reveal changing momentum?

Applying this rule can be humbling, even painful. When you really work at immersing yourself in the realities of a past situation—the information available at the moment; the time constraints under which leaders were working; and, above all, the psychological, organizational,

> *In synthetic history, imagination matters, but knowledge of the facts matters more.*

and social pressures they faced ("What will people think?")—you may well be forced to admit that under those circumstances, you might have made exactly the same mistakes your predecessors made.

But that's part of the value of synthetic history. Living through those kinds of high-pressure decisions in retrospect is a way of preparing yourself for the similar challenges you'll face next week or next year. You may still make a misstep when forced to decide on the fly, in real time. But having lived through a number of decision points through the enhanced video replay that is synthetic history increases your chances of making the right call when the real game is on the line.

Sinofsky did in fact challenge Microsoft's direction in an e-mail to the boss. But in response, Bill Gates did *not* march down to Sinofsky's office and chew him out for diverting his attention from Windows. Nor did he, in passive-aggressive fashion, simply delete Sinofsky's message after reading it.

Gates read it, and he got it. He understood that Sinofsky was describing a potential Microsoft-killer—that through a fortuitous confluence of good luck, the hiring of smart people, and his own willingness to listen, he actually had the opportunity to witness the moment of origin of a great new destructive force and risk harbinger. Gates's risk antennae must have been operating at a high frequency.

Recognizing the early warning signs of risk involves an extreme sensitivity to the early weak signals that are drowning in noise and that are so easy to ignore. But recognizing the new risk his business faced didn't make Gates's decision about how to respond an easy one. The upstart company called Netscape, which was responsible for the digital infrastructure on Cornell's campus, appeared to be on to something. But Gates had been around the block. He knew full well that most high-tech start-ups, however promising, impaled themselves on their own mistakes in their early years. He'd seen too many great launches sputter in the haze of a half-baked, unconvincing follow-through. The odds were much better than 90 percent that these Netscape guys would crash into a wall of their own creation. Why distract a Microsoft organization that he had spent the last twelve months fine-tuning to get the Windows launch right?

On the other hand . . . these students were living in a different world, in a different way. That world was growing very quickly, not just at Cornell but on college campuses and high-tech enclaves around the country. What should he do?

Fortunately for Gates, this wasn't the first time that a great high-tech company had found itself staring at a scary crossroads. Gates had learned from a great teacher how to think about these painful decision points when a technological or business model discontinuity looms.

THE International Business Machines Corporation was founded in 1914. For a generation, its business was mostly calculators of various kinds—large, bulky, expensive, and essential.

By the 1930s and 1940s, IBM had emerged as the gorilla in its game. Under the smart and aggressive leadership of Thomas Watson Sr., the company more than thrived, it dominated. Watson understood his industry well. He knew that technology was wonderful, but he also knew it was the customer that mattered and the sales force that drove success. Guided by those two principles, his business *stayed* superdominant through the high-growth years of the 1950s.

In 1953, Sperry-Univac introduced the first commercial computer. The early computers crunched numbers just like calculating machines, but they were clunky and expensive and unreliable. IBM's knowledgeable sales reps sneered. But not the CEO's son, Tom Watson Jr. He looked beyond the cost and the clunkiness and saw a potential IBM-killer. He raised the alarm within the company.

This can't have been easy. Just ten years earlier, Watson senior had famously declared, "I think there is a world market for maybe five computers." It's never fun to disagree with the boss in public. It's even worse when he happens to be your father.

After huge arguments and heated debates, Watson junior got his father and IBM's senior managers to invest research dollars both on calculating machines *and* on computers. Think of it as building an ark, just in case those clouds on the horizon presage the flood of a lifetime.

Watson pursued a classic strategy of *double-betting.* It's a large-scale variant on the familiar strategy from games such as blackjack and horse racing where a gambler hedges his bets by putting money on two or more outcomes, thereby boosting the odds of a winning payoff. Or as Yogi Berra said on more than one occasion, "When you come to a fork in the road, take it."

IBM's genes led it to try to dominate in anything it did, and it applied that aggressive attitude to the new field of computers. Within a decade, the computer industry had grown into a real and important business, and IBM was its leader. In 1964, it launched the new IBM 360, which changed the model of computing and would cement IBM's dominance for the next two decades. Or so the company thought.

In the 1960s, an irritating upstart named Ken Olsen came along, created something he called a minicomputer (as big as a refrigerator but one-tenth the size of IBM's mainframes), started Digital Equipment Corporation (DEC), and began attracting hordes of customers. For most of the leading mainframe makers (including the famous BUNCH— Burroughs, Univac, NCR, Control Data, and Honeywell), Olson's refrigerator looked like an inelegant, overgrown toy. Not to Tom Watson Jr. What *he* saw was *another* IBM-killer. He saw that he had to double-bet again.

He did. By the end of the 1970s, IBM was number one in mainframes and number two in minis as well (and nipping at the heels of DEC).

By the early 1980s, IBM was the most admired company in the world. Everybody talked about it (just as everybody talks about Toyota today). Everybody wanted to be like IBM. But few studied it as obsessively as Bill Gates. Gates borrowed his technology from Xerox PARC (just as Steve Jobs had done), but he borrowed his strategy from IBM. He learned how IBM had cracked the "absolutely closed" Japanese market;

how IBM owned the customer relationship; how IBM had come to dominate every segment. But most of all, he learned that the triumphant IBM of the early 1980s was the result not of a smooth march to victory but of a series of near-death experiences.

The French statesman Georges Clemenceau, who helped forge the Allied triumph in World War I, once remarked, "War is a series of catastrophes that results in victory." Bill wanted to be on the victorious side. So for him the single most important part of the IBM playbook was double-betting—the surest way of turning catastrophe into victory. He saw that in the computing world, technology made you very rich, and then it killed you. Unless you knew enough to double-bet.

So double-betting became a core skill for Microsoft. In the early 1980s, it double-bet on PC applications and Mac applications. In the late 1980s, it double-bet on OS/2 and Windows.

Which brings us to 1994, the fateful trip to Cornell, and the dawning realization that the new wired world could be a Microsoft-killer. There might be only a 5 or 10 percent chance that Netscape would win. But if it did, it could cost Gates his whole company. This meant Microsoft had to take the threat seriously. (Statistics show that the chance that your home will catch fire this year is only about 1 percent. Would you go without fire insurance? Most of us insure our homes against fire more diligently than we insure our businesses against strategic risks.)

On December 7, 1995, Gates called together his troops and delivered his famous Pearl Harbor Day speech—one of the most remarkable addresses in corporate history. In a nutshell, the message was this: *The Internet is here, it is everything, and we will build the Internet into everything we do. We will develop the leading browser and we will make* all *our products Internet-compatible, Internet-ready, Internet-savvy.*

The already huge organization (more than 17,000 employees) turned on a dime. Microsoft didn't jettison Windows—it continued to develop products and services in support of the operating system franchise—but it double-bet by investing heavily in Web-based applications. As the Internet grew, Microsoft was able to grow with it. The company not only survived the transition but had some of its best growth years ever as a result. It had turned its biggest threat into its biggest opportunity.

There are two points especially worth noting about the Microsoft Internet story. First, both top executives and middle managers play vital roles in dealing with transition risk. Gates's deep understanding of risk, his knowledge of history, and his readiness to invest in double-betting even when the threat posed by Netscape might have appeared remote were all crucial to Microsoft's success. But Steve Sinofsky and his fellow managers were equally crucial. Middle managers extend a company's antennae to the frontiers of the competitive arena. Through their constant contacts with customers, competitors, suppliers, distributors, and other outside sources of information, they hear about potential discontinuities when it's still early enough to prepare for the shock. So CEOs who aspire to master risk will listen attentively when middle managers are delivering troubling news. The sooner they absorb it, the greater the opportunity to transform it into good news.

Second, the threat of the Internet arose at precisely the moment of Microsoft's greatest power, profitability, and fame—just as the Windows franchise was solidifying the company's leadership position in computing. That's how risk often works.

This is true for many reasons: psychological (when you are flying high, you tend to let down your guard), competitive (the industry leader is always the target for the most potshots), managerial (in a very successful company, everyone is running at top speed just keeping up with growth; no one has time to imagine tomorrow's dangers), and structural (a successful company tends to get complex, bureaucratic, and slow).

> *Your moment of maximum success is your moment of maximum danger.*

It's another lesson for the aspiring shaper of risk: Whenever you feel tempted to relax or even be a bit smug, *that* is the time to be most nervous and to redouble your vigilance.

Transition risk has been spreading from its traditional niche in the high-tech industries to infect a wide range of business types. Over the past ten years, one industry after another has been revolutionized by the emergence of new technologies affecting manufacturing, marketing, customer service, and other traditional processes. As a result, non-tech companies will increasingly find opportunities to use double-betting as a risk-control and new-growth-search strategy.

More Synthetic History:
Netflix Versus Blockbuster

Most important, remember that technology shift isn't the only kind of risk that calls for double-betting. Sometimes the risk involves a combination of business design and technology. When a new business model emerges, smart double-betting may be necessary to save your company. It's a lesson Blockbuster *could* have mastered—but that it learned in time only in the world of synthetic history.

It's 1999. Internet fever has infected countless companies in almost every industry. Some businesses, such as bookselling and financial services, are already experiencing the early stages of an online revolution. Others, including grocery retail, are witnessing speculative attempts at creating new Internet-based business models that will prove, at least for the time being, illusory—remember Webvan? Unfortunately, distinguishing the true revolution from the flash in the pan is a lot easier in retrospect than in real time.

In the home video business, the Internet upstart is Netflix, which is challenging industry giant Blockbuster with an online rental model. Netflix offers customers several advantages over Blockbuster: the speed and ease of choosing videos online (as opposed to searching the aisles of a local store); access to a vast library that includes tens of thousands of movies and other programs (as opposed to the limited selection available at any one Blockbuster outlet); quick, reliable home delivery and return via postage-paid mail (as opposed to having to drive back and forth to the store when renting and returning videos); and, most important, the freedom to keep any video for an unlimited time period (as opposed to the three-day window enforced by the despised late fees charged by conventional rental outlets).

As of 1999, Netflix has just over 100,000 subscribers and revenues of a mere $5 million, as compared to Blockbuster's $4.4 billion. Blockbuster's management takes a wait-and-see attitude toward Netflix.

That is, until 2000. In that year, Netflix takes several giant leaps toward being a serious player in the video rental business. The subscriber base almost triples, to 292,000. Revenues increase more than seven times, to just shy of $36 million. And favorable press coverage is causing thousands of Blockbuster customers to open Netflix accounts every month.

The Fork in the Road

Blockbuster's leaders decide to wait no longer. In March 2000, they announce plans to launch their own online rental service, Blockbuster Online, designed along much the same lines as Netflix. However, Blockbuster has some significant advantages over its upstart rival, including vastly better brand-name recognition, the largest existing customer base in the industry, a network of more than 5,000 stores in the United States, and positive relationships with the big movie studios, for whom Blockbuster has long been a major customer.

To maximize the value of its head start, Blockbuster plans a smart integration of its online and offline operations, giving customers the freedom to move between them at will. An online member who wants to return a movie to the local store is free to do so—and if she spots a DVD on the new-releases shelf while she's there, she can rent it as part of her online subscription. As for those late fees, they are a thing of the past. "Frankly, we hate to see them go," says one Blockbuster executive, "but in the long run, our revenue stream will be healthier and more sustainable, since it will be built on a base of happier customers."

All in all, it's a very attractive proposition. And Blockbuster follows up the launch with a series of additional steps to expand its customer service offerings and solidify its position as the movie rental leader. In January 2002, it begins offering customized product recommendations using off-the-shelf, "collaborative filtering" software linked to its enormous database of individual movie rental histories. In October 2003, it launches an attractive loyalty card program, providing members with discounts on Blockbuster products and services, further solidying its relationship with its customer base.

Blockbuster's moves take the wind out of Netflix's sails. The subscriber growth that Netflix had been counting on never materializes. By contrast, Blockbuster experiences a tremendous surge in members, and by 2004 its online revenues amount to over $2 billion—about one-quarter of the company's total turnover.

Early the following year, Netflix throws in the towel. The announcement that Blockbuster has purchased the assets of the once-promising company merits little more than a few column inches on newspaper business pages. Other stories in 2005 and 2006 grab much more attention from the worlds of media and entertainment, with headlines such as "Blockbuster Leverages Vast Movie Rental Database in Marketing Deals with Hollywood Studios" and "Already Dominant in Rentals, Blockbuster Seizes Lead in New Movie Download Business."

That's how it might have been. Unfortunately for Blockbuster, that's *not* how it was.

As Netflix grew through the early 2000s, Blockbuster's senior managers held back from double-betting. They, like so many before them, simply failed to take the threat of a new competitive business model seriously. "Video rentals are an impulse decision," they said. "Most people aren't movie aficionados with a list of films they want to punch up online. They prefer to browse our shelves and pick a movie for the weekend that way." Of course, Blockbuster was also reluctant to give up those easy, pure-profit dollars from rental late fees. And when the dot-com boom went bust in 2001, that simply reinforced the feeling that Netflix's success might be illusory. As late as August 2002, a Blockbuster spokesperson dismissed the Netflix customer base as "a niche market."

As Blockbuster held back, the numbers of Netflix subscribers kept growing: from 292,000 in 2000 to 456,000 in 2001 and then to almost 1.5 million in 2003. Those growing Netflix legions weren't all serious movie buffs, either. One Netflix customer, who describes himself as a casual movie viewer, describes his experience this way:

> The convenience and service quality are very impressive. I love being able to browse the online Netflix movie library and add pictures to my queue whenever I have a few minutes to spare. I find my tastes expanding because it's so easy to try something new. I still like watching the latest releases, but now I've also started catching up on classic films of the fifties and sixties that I'd never gotten around to seeing. When I drop one DVD in the mail, I find that I usually get the next one from my queue in just two days. And Netflix periodically queries me via e-mail about delivery speed, which makes me feel they really care about keeping service quality up to snuff. Frankly, I can't imagine why I would ever switch back to Blockbuster.

Revenues at Netflix grew steadily, surpassing $250 million in 2003. It was still a modest figure compared to Blockbuster's revenues of almost $6 billion. But it was big enough for Wall Street to take seriously. Beginning in 2003, stock in Netflix significantly outperformed shares of Blockbuster.

It wasn't Blockbuster but Wal-Mart that launched the first attempt to steal Netflix's thunder, opening its own online rental business in June 2003. Not until August 2004—nearly five years after Netflix and fourteen months after Wal-Mart—did Blockbuster announce plans to leap into the online rental market in a move that many analysts viewed as too little, too late.

By mid-2006, Netflix boasted 5.2 million online subscribers, while Blockbuster had 1.4 million. (Wal-Mart's effort made little headway and was shut down in June 2005.) In January 2005, Blockbuster had finally been forced by customer pressure to eliminate its late fees. But because of the huge head start Netflix had been allowed to build, this move had relatively little impact on the competition between the two companies—except to eliminate over $400 million in annual revenues from Blockbuster's coffers.

Today, other companies—not Blockbuster—are maneuvering to position themselves as the next decade's leaders in entertainment distribution. AOL, Amazon, and Apple are all offering online movie download services, with Wal-Mart ready to follow suit. Apple has partnered with Walt Disney to offer movies for viewing on its video iPod device (and, within months, through streaming video on living-room TV sets) and in the first week of availability, with just seventy pictures to choose from, the partnership sold 125,000 movies. And Netflix itself is moving up the value chain with co-production and marketing deals for independent movies, including a fifty-fifty partnership with Roadside Attractions to acquire and release a Sundance romance picture.

If Blockbuster continues to respond sluggishly to new technology threats—in real as opposed to synthetic history—the company may not survive the next couple of discontinuities that hit its industry.

WHY DOESN'T EVERYONE DOUBLE-BET?

At the end of the day, it doesn't much matter whether the risk comes from a brand-new technology or a change in business design that has little to do with technology. Double-betting provides the insurance to protect your business and open a potentially major source of new growth.

Yet the track record of companies faced with transition risk is not encouraging. Most of them did not double-bet. In the last three decades, across numerous technology and business model shifts, the fraction of companies that made a successful transition averages no better than 25 percent.

Consider, for example, the sequence of transitions in computing technology during the second half of the twentieth century. Of all the manufacturers of calculating machines, only one made a successful transition to mainframe computers (IBM). Of the eight major manufacturers of mainframes (including GE, RCA, and the so-called BUNCH), only one made a successful transition to minicomputers (IBM). And out of six major minicomputer companies (including HP, Wang, Prime, Data General, and DEC), only two successfully transitioned into PCs (IBM and HP).

For another example, consider steelmaking. Seven companies dominated the old integrated steel mill business—USX, Bethlehem, Inland, Jones & Laughlin, Armco, National, and Ford. Of the seven, only USX has made a transition into the industry's next phase. As you consider more industries (see Figure 3-2), the successful transition rate is usually no better than one in five.

FIGURE 3-2

TRANSITION RISK: PERCENTAGE OF MAJOR COMPANIES THAT SUCCESSFULLY TRANSITIONED INTO THEIR INDUSTRY'S NEXT PHASE

Mainframe companies	13%
Department stores	11%
Minicomputer companies	33%
Integrated steel companies	13%
Discount stores	11%
PC companies	20%
Home improvement stores	14%
PC software companies	30%

Source: *Oliver Wyman analysis*

We don't have to go back five decades to see how many companies have been saved or destroyed by double-betting or the failure to double-bet. Just the past decade gives us evidence enough (see Figure 3-3).

FIGURE 3-3
A DECADE OF DOUBLE BETS MADE OR MISSED

YEAR	MADE	MISSED
1992	Lotus double-bets on Notes	
1994	IBM double-bets on services	
1995	Microsoft double-bets on the Internet	
1997		Motorola doesn't double-bet on digital
1998		Detroit doesn't double-bet on hybrid
1999		Blockbuster doesn't double-bet on Netflix
2001		Sony doesn't double-bet on iPod

Why doesn't every company facing transition risk employ double-betting as its insurance policy? What stands in their way? Two contrasting stories provide a big part of the answer.

In 1997, Motorola faced one of those critical forks in the road that its synthetic history so clearly reveals. Motorola faced a simple question: whether to stick with analog cell phones or shift to digital. Nokia, which had just shed all of its non–cell phone businesses (lumber, rubber, hotels, etc.) to focus on cell phones, was shifting to digital and doing it very quickly.

Most people at Motorola knew they had to make the shift, but the leadership of its cell phone business resisted. They'd invested too much money in analog (where Motorola was the big leader) and perceived too much uncertainty about digital. These factors made it tremendously difficult for Motorola to double-bet in 1997.

Moreover, by any measure, Motorola was looking extremely success-ful. From 1993 to 1996, Motorola was on a tear. Sales, earnings, and stock price were all growing rapidly. Everyone was productively busy—and when you're really busy, you don't have much energy to think of other things, even if they're the things that matter most. Things were going better than ever. "What strategic risk?" the cell phone leaders must have asked. "We don't see it in the numbers."

So the managers at Motorola who *knew* that they should double-bet didn't raise enough of a ruckus to force the issue. And when you don't raise enough of a ruckus, inertia wins.

Inertia won and Motorola lost. By 2000, Nokia was the world's cell phone leader.

The Motorola story shows again that strategic risk is highest when your success is greatest. That's precisely the point where you are least able to see the risk and least inclined to do anything about it.

Lotus was in a similar position in 1992. After a tough spell in the late 1980s, Lotus was back. Its new version of Lotus 1-2-3 was taking the spreadsheet market by storm, grabbing 70 percent of the global market. Revenues, profits, and stock price could not be doing better. This was ex-actly the moment of maximum risk.

The risk came from Windows. The world was shifting from MS-DOS to Microsoft applications that ran on Windows. And because Lotus had failed to double-bet on a Windows version of 1-2-3 five years earlier, it was in no position to respond.

Jim Manzi, CEO of Lotus, understood what was happening. As insurance against exactly this turn of events, Manzi had funded a Skunk Works effort to develop Lotus Notes, the first major collabora-tive software program. Customers loved it and it grew very quickly. However, in 1992, Notes was still a tiny business compared to Lotus 1-2-3, and the organization strongly resisted putting its efforts behind Notes.

At Motorola, dozens of managers saw the double-bet problem clearly, but the leadership of the cell phone business resisted. At Lotus, it was the opposite: Manzi saw they had to double-bet, but most of the management team didn't. Manzi argued, persuaded, cajoled—all to no avail. People were just making too much money and having too good a time in the current business to think about investing in what was seen as an insignificant start-up.

In the summer of 1992, Manzi organized a series of lunches with each of his company's top managers. At each lunch, he made the case for an urgent investment program in Lotus Notes, and he asked the manager to make a decision: either back Manzi on Lotus Notes or leave the company.

Most left. Manzi had to change practically his entire senior management team, knowing he needed a cohesive group to make the double-betting strategy work.

The new Lotus management team did make it work. While Borland, WordPerfect, and other software makers that had failed to anticipate the discontinuity caused by the Windows juggernaut had lost 90 percent of their value by 1995, Lotus's value rose from $1 billion to $3.5 billion by 1996, thanks to the explosion of interest and revenues created by Lotus Notes.

These two stories illustrate the several factors standing in the way of double-betting. One is *failure to face reality*. The human tendency to turn a blind eye to risks leads companies to fail to act in time. Sometimes the threatened company simply can't believe that the new technology is for real. Louis B. Mayer of MGM said that television would never amount to .anything. Ken Olsen of DEC said the PC was a toy. Hollywood in the 1980s thought that videocassettes wouldn't grow. The music industry in the late 1990s thought the same thing about MP3s. Motorola's executives believed that analog telephony was just fine—who needed digital? This is human and understandable. If you've devoted your whole career to developing, marketing, and defining a particular technology or business design, how can you see its weaknesses or understand how some upstart might swiftly replace it?

The second stumbling block is *misplaced strategic logic*. Sometimes the threatened company recognizes the power of the new technology but wants to avoid the cannibalization of its old product. Unfortunately, this logic often produces the curious result that everyone else invests in the new technology *except* for the threatened firm. It's painful to cannibalize your own business. But is it any better to have someone *else* do the devouring? If you do it yourself, you can at least handle it in a way that optimizes the transition for your people from yesterday's business to tomorrow's.

The third factor is *fear of spending.* The threatened company believes in the new technology and wants to invest in it. But they also believe they can't afford to invest because it's expensive and would blow their R&D and capital expenditure budgets.

Some go so far as to claim, "You can double-bet your way to bankruptcy."

Yes, you can. And you *will* double-bet your way to bankruptcy if you double-bet unthinkingly, without checking to see whether the risk you perceive is a false positive, an apparent threat that isn't real.

> *Double-bet only when you don't know, and can't know, which alternative will win.*

The good news is that you can detect the false threats, usually fairly quickly and cheaply. Here are a few examples.

In the early 1990s, everyone was swept up in cable frenzy. The phone companies thought they had to overbuild the cable companies to protect themselves. But four months of research (actually done independently by several different organizations working from the same fact set) showed that there weren't enough new video applications, that there wouldn't be for years (because the developer community was just too small), and that in any case consumers wouldn't pay enough to cover the cost of the overbuild. Most companies got the message and didn't waste billions double-betting on the cable overbuild.

In the late 1990s, B2B exchanges (online networks for buying and selling raw materials, parts, manufacturing services, and the like) were all the rage. Some were predicting this trend would balloon into a $100 billion business within a few years. Manufacturers worried, and distributors worried even more. But if you'd spent a few weeks doing a fundamental analysis of the B2B exchange proposition, you would have discovered that there were several qualifying factors (such as specs, logistics, exchange rates, contract terms, etc.) necessary for a product to be appropriate for sale through a B2B exchange. The absence of even one would rule out the B2B exchange application. The conclusion: There was no way this business would mushroom as predicted. It didn't.

Webvan, the online grocery-delivery service, was launched in 1999. The concept made lots of grocers very nervous, especially since $800 million of venture money said it was a good idea. But once you calculated the economics of conventional shoppers using their own gas, time, and vehicle depreciation, and determined how much more efficient a stand-alone delivery company would have to be to overcome that disadvantage, you realized that Webvan simply couldn't get there. Sure enough, the company folded in two years.

In every case, it was possible *at the time* (not just with benefit of hindsight) to determine that the threat was false. You *could* know—and you didn't need to double-bet.

PROFILES IN COURAGE

For all the reasons we've cited, double-betting is psychologically the trickiest weapon in the risk-management arsenal. It's almost painfully difficult to pull off. Imagine the conditions within which a smart group of people has to make this decision:

1. You are part of a very successful, financially secure company.

2. Your basic business model has a lot of momentum behind it.

3. Your market is far from saturated; the growth ceiling is many years away.

4. You're exquisitely aware of the operational challenges of running your current business model, and you want to keep your people focused on those challenges.

5. At the time of decision, you don't know and often *can't* know whether the new model will work.

6. By contrast, you *do* know that double-betting will wreck your financial statements in the short term.

7. Double-betting means mobilizing your most talented people, running ninety-hour workweeks (and then some), and operating under conditions of extreme emotional intensity.

So try explaining this suggestion to your boss: "We're going to take our thirty best people and work them to death for the next year to protect against a threat that might not happen." You don't have to work hard to imagine what the boss will say. It's the toughest decision in business to make. That's why double-betting usually doesn't happen.

It takes smarts and guts to push back against the business climate that makes double-betting so difficult to advocate, much less do. But done right, it's the most valuable risk-reversal tool a leader can wield—and often the greatest growth opportunity a company can find.

De-Risk Your Business

1. How soon might your own business confront transition risk? What risks of this kind do you see on the horizon right now? Do they grow out of technological innovations, changes in business model, or a combination of the two? How do you think you organization will react?

2. Create a little bit of synthetic future history related to the business you help to run. Imagine and sketch out a few moves, decisions, countermoves, responses, twists, and surprises that illuminate possible trails you might take in the years to come. Start by looking backward. Think about the last three years, and write out three alternative, completely different *past* synthetic histories.

3. Looking at the synthetic histories you've created, consider the answers to these questions: What were the key decision points, events, actions, and interventions that caused things to turn out the way they did? What role did chance play in shaping outcomes that, in retrospect, appear inevitable? How could things have been different?

4. Finally, shift your gaze back to the future. Write out three *very different* synthetic histories, event after event after event, tracking your business over the next twenty-four months. This one exercise will force your mind more deeply into the future than anything else you can do. Seeing those forking pathways, what decisions should be made differently today?

CHAPTER FOUR

Unbeatable

Surviving the Arrival of the Unique Competitor

T HERE's NOTHING like coming face to face with a uniquely powerful competitor to get your juices flowing. Just ask basketball great
Bill Russell.

In 1956, Russell graduated from the University of San Francisco and
began playing center for the NBA's Boston Celtics. Russell was a remarkable player with a special knack for enabling his teams to win. It was true in
high school and in college, and now it was happening at the Boston Garden. He played for the Celtics during the team's 1956–1957 championship
season and then led the Celtics to championships in 1959 and 1960.

In 1959, Wilt Chamberlain entered the league, playing first for the
Philadelphia and San Francisco Warriors and then, starting in 1964, for
the Philadelphia 76ers.

Wilt was very different from Russell. Russell was 6'10", but Wilt was
7'1". Russell weighed 225 pounds, but Wilt weighed 50 pounds more.
Taller, with a longer reach, and more powerful, Wilt was a defensive machine (he could block shots better than anyone) and a scoring machine
(50 points a game was almost routine for him; in one legendary game he
scored 100). The smart money said: *You can't beat Wilt. He'll kill you. There's
no way to survive in a Wilt Chamberlain world.*

Sure enough, Wilt was named NBA Rookie of the Year and Most
Valuable Player in 1960, just the first of four MVP awards he would win.
Wilt loomed over the league, a unique competitor if ever there was one.
What was Russell to do?

Russell spent a lot of time wrestling with the dilemma posed by his
rival. The conventional wisdom was that nobody could beat Wilt at the
vertical game—he was just too tall, too big, and too strong. All of which
was true.

115

Herb Scharfman/Time & Life Pictures/Getty Images

"I got to his favorite spot first."
The Celtics' Bill Russell denies yet another shot to the Sixers'
taller, stronger Wilt Chamberlain.

As Russell thought about this, he noticed something funny. "How much," he asked, "of the game of basketball *is* vertical?"

Russell started doing some simple calculations. In a typical NBA game, each team takes about 80 shots, so there are 160 shots in all. Each shot takes 2 to 3 seconds. There are also about 80 rebounding opportunities, one for each missed shot. Each lasts about 1 to 2 seconds. All those vertical moves take a total of about 500 to 600 seconds, or about 8 to 10 minutes out of a 48-minute game. The other 40 minutes are horizontal. And in the horizontal game, the questions and the challenges are different. It's not about who can jump higher; it's about what position a player can get to before his opponent does. What position can he bias his opponent toward, to get him out of his comfort zone?

In his book *Russell Rules*, Russell explains what he did with this new insight. "Wilt played vertical, I played horizontal. I got to his favorite spot first. That annoyed him. I covered so that he'd have to shoot from an angle he didn't like." Russell played a different game, a different way.

> *When you can't beat a unique competitor at his own game, invent a different game instead.*

Wilt always scored more points. *But the Celtics always seemed to win.* They took home NBA championships in 1961, 1962, 1963, 1964, 1965, 1966, 1968, and 1969. The smart money said you couldn't beat Wilt, but Russell proved them wrong.

MEETING THE UNIQUE COMPETITOR

In 1962—six years after Bill Russell came to the NBA—Sam Walton opened the first Wal-Mart in Rogers, Arkansas. As with all openings, there were lots of glitches and a few missteps, but the low prices brought people in, and they kept coming.

With every passing year things seemed to accelerate. Wal-Mart quickly learned the secrets of successful retail. Soon they were unsurpassed at aggressive buying, brilliant inventory management, and saturating a county with stores to get an unbeatable cost position.

In the late 1960s, Sol Price introduced a new format, Price Club, that was even cheaper than Wal-Mart. It put a big scare into Sam Walton; someone had taken his formula and beat him at it. After agonizing over it, Sam did what he had to do: he started a new business—Sam's Club—to compete directly with Price Club. It worked. Now Sam Walton had two growth engines to manage. The learning rate just got higher.

Wal-Mart developed many new techniques. It became incredibly good at logistics, at information technology, at gathering and using customer information. In many areas, it *was* the market, which meant that Wal-Mart knew much more about what was happening than manufacturers, distributors, or any other retailers. In 1980, Wal-Mart sold $1 billion worth of goods. In 1992, it sold $43.9 billion.

As Wal-Mart expanded into one county and state after another, competing retailers at all levels across the country felt the shock. First to suffer were local retailers—owners of individual department stores, houseware and hardware stores, toy stores, clothing retailers, and general discounters. When Wal-Mart moved in, even a business with generations-deep roots in a community soon found its customers abandoning the familiar Main Street shopping experience in favor of driving an extra fifteen minutes to the big-box discounter just outside the town limits—all for the sake of those "everyday low prices" on everything from shampoo and paper napkins to jeans for the kids. In a year or two, the Main Street stores were being shuttered.

Next it was the turn of the regional discount retailers—venerable companies such as Bradlees, Ames, and E. J. Korvettes, which had built thriving businesses in postwar America selling tons of goods at just-below-department-store price points. Wal-Mart's prices were consistently lower—not by much, but enough to notice—and the selection was bigger, the stores were brighter, and the inventory was fresher. One by one, the regional chains began to fold under the onslaught of this unique competitor.

By the 1980s, Wal-Mart's impact was being felt nationally. Companies such as Sears and Kmart, which had once dominated America's retail landscape, were feeling the pressure. The closest analogy to Wal-Mart, Kmart, which had burst onto the scene at exactly the same time as Sam Walton's chain, fought back for a while, then went into bankruptcy.

Now the fearsome prowess of the marketers, cost cutters, and logistics geniuses at Wal-Mart had become conventional wisdom. The smart money said: *You can't beat Wal-Mart. They'll kill you. There's no way to survive in a Wal-Mart world.*

PLAYING A DIFFERENT GAME

Target Stores grew up in the shadow of Wal-Mart. The first Target was opened by parent Dayton Company in suburban Roseville, Minnesota, in 1962—the same year Wal-Mart was born. The new discount chain grew nicely through the 1960s, though at nowhere near the pace of Walton's company.

Bob Ulrich joined Target right out of college as a merchandising trainee in 1967. Born in Minneapolis and a graduate of the University of Minnesota, he was a quiet, serious, head-down young businessman eager to learn about the world of retailing. He worked very hard, observed customers closely, and noted what they did and did not respond to. He also learned that no matter how smart, intuitive, and successful you are at merchandising, if you weren't really good at operations, you would never really win at the retailing game.

One other thing about Ulrich was unusual. Every retailing organization has its revenuers (natural-born sellers who live to move merchandise) and its cost cutters (who think costs are the devil and live to trim expenses). Bob Ulrich was a revenuer and a cost cutter rolled into one. This gave him a big advantage over others in his field. If you understand how tough the cost world is, you can really appreciate how powerful it is to have unique merchandise to offer—merchandise that the customer can get nowhere else and that will bring the customer to your store. Bob Ulrich realized that it was in these precious pockets of non-overlap that most retail profits were made. It was a crucial insight that would serve him well when the task of managing the unique risk posed by Wal-Mart landed on his desk.

Ulrich worked his way up the ranks of the organization and became president of Target in 1984. He was named CEO of Target's parent company (then called Dayton Hudson) in 1995. Even as he rose through the corporation and developed his astute merchandising sense, he retained his taciturn, spotlight-shunning midwestern personality. This often worked in his favor. For example, during conferences with Wall Street analysts, Ulrich habitually deferred questions to trusted lieutenants, which prompted much admiration for his modesty and team spirit. To this day, Ulrich is perhaps the least widely known of the world's great CEOs. One suspects he likes it that way. One directory of business biographies—while referring to the "genius of Robert Ulrich"—offers only the following personal data about him: "Family: Son of a 3M executive (name unknown); married (wife's name unknown; divorced); children: two." More detail is available about most people in the federal witness protection program.

But if Ulrich kept a low profile, Wal-Mart and its charismatic founder

Sam Walton did not. By the time Ulrich took the reins at Dayton Hudson, everyone in the world knew Wal-Mart and talked about it incessantly. It had evolved into an incredible economic machine, destroying competitors everywhere. Retailers around the country were desperately seeking refuge from this unprecedented juggernaut through consolidations or other last-ditch strategies.

If Target had followed the lead of some other retailers and simply tried to out-Wal-Mart Wal-Mart—competing head to head on price—its chances of survival would have been pretty slim, probably no better than 10%. But Bob Ulrich had come to understand that not every customer is or even wants to be a Wal-Mart customer. Many shoppers look for different things in a discount retailer. Deciphering those people and responding to their needs might make it possible to play a different game, a game that Wal-Mart might not dominate.

Target had long tried to play its own game. As far back as the 1970s, it was being described as an "upscale discounter"—a discounter with a difference. It found and served a layer of customers just above the Wal-Mart layer and just below the department store layer. This alone improved Target's odds of survival—perhaps to 20%. But under CEO Bob Ulrich, this strategy of "playing a different game" ratcheted up several notches.

One of Ulrich's tactics was to explode the traditional assumption that low price had to mean generic, undistinguished products. Just as Japanese automakers such as Toyota and Honda had exploded the traditional assumption that an economy car had to be poorly made, Ulrich and Target set out to combine discount prices with high style by developing merchandise lines that were not expensive but had flair, chic, and great design—a whole series of qualities that Wal-Mart didn't offer.

This was a path that grew, in part, from the history of Target's parent company. As the owner of Marshall Field's, an upscale department store chain, Dayton Hudson had long valued high fashion as a driver of customer traffic. (The main reason Ulrich always used to cite for hanging on to those grand old stores—until he finally sold them in 2004—was the fashion ideas and contacts they helped generate for Target.)

But great design is also a personal love of Ulrich's. He collects carved wooden masks and figures from Zaire, serves as a hands-on director of the Minneapolis Institute of Arts, and reportedly helped an architect design a Frank Lloyd Wright–style home in the city's suburbs. So the counterintuitive notion of infusing style into a discount store's DNA may have come naturally to Ulrich.

But how to do it? Famous designers don't come cheap—unless you get the timing exactly right. Ulrich wanted to offer spiffy goods to his "guests" (Target-speak for customers) but did not want (and, in a Wal-Mart world, could not afford) to overpay. So Target astutely focused on brilliant designers who were temporarily down on their luck. Remember Disney back in the late 1980s? As the movie studio worked to refurbish its faded image, it applied a motto of "creativity and discipline" to every corner of its operations, including the signing of stars. The strategy was to look for movie stars with great names who had appeared in a recent string of flops and could therefore be signed at a reasonable price. Talented actors such as Bette Midler, Alan Arkin, Richard Dreyfuss, and Nick Nolte soon appeared in Disney pictures. Their careers were revived and Disney created a series of hits—at very low cost. Target used the same approach. Both companies were, after all, in the entertainment business.

When Isaac Mizrahi's financial backers pulled out in the 1990s, Target stepped in with a design and merchandising deal. When Mossimo Giannulli was down in 2000, Target was there. By the late 1990s and early 2000s, Target was offering designer apparel from Mizrahi, sportswear from Mossimo, housewares designed by famed architect Michael Graves, chocolates from Philippe Starck, wines from Andrea Immer, outdoor items from Stephen Sprouse, maternity wear from Liz Lange, bedding from Amy Coe, and distinctive merchandise from many others. The whirlwind of designer names won countless headlines for Target and boosted the company's odds of surviving in the Wal-Mart space to the neighborhood of 30%.

Rather than just choosing off-the-shelf goods by these designers to stock at Target, Ulrich and his product development team worked with them to create unique lines available only from Target. He hired Robyn Waters, a shrewd marketer who had once aspired to being a grain trader in the futures markets but got hooked on merchandising as a fashion coordinator for the Donaldson's chain. (She has since left Target to launch a design consultancy.) Waters made her 3H Design Theory part of every conversation with a Target designer: Head is the need that drives a purchase, Handbag is the value that the item and its price represent, and

Target's flair, style, and exclusivity.
Target has differentiated its stores and its offerings by commissioning
well-known designers to create unique clothing and houseware lines,
and by making a splash at runway fashion shows.

Heart is the emotional magnet created by great design. When all three are maximized, the result is a perfect Target product.

Waters's favorite example is, of all things, a kid's sippy cup designed by Philippe Starck. Here's how she tells the story:

When he first suggested that Target produce a sippy cup on a pedestal that looked like cut crystal and had two handles like a loving cup, the buyers were like, "I'm sorry, but that's not what a sippy cup is. A sippy cup should not be on a pedestal." But why not? I just had coffee with a woman I used to work with at Target. Somehow the sippy cup came up. She still has it. She remembers who gave it to her. When she sets a nice table for dinner for her family, she puts that cup at her little girl's setting. It's this special thing. It's just a $3.49 plastic sippy cup, but it represents so much more.

Target's unique offerings weren't restricted to artsy designer goods. The company also partnered with little-known suppliers to transform local, niche products into national brands. A Target buyer discovered ecologically sensitive Method soaps and detergents in a little store in San Francisco. Today, Method products are sold at Targets around the country. And Target continues to work with big companies to create proprietary product lines just for its customers, such as a collection of all-white consumer electronics created by Sony.

Through this whole process, Target was being run with the heart of a merchandiser but the soul of a discounter. Both sides of Ulrich's personality got a good workout.

Target streamlined its operations, cutting costs by $350 million during Ulrich's first four years in office. Ulrich won a reputation as a hard-nosed manager famous for demanding accuracy, efficiency, and intense competitiveness from his staffers: "Bullet Bob," known for his motto, "Speed is life." All this and chic style too—creativity and discipline. It works. And the strict price discipline helped boost Target's survival chances still further—call it **40%**.

People around the country began to talk about Target. They noticed the anomaly—a discount store with great low prices comparable to Wal-Mart's, but with unique product offerings and a stylish flair that conventional wisdom had decreed could *never* be provided at discount prices. It was an iron law of retailing: You could offer customers *either* low prices *or* exclusive, up-to-the-minute merchandise—but never both. Target seemed intent on repealing that law. It startled people in a delightful way, much as the Japanese carmakers had done.

The buzz about Target began to grow. Under Bob Ulrich, Target found clever ways to stimulate even more buzz. Fun, innovative retailing ideas from Target seemed to hit the front pages every few months. In 2002, Target docked a 220-foot-long ship filled with holiday gift items for sale off Manhattan's trendy Upper West Side, garnering reams of local and even worldwide publicity. In 2003, Target opened a temporary

Isaac Mizrahi boutique for six weeks in Rockefeller Center. In the summer of 2004, Target "Deliver the Shiver" trucks sold air conditioners in SoHo, with salespeople ensconced behind red velvet ropes like those used to control crowds outside the hottest downtown dance clubs. (They sold 1,000 air conditioners at $75 each.) Target bought 23,000 square feet of billboard space on nine signs at 7 Times Square, one of the world's most famous and visible advertising venues. And when a remodeled Museum of Modern Art (famous, among other things, for its collection of stylish contemporary product designs) opened in late 2004, Target sponsored free admission every Friday night.

By 2003, poll results showed that 96 percent of all Americans recognized Target's red-and-white bull's-eye logo, a higher level of recognition than the Ralph Lauren Polo pony. When the good news was delivered to Ulrich by Michael Francis, Target's senior vice president of marketing, Ulrich urged him to track down the remaining 4 percent of the populace and find out what the company was doing wrong. "And he wasn't kidding," Francis says. The fame lifted Target's odds of surviving just a little more—call it **50%**.

Once customers are lured into a Target store by ads or favorable publicity, the merchandise selection usually does the rest. One young woman describes Target as "the only discount store I would go to," and explains why:

> I like what they've chosen for me to look at. Their selection is very thoughtful—they have a good sense of the customer and what she might want. The clothes have cute style and are very of-the-moment—what I call "throwaway fashion," clothes I can have fun with for a season or so and then replace with something new. It obviously works for me, because I always end up buying stuff I didn't anticipate needing.

Another frequent customer, this one a middle-aged mother, emphasizes the experience of shopping at Target:

> I don't want to feel depressed after I've been out shopping. That's why I go to Target. It's brighter and cleaner than other stores, and the displays are neater and better organized. So are the checkout lines. At

Target, there always seem to be plenty of registers open, and the lines are short, but at other discount stores, you never know what to expect.

I guess I'm really becoming a Target fan. Now I usually visit the Target Web site before I go shopping, just to anticipate what I'll be seeing in the store. But once I get there, I usually end up buying a few extra things—the displays are pretty eye-catching.

A significant fraction of Target shoppers turn into proselytizers for the company. Visit the Slave to Target blog (www.slavetotarget.blogspot.com) and you'll meet two self-described Target addicts, a pair of stay-at-home moms who religiously scour the aisles for items ranging from the useful (a water purifier, a baby movement sensor) to the unusual (carnivorous plants) to the stylish (a pink leather laptop carrier with a black-and-white polka-dot lining). Other Target fans visit the Web site to describe their own adventures in shopping at their favorite store.

For Target, flair, style, and exclusivity don't come *instead* of perfect operations. They come *along* with perfect operations. Target's bar code scanners check all items in the store and send signals to warehouses indicating which items need to be replenished. Shelving error rates are monitored meticulously. To make workers' lives easier and their workday more efficient, storeroom shelves are organized with cardboard containers arranged by bar code. The goal is to drive error rates below 3.0 percent. (Some employees are already down to 0.2 percent.)

All employees are graded on service performance through a simple system of green (good), yellow (alarming), and red (bad). When there are too many reds, managers focus on the store to work on the issues, and return at eleven-day intervals until the problem is solved.

Rapid service is another hot-button issue for "Bullet Bob" Ulrich. Target has implemented a one-plus-one checkout standard: It's acceptable to have one person being served and one person on line—but no more. As a result, speed through the line has been improved by 25 percent in the past three years.

Managers and employees huddle every morning to focus on the issues of the day and to promote recognition for outstanding performance. The belief is that "employees are the managers of the brand," and if you don't invest in them, you're not investing in the brand.

Investment means time, effort, and systems. For instance, every grocery aisle has a red phone at one end, which a customer can use to get help finding something. (One frequent Target shopper we spoke to was especially appreciative of the red phone: "I love to use it. It gets people there within sixty seconds—boy, do they come running!") Everybody from shop clerk to manager knows when the red phone is used, how often, and how long it takes to answer the question. Over time, the displays and the signage keep improving so that red phone usage keeps going down.

Throw in the intense focus on service improvement, and Target's odds for surviving in the face of Wal-Mart go up still higher—perhaps to **60%**.

Bob Ulrich is still pursuing his personal holy grail of "non-overlap." Although 70 percent of Target's stores are in markets where there is a Wal-Mart, only 30 to 40 percent of the merchandise assortments overlap. And Ulrich aims to make that overlap even smaller in the future—not just in terms of the goods on offer but also in terms of presentation. Looks and visuals are critical, both to be clear and easy to read for the guests and to emphasize the qualities that make Target unique. Stores are redesigned and updated every three to four years, with specific product categories shrinking or growing in response to changing demand. This is unheard-of frequency for a discounter. But it's all part of playing a different game, in a different way, and creating the maximum non-overlap with everybody—not just Wal-Mart but other retailers as well.

When you ask Bob Ulrich to discuss the store departments he's still not satisfied with, his response is revealing. After some thought, he mentions live plants and automotive products. Why? Because in those areas, "our presentation is not distinguished; *we look like everyone else*" (emphasis added). That generic quality, taken for granted by most retailers (are there really that many different ways to display rhododendrons?), is simply unacceptable at Target.

Ulrich's strategy of constantly seeking ways to look like nobody else has proven extremely lucrative for Target. While discounter bankruptcies have become common in a Wal-Mart world, Target has been growing earnings at 17 percent. For the past several years, Target's revenue growth, same-store sales growth, and earnings growth have exceeded Wal-Mart's.

"You can't survive a unique competitor" is the rule of thumb—and it's usually a wise one. You certainly can't if you play their game their way. But if you focus on creating the maximum degree of non-overlap, if you choose to play a *different* game, you and your customers can do extremely well in a world where other competitors are being defeated by an "unbeatable" force such as Wal-Mart.

What is an unbeatable risk for others turns into a growth opportunity for you so long as you stay obsessed with playing that different game in a different way. As Bob Ulrich has said in answering the umpteenth question asked him about Wal-Mart: "Yes, they are the biggest company in the world, and yes, we feel threatened by them. But, if we do our job every day, there's still a niche and a need for Target."

As Target grows, the company's risk story continues to evolve. One of the chain's major growth areas is the new SuperTarget stores, which include full-sized grocery stores and are broadly comparable to Wal-Mart's Supercenters. By 2005, there were 136 SuperTargets, and Ulrich was planning to open more at a rate of forty per year, representing some 40 percent of the company's projected future growth.

But playing in the notoriously competitive, low-margin world of groceries poses a range of new challenges. Customers shopping for family-sized packages of ground beef or cases of soda or twelve-packs of toilet paper are focused above all on price. And here Target's carefully groomed image of style and flair may be a liability rather than an asset. "Customers don't realize that our prices are low," Ulrich says. "For that reason, the biggest marketing challenge for SuperTarget is price perception in the grocery area."

The solution to Target's current dilemma as a discount grocer with creative pizzazz will have to be multifaceted. Broadening the range of private-label brands (including both upscale and value brands) and boosting their share of the customer's shopping basket are two elements in the company's current strategy. Another is enticing customers to visit Target stores more often—for example, by improving the selection of health and beauty aids, and expanding pharmacy services. The latter initiative is being boosted by a much-praised, unique new design for Target's prescription drug packages, featuring easier-to-read instructions, color coding for different members of the family, consistent and clear new warning graphics, and a host of other small but significant innovations—for example, avoiding the word *once* in dosage instructions, since it means "eleven" in Spanish.

These moves are aimed at subtly changing the customer's perception of Target. The new message: *Yes, Target is still a store where kicky clothes and unique housewares can be found at surprisingly affordable prices. But it's also a great place to drop in two or three times a week for low-priced staples and health necessities.* Navigating this shift in focus—and keeping *both* images vibrant—is one of the biggest risks Ulrich now faces. It's one he'll need to master with all the finesse he's previously demonstrated if Target is going to mount a serious challenge to Wal-Mart in the grocery arena. Pulling it off will surely boost Target's chances for sustained success— probably up into the range of 70%.

The smart money isn't betting against the quiet Minnesotan.

DETECTING THREATS ON THE HORIZON

At any given time in business history, there are only a few unique competitors on the business landscape. (Figure 4-1 provides a historical perspective on some of the dominant unique competitors of the past century.) Right now, the most powerful ones fall into two categories. The first is firms such as Wal-Mart, Microsoft, Progressive, or Southwest Airlines, whose business design has enabled them to sweep through broad swaths of competition, rapidly achieving dominance in one marketplace after another. The second is emerging nations such as China or India, which parlay low-cost labor and an improving infrastructure into a strong competitive force in manufacturing and service industries.

If you create a sufficiently sensitive early warning system to detect emerging threats, you'll give yourself the greatest lead time to manage unique competitor risk.

When a unique competitor enters your business, the results can be devastating. You can lose half your value, or all of it. Just ask

128

Borland, WordPerfect, Ashton-Tate, Bradlees, Ames, or any PC maker, carmaker, manufacturer, or software company.

FIGURE 4-1
Unique Competitors

Ford	1910s
U.S. Steel	1910s–1960s
Standard Oil	1930s
General Motors	1950s
IBM	1970s
Microsoft	1990s
Wal-Mart	1990s
Dell	1990s
Starbucks	1990s
Southwest Air	1990s
Tesco (UK groceries)	1990s
Google	2000s
Progressive Insurance	2000s
Chinese manufacturers	2000s
Indian software companies	2000s

The risk is big, severe, and potentially total—but never sudden. There are always signs. For those who know how to look, the signs, though small, are unmistakable—like the cluster of thunderstorms that drifts over a patch of warm water in tropic seas, which is the point of origin for a hurricane that may drown miles of coastline and drive tens of thousands from their homes. Those points of origin can be seen early enough to change your business design to survive, and thrive.

It's important to continually map the moves of major companies in and around your marketplace. For example, here is the record of how Southwest Air gradually expanded its service area during the last quarter of the twentieth century:

- 1975: Southwest flies to four cities in Texas.
- 1983: Additional Texas locations added plus California, the Southwest, and initial forays into the Midwest. Easternmost penetration: New Orleans. Total destinations: **22.**
- 1990: Further penetration into the Midwest. Easternmost penetration: Detroit. Total destinations: **33.**
- 1995: Initial penetration of northwestern and northeastern states. Easternmost penetration: Baltimore. Total destinations: **45.**
- 2000: More northeastern and northwestern cities added, along with five cities in Florida. Easternmost penetration: Boston. Total destinations: **60.**

This is an unmistakable pattern, one that creates early warning signals and the lead time needed to prepare a response.

The same is true in discount retailing. Any competitor who had tracked the expanding circle of Wal-Mart stores during the 1980s and 1990s on a map of the United States would have been able to anticipate and predict when this retailing competitor would arrive on his or her doorstep. Originating in Arkansas, that circle expanded at a rate of seventy miles per year. Any discount store could have calculated when it would arrive in their business area. Many major retailers failed to do so. A handful, including Target, recognized what was coming and responded in time.

CHANGING THE EQUATION

Another crucial countermeasure is creating non-overlap—places where you can play a different game than the unique competitor.

Target and Bill Russell aren't the only ones who have faced the risk of a unique, supposedly unbeatable competitor and invented a different game to win. Some of the best examples come from the same domain as Target. In a Wal-Mart world, stores such as Kohl's, Aldi, Dollar, and Whole Foods are more than holding their own. Each of these chains has created its own area of non-overlap. Each has invented a different game and a different way to play, and each creates excellent financial results in a difficult retailing environment.

You may not face an unbeatable competitor in your industry (for the moment), but look closely at the companies that have beaten unique competitor risk and how they have done it. They may give you some ideas for managing your own competitive equation differently—creating more non-overlap, inventing a different game, playing a different way, at least in some parts of your business. These are moves that could change your overall risk equation by creating pockets of high return and low risk inside the overall fabric of your enterprise.

TARGET'S DE-RISKING MOVES

Let's take a moment to look back at the moves Target made that have enabled it to thrive in a Wal-Mart world:

- Play a different game: define a different customer base, product mix, brand image, and business model from that of the unique competitor.
- Streamline the system: minimize fixed cost and maximize efficiencies to reduce financial risk.
- Pursue non-overlap: look constantly for ways to differentiate your product and service offerings from those of the unique competitor.
- Get stylish on a budget: partner with high-fashion brands that are temporarily available at reasonable prices.
- Build buzz to get customer attention out of proportion to your company's scale.
- Use technology and rigorous employee training to hone unbeatable service.

A Whole New Ball Game:
Mike Leach Tilts the Playing Field

Bill Russell was one of the first sports figures to divine the secret of defeating a seemingly unbeatable competitor. He wasn't the last. In every sports era, there's an individual performer, a team, or even a group of competitors that are generally deemed unstoppable—until someone comes along, finds a way to redefine the nature of the competition, and steals their thunder.

The latest example is Coach Mike Leach, who has transformed lowly Texas Tech in Lubbock, Texas, into a football powerhouse that competes on an equal footing against richer, more famous teams such as Texas, Oklahoma, and Texas A&M, which can afford far more aggressive player recruiting strategies. Year after year, Leach's roster is filled with players that other teams haven't bothered to recruit. Yet Leach's Tech teams have won thirty-nine games in his first five years (a school record), appeared in five bowl games in that stretch (another first), and have set more than 150 team and individual records.

Results like these would probably be impossible if Leach tried to compete with the major teams on their own terms. So he doesn't. Instead, he devises tactics that most coaches find weird and often infuriating—but which nothing in their training has prepared them for. Rather than striving for a "balanced attack," in which runs and pass plays are about equal in number, each supposedly setting up the other, Leach calls for pass after pass, spreading throws around the entire field and using every possible player as a potential receiver. Rather than trying to eat up the clock on offense, he speeds up the action (Texas Tech once got off six plays in one 21-second stretch against Alabama) using sideline passes followed by quick steps out of bounds to trade time for field position. He lines up the offense not in a tight row but with as much as five to seven feet between players, which confuses the defenders (who are forced to spread themselves equally far apart), forces the opposition's 300-pound linemen to wear themselves out running all over the field, and makes player movement easy for his quarterback to see, read, and respond to in real time.

As a result of Leach's relentless experimentation, Texas Tech teams have posted some unusual line scores. The first halves of their games tend to be highly competitive, with halftime scores like 14–10 or 21–13. Then, as if Leach and his offense suddenly "solve" the defense by discovering its hidden weakness, Texas Tech explodes, often reeling off five or six consecutive second-half touchdowns and winning games going away, by final scores like 65–10 or 75–21.

Coach Leach inspires strange reactions from his counterparts at other teams in the league. Here's how his agent, Gary O'Hagan, explains it:

He makes them nervous. They don't like coaching against him; they'd rather coach against another version of themselves. It's not that they don't like him. But privately they haven't accepted him. You know how you can tell? Because when you're talking to them Monday morning, and you say, "Did you see the play Leach ran on third and 26?" they dismiss it immediately. Dismissive is the word. They dismiss him out of hand. And you know why? Because he's not doing things because that's the way they've always been done. It's like he's been given this chessboard and all the pieces but none of the rules, and he's trying to figure out where all the chess pieces should go. From scratch!

Mike Leach has figured out the secret of beating the unique competitor: If you can't beat the other guy at his game, play a different game instead.

De-Risk Your Business

Here are some questions that can help you to be prepared for the advent of a unique competitor in your own business arena—or to fend off the onslaught from a unique competitor that has already arrived.

1. Does our business design have an early warning system in place to identify powerful new competitors as they arrive on the scene? Does our organization have a forum in which our people on the front lines—salespeople, customer service reps, supply chain managers, distribution managers, and so on—can bring new competitive threats to the attention of our leadership? Do we have a mind-set that encourages people to take such threats seriously, even when they may appear distant or insignificant?

2. Is there a unique competitor already operating in our business space or in any adjacent space? If we analyze the unique competitor's complete business design in as much detail as possible and compare it to our own, what are the most important differences that give the unique competitor its advantage?

3. How can we adjust our own business design to create meaningful differences compared to the unique competitor? What assets do we own that could enable us to offer customer benefits that the unique competitor would be hard pressed to match? These assets could be tangible (facilities, equipment, products, information systems) or intangible (market knowledge, product expertise, brand image, customer loyalty).

4. Most difficult of all, what unspoken assumptions about our business stand in the way of creating a new and different game in which we can out-compete the unique competitor? If we spend time brainstorming the ten facts about our industry that "everybody knows" are true, then examine each one and turn it on its head—the equivalent of "going horizontal," as Bill Russell did when he took on Wilt Chamberlain—which of those ten facts can be changed to create a new business design tailored to our strengths?

CHAPTER FIVE

Powerful, Proud, and Vulnerable

Rethinking Your Business Design to Protect Your Brand

IN THE 1960s, Plymouth was one of the top auto brands in the world. Today, Plymouth doesn't exist.

From the 1930s to the 1970s, the name Pan American symbolized the best of air travel—efficiency, glamour, sophistication. There aren't many of those qualities left in air travel. And there's certainly no Pan Am.

Similar fates have befallen a host of other once-great brands, from Lucky Strike to Pepsodent to Brylcreem. (You can probably still hum their advertising jingles, decades after they fell silent forever.) Just consider a partial list of the well-known, powerful, once-profitable, once-impregnable brands that have plummeted in value or even disappeared (Figure 5-1).

Brands originate as an attempt to escape from risk. Consumers and even corporate buyers like brands because they offer a guarantee of quality. As *The Economist* once observed, "A book-buyer might not entrust a company based in Seattle with his credit-card number had experience not taught him to trust the Amazon brand; an American might not accept a bottle of French water were it not for the name of Evian." And companies like brands because they not only create a price premium, a volume premium, and positive word of mouth but also offer partial protection from competition—or at least appear to do so. At their peak, brands always seem impregnable. In their glory years, the idea that great names such as Plymouth, Pan Am, and Schlitz would simply disappear would have seemed laughable.

FIGURE 5-1

BRANDS THAT HAVE FALLEN FROM GLORY

Kmart	Howard Johnson	Pepsodent
Polaroid	Oldsmobile	Zenith
Cutty Sark	Schlitz	Plymouth
Bulova	Sony	Keds
Maytag	Levi's	Canada Dry
Blockbuster	A&P	Gateway
Pinch	Reader's Digest	7-Up
Norelco	Baldwin Pianos	Brylcreem
Winston	Hawaiian Punch	Wise
Rheingold	Fiat	Pabst

Therein lies the risk. The very strength of a great brand infects the thinking of its owners, leading to misjudgments that are often fatal. Companies overrely on their brands. Thinking they are invulnerable, they underinvest in them, treating brand value as an inexhaustible bank account that needs little replenishing, no matter how many checks are drawn against it, or squander money on "brand investments" that actually do little to support the brand. They ignore or misunderstand the vital interrelationship among brand, product, and business design that, as we'll see in this chapter, determines the long-term value of a brand.

As a result, brand risk mounts—usually in ways that even smart, hardworking business practitioners fail to recognize. Jeremy Bullmore of the WPP Group spoke for many executives when he remarked, "Brands are fiendishly complicated, elusive, slippery, half-real/half-virtual things. When CEOs try to think about brands, their brains hurt."

Brand risk can strike in two basic forms: brand collapse (very dramatic, very clear) and brand erosion (slower, more subtle, but just as costly). Brand collapse strikes overnight, as when a widely publicized problem with product tampering, quality breakdown, or a corporate scandal wreaks havoc with the image of a brand. When managed well, collapse can lead to survival and strengthening (after its cyanide capsule crisis, Tylenol emerged stronger than ever). When managed poorly, collapse can lead to oblivion (as with Arthur Andersen). In other cases, brand value suffers a slow but devastating long-term erosion. And today, such erosions are more common and more expensive than ever before.

BRAND EROSION: THE SONY STORY

To illustrate the process of brand erosion, let's consider what happened to Sony.

When you traveled around the world in the 1980s and 1990s, you'd see the Sony logo everywhere. It inspired a strong set of feelings. The brand stood for the people who'd invented the Trinitron, the Walkman, the PlayStation, and other electronic marvels. The name meant innovation, perfect quality, and leadership. It was number one in the minds of electronics buyers—a name for which you would pay a price premium of 40 percent or even more.

In practical terms, that meant a predictable pattern of customer behavior in response to that Sony logo. Picture a recent college graduate walking into an electronics store in September 2000 to buy a DVD player for her first apartment. She sees several brands on sale, of which the Sony is the most expensive. Maybe she picks a model on her own, or maybe she calls her friends for advice. Either way, the decision is likely to be heavily influenced by that Sony brand: "Might as well pay a few bucks more for the player I *know* will work for the next couple of years."

Multiply that decision by millions of consumers, and you have a major financial impact, one that can be measured and valued. Interbrand, a branding consultancy, periodically produces estimates of the value generated by the world's leading brand names. In 2000, Interbrand estimated that the four letters in the Sony name carried a brand value of $16.4 billion, which ranked twentieth on the list of the world's top brands.

Then something happened. The value premium that Sony products had earned over the years began to dissipate.

Sony's sphere of competition started to change. Sony used to compete with Panasonic, Philips, Samsung, Toshiba, and other consumer electronics makers. Then new names entered the battlefield, including Microsoft, Apple, and Hewlett-Packard. Retailers such as Best Buy, Wal-Mart, and Circuit City began to develop brand strength that rivaled that of Sony and other manufacturers. The same happened with online distributors such as Amazon. Customers began to wonder, "Do I need to pay more for a DVD player from Sony? Probably not—if Best Buy sells this no-name machine, it's probably okay."

As they bent the loyalties of customers to themselves, the retailers sought out new manufacturers eager to demystify the leaders' brand magic, selling competently made goods for very low prices.

Apex is a case in point. This Chinese manufacturer of DVD players didn't need to spend hundreds of millions in advertising. It just needed to make a deal with a couple of big retailers that were eager to have low-price-point goods to sell.

Apex started selling DVD players in 1999, when Sony's share of the DVD player market was 20 percent. Four years later, Apex had a higher share (15 percent) than Sony (13 percent). And Sony's price premium had collapsed from 44 percent in 2000 to 16 percent in 2004.

By 2004, that same college grad wasn't likely to choose the higher-priced Sony DVD player. Instead, her thinking was more likely to go like this: "Look how much more the Sony player costs—$200 next to this $49.99 brand from some company I've never heard of. But my best friends from college got the cheap player and they said it works fine, at least for a while. It might break in a year or two, but then I can get a new one and still be spending less than I would have spent on my first Sony. And two years from now, whatever I buy today will probably be obsolete anyway. I'm going for the bargain brand."

The multidimensional force that was reshaping competition in the electronics sphere applied unremitting pressure to the Sony brand, like a set of steel plates pushing in from several directions. Brand risk intensified, and the erosion of brand value reflected the erosion that was taking place inside the mind of the customer (see Figure 5-2).

FIGURE 5-2
SONY BRAND VALUE, IN $BILLIONS

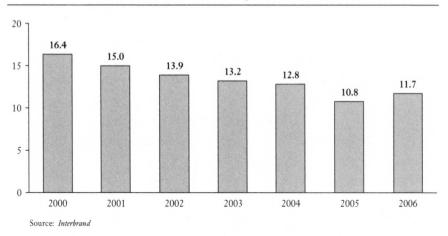

Source: *Interbrand*

Sony was still a good brand, but it didn't seem to be so special any-more. The allegiance of the Sony customer, once one of the strongest bonds in all of commerce, had begun to fray.

FORD HITS THE HEADLINES

Sometimes, as with Sony, brand erosion starts quietly. Sometimes, as with Ford, it starts with a dramatic, public crash. In 2000, Ford had a calculated brand value of $36 billion. Then the Firestone-Explorer crisis struck.

In February 2000, Houston television station KHOU reported on a series of little-known auto safety lawsuits. The lawsuits suggested that exploding Firestone tires mounted on Ford Explorer SUVs had caused some thirty deaths due to vehicle rollovers.

At first, both Ford and Firestone (as well as Bridgestone, Firestone's parent company) denied accountability, blaming each other for the problem. Journalists around the country began to investigate, and re-ported deaths involving Firestone-Explorer rollovers mounted, ulti-mately reaching a total of 271. Finally, in August, a month before highly publicized Senate hearings into tire safety began, Firestone acknowl-edged the problem and took the extraordinary step of recalling 6.5 mil-lion tires, the largest auto safety recall in history.

Making matters worse, documents from Firestone and Ford suggested that both companies had been aware of fatal accidents caused by a combination of tire tread separation and top-heavy SUVs but had done nothing to alert drivers (an allegation that Ford has always denied). The brand images of both Ford and Firestone took heavy hits.

As in Sony's case, enormous pressure on the Ford brand came from several directions, including not only the rollover tragedy but also the decline of the Taurus (whose success had so strongly propelled the brand and the company in the 1980s and 1990s), the downgrading of Ford's debt, and the company's increasingly unpopular lineup of cars, which took increasingly large discounts to sell.

The Ford brand had been the single most valuable brand in the automotive world. Now it experienced a world-class collapse (Figure 5-3).

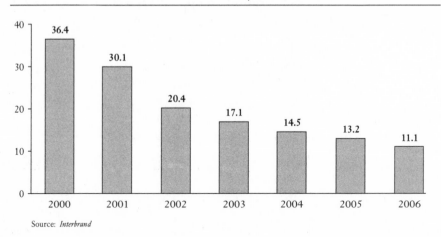

FIGURE 5-3

FORD BRAND VALUE, IN $BILLIONS

Source: *Interbrand*

Will Ford pull itself out of harm's way, or will the fall continue?

TODAY'S BRANDS: MORE VULNERABLE THAN EVER

No one is predicting the imminent demise of Sony or Ford. These companies are too large and powerful to succumb to the series of painful setbacks they've suffered in the past three years. But the companies' current struggles to re-build their brand images should never have been necessary.

Recent years have seen a startling increase in the numbers of brands whose value has fallen dramatically. One recent study finds that of customers describing themselves as "highly loyal" to a particular brand, nearly *half* re-ported they were no longer loyal to the same brand just one year later.

From 2000 to 2005, Interbrand's Top 100 brand rankings included fifty-seven brands that

Even the strongest brands are vulnerable to the insidious and debilitating threat of brand risk— today more than ever.

appeared on the leader board in each of the six years. Of those fifty-seven, some 40 percent experienced significant loss of brand value (examples are provided in Figure 5-4). Brand risk is real and getting more pervasive.

FIGURE 5-4
FIVE-YEAR DECLINES IN BRAND VALUE, IN $BILLIONS

	BRAND VALUE 2000	BRAND VALUE 2006	VALUE DECLINE
Levi's	3.8	2.7	29%
Duracell	5.9	3.6	39%
Xerox	9.7	5.9	39%
Microsoft	70.2	56.9	19%
Ford	36.0	11.0	69%
Sony	16.0	11.7	27%
VW	7.8	6.0	23%
Nokia	38.5	30.1	22%
Disney	33.5	27.8	17%
Kodak	11.8	4.4	63%

Source: *Interbrand*

Today's escalating levels of brand risk can't be blamed on incompetent brand managers. The fact is that brand risk management today has become more subtle and complex than in the golden 1980s and early 1990s. Once thought of as relevant primarily in packaged goods, branding has become vitally important in almost every business segment, as indicated by the explosion of ad spending to build brands in segments such as telecom, pharmaceuticals, retailing, and financial services, and in both the B2B and B2C spheres. There are correspondingly many possible models of brand investment based on complex and highly variable combinations of industry, brand, and market conditions—all of which makes brand risk management a trickier discipline than it was a decade ago.

BEATING BRAND RISK: THE GOLDEN TRIANGLE

Author James Surowiecki offers a useful insight into what has been happening in the contemporary brand universe:

> If once upon a time customers married brands—people who drove Fords drove Fords their whole lives—today they're more like serial monogamists who move on as soon as something sexier comes along. Gurus talk about building an image to create a halo over a company's products. But these days, the only sure way to keep a brand strong is to keep wheeling out products, which will in turn cast the halo. (The iPod has made a lot more people interested in Apple than Apple made people interested in the iPod.)

The point is not that brands are dead or have become valueless. But brands *alone* have less power to create and retain loyal customers than they once did. As long as you think of brands as merely sending a signal about positioning or image, you cannot solve the brand risk problem. Today, investing in your brand requires *building and servicing great products and developing a great business design* that is consistent with and supports *a relevant and appealing brand signal*. The three crucial elements are interlinked in what we call the Golden Triangle of brand value (Figure 5-5).

FIGURE 5-5

THE GOLDEN TRIANGLE

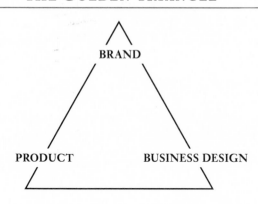

Today, business design, product, and brand signal are three inseparable actors in the drama of brand risk. Tired products help a brand erode more quickly. The wrong business design (especially in arenas such as service, distribution, quality, innovation, design, information, and customer experience) can do the same.

The reverse is also true. Declining brands can be rejuvenated by great products, and even more powerfully by great business designs. Striking examples include the Apple brand, the iPod product, and the iTunes store business design; the Toyota brand, the Prius product, and Toyota's business design for its hybrid line; and the Lexus brand, the Lexus product, and the Lexus business design of a separate and highly specialized dealer network.

The process begins with knowing *why* the brand is eroding. This usually requires a detailed deciphering of your brand's strengths and weaknesses, measured against the characteristics that are the most important to your customers. To perform this *brand risk analysis*, you first need to determine the true equity elements of your brand. Think about any brand you own. What are the five to seven equity dimensions that matter most to your customers? (For help in naming them, see the sample dimensions listed in Figure 5-6.) Then try to rank these elements in order of importance to your customers. Quantify the *relative* importance. Finally, find out how your brand scores with your most important customers, compared to your strongest competitor. The result may be a very revealing look at a looming brand risk in your future.

Once you've identified the problem, you can begin attacking the erosion with a radically altered, restructured investment program that includes improvements in the product, the business design, and the way you communicate the brand signal itself. All three points of the triangle are essential to halt and reverse the risk of brand erosion.

FIGURE 5-6
Sample Brand Equity Elements

Trustworthy	Provides good service
Fast	Family-friendly
High in quality	Prestigious
Saves me money	Fashion-forward
Saves me time	User-friendly
Flexible	Safe
Luxurious	Fun
Innovative	Technically sophisticated

Samsung: Investing in the Brand by Investing in the Business Design

Samsung provides a prototypical example of brand risk, and of how smart management can mitigate the risk and then reverse it by changing the brand investment pattern. Let's start with a little time travel back to the recent past.

The year was 1997. Korean electronics giant Samsung owned a brand associated in the consumer's mind mainly with low-end TVs, microwave ovens, and videotape players. Samsung meant "cheap." In the tradition of the Korean *chaebol* (conglomerate), Samsung's managers were focused on continually boosting output and sales revenues, even as prices for their rapidly commoditizing products fell and profits dwindled.

Jong-Yong Yun is CEO of Samsung. Soft-spoken and unimposing, he is nonetheless known for his willingness to tackle tough decisions and take the heat for his choices. Though his educational background is a B.S. in electrical engineering from Seoul National University, Yun is a humanist at heart: He studied engineering, he says, because "Korea was a poor country then, so I knew that if I majored in philosophy I would not have a job." And at times he speaks as if his job at Samsung is merely a way station in preparation for a more meaningful life quest. "I want to lead Samsung Electronics to become one of the best companies in the world," he has said. "When this goal is achieved, I want to visit historical and cultural sites around the world to pursue my study of philosophy." Perhaps this broader perspective helped Yun grapple with the complex interactions among business design, product, and brand signal that underlie the Samsung brand risk story.

In 1997, as Yun surveyed the carnage wrought by the recent Asian financial crisis (massive risk made manifest) and considered the realities facing his own company, he saw that the risks it faced were extremely serious. Samsung was heading toward decline and unprofitability because of powerful retailers and rapid commoditization—its products were too much like those made by a dozen other companies. What's more, the brand stood for cheap products. There was no basis for demanding a price premium—in fact, Samsung's strategy focused on low prices, constantly getting lower. Powerful buyers, insignificant product differences, and lack of brand uplift combined to eliminate profits and weaken the company.

Brand risk is difficult to quantify. But if Yun had wanted to calculate the chances that the Samsung brand might stave off a full-blown value collapse within the next five years, he might have come up with a number in the range of **40%**—a very uncomfortable place to be.

It is hard to see your risk story clearly in times of great success. It is even harder to see your *true* risk story in times of great crisis. But Yun, Samsung's philosopher-king, had the rare gift of clear vision, clear hearing, and the willingness and will to act.

Recognizing the enormous risk of Samsung's weak and eroding brand (conditioning a whole generation of consumers to think the wrong things about Samsung), Yun decided to tackle the issue of brand risk head-on: "If we keep selling low-end products, it damages our corporate image.... We believe that 5 to 10 years from now, our future will depend on our brand equity."

Yun recognized the crucial importance of *innovation* and *speed to market* as brand components in the world of consumer electronics, where new devices retain their full value only for a matter of quarters or even months. These characteristics had to become part of the Samsung brand, and it wouldn't be enough to try to convince consumers through clever advertising or publicity stunts. The underlying business design had to change as well.

In response to Yun's leadership, the firm began pouring major resources into R&D, positioning Samsung to launch new cell phones, TVs, music players, and other products at a faster rate than rivals such as Sony and Panasonic. As a direct result, Samsung has become a technology leader rather than a follower. For example, it was Samsung (in partnership with a state-run research institute) that developed WiBro, the new high-speed wireless technology that is eight times faster than conventional cellular systems, and much cheaper. By the end of 2006, Korea is expected to be the first country to adopt the WiBro standard.

Samsung also moved to change the balance of power between engineers and designers in favor of the designers. With the help of the Art Center College of Design in Pasadena, California, the firm opened an in-house design school, where Samsung designers, marketers, and engineers began taking six-day-a-week classes in cutting-edge design techniques. It created design centers in every major market, the better to capture local customer trends. For example, Samsung opened studios to design cell phones in Seoul, San Francisco, London, Tokyo, Los Angeles, and China.

The company also took dramatic steps to convey to its employees and to outside stakeholders the seriousness of its new commitment to product quality. When customer complaints about Samsung wireless phones began to multiply, the entire product inventory—almost $50 million worth of goods—was piled up in a factory courtyard. Workers wearing headbands with the slogan "Quality First" were ordered to smash the phones and toss them into a bonfire. "Before it was over," one account has it, "employees were weeping." It was a shocking moment, one that conveyed an unmistakable and unforgettable message.

Yun's commitment to quality, forceful promotion of an aggressive R&D agenda, and forward-leaning design program probably helped boost the odds for survival of the Samsung brand into the neighborhood of 60%.

Making these changes in the business was tough, yet other changes in the business design were even tougher. They involved some painful choices. Samsung's shift in direction generated some costs that were far from obvious. For example, after Yun announced the new focus on high-style products, the firm decided it would no longer offer its old, "cheap" TVs. It pulled older TV models from European markets months before the more expensive digital TVs were available. "TVs are the face of Samsung Electronics," Yun explained. Deliberately passing up months' worth of easy revenues produced shock waves both internally and externally; it sent an unambiguous message to the customer and to the organization, and heightened the urgency to complete the transition. But Yun recognized that this move was an essential investment in creating a clear and genuinely new brand image for Samsung, which would be far more profitable in the long run.

A second tough business design decision was made in 2000. Yun saw that selling at Wal-Mart was not consistent with the brand he was creating. Samsung decided to pull its products out of Wal-Mart—the world's largest and most powerful retailer—and shift volume and focus to stores such as Best Buy and Circuit City.

It takes real courage to bite the bullet this way. The short-term price is obvious. The long-term benefits, though much less obvious, are huge. Yun's choice to forgo the easy but dangerous revenues from old-look products in deep-discount channels improved Samsung's brand protection numbers by another few points, raising the odds for success up to some **70%**.

Targeted and aggressive brand-messaging efforts—the third point of the Golden Triangle—accompanied the product and business design moves. Samsung increased its spending on branding and marketing to some $3 billion per year, launched a two-year product placement agreement with New Line Cinema, and signed on as a partner for the Olympic Games. Samsung products have turned up in movies such as the *Matrix* series and in co-marketing programs with elite fashion and design magazines and sites such as *Vogue* and Style.com. These brand-messaging efforts would have had minimal impact if not for the reinvention of the underlying product and business design realities. But in combination with that effort, they helped improve the company's brand survival odds to somewhere around **80%**.

Today, with the benefit of a new brand image, a constant stream of great products, and a very different business design, Samsung is poised to challenge Sony for the overall lead in the consumer electronics marketplace. From 2000 to 2004, Samsung's sales more than doubled, from $27 billion to $55 billion. Today, with a market capitalization of $98 billion, Samsung is the world's most valuable non-U.S. technology company.

Brand value has tracked the same upward climb, and Samsung has leapfrogged its chief rival. In 2006, Sony's brand was worth $11.7 billion, Samsung's $16.2 billion (Figure 5-7). What's more, Samsung products are beginning to enjoy the price premium once owned by Sony. For example, Samsung handsets now sell at prices 44 percent higher than comparable models produced by rival firms.

FIGURE 5-7

SAMSUNG BRAND VALUE, IN $BILLIONS

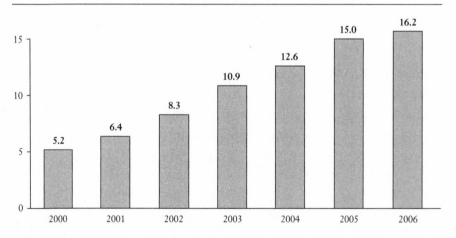

Samsung has made many moves to de-risk its business design. It focused on factory flexibility, to produce a wide variety of products in the same facilities. It entered into a broad technology-sharing agreement with Sony, to reduce the risk of technology lags. And it did numerous market tests to make certain that its development efforts were on target.

But its most important moves were the combined actions taken on product, brand, and business design, actions that reversed the brand erosion of the 1990s and launched one of the great brand growth stories of the 2000s.

THE ART OF BRAND LAYERING AT SAMSUNG AND ELSEWHERE

Isn't Samsung's drastic shift in brand image a high-risk maneuver? Didn't the company run the risk of losing the brand attributes that had contributed to its initial success while failing to make the transition to a new and even more valuable set of attributes?

Yes, that possibility exists. Any move to change your brand's meaning is inherently risky. So risk shapers such as Jong-Yong Yun limit the risk through the process of *brand layering*: making investments at all three points of the Golden Triangle that are designed to add positive attributes to your brand image that are consistent with and build upon its existing positive attributes.

By the time Yun decided to launch his brand makeover in 1997, Samsung had already grown to be one of the world's biggest electronics companies, and there were some positive brand attributes to build upon. Yes, Samsung meant "cheap." But it also meant "affordable," "reliable," and "proven technology." Every time a customer purchased another basic but perfectly acceptable Samsung TV or VCR or even rice cooker, those positive attributes got a little stronger.

It would have been absurd and highly risky for Samsung to try to completely upend its familiar brand image—for example, by trying to transform itself into a source for high-end, ultra-sophisticated, specialized, and expensive electronics gear. Instead, Yun and his team set about layering a series of positive new attributes on top of the familiar ones, adding qualities that were fresh but not fundamentally contradictory. Samsung products are still affordable, reliable, and so on. But increasingly they are also cleverly designed, versatile, stylish, and at the leading edge of current technology—and not quite as cheap as before.

This process of altering the brand through layering has been quite conscious and deliberate. Today, Samsung's leadership team is planning

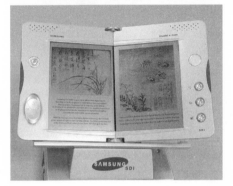

Rainer Jensen/dpa/Landov/JOCHEN ECKEL/Bloomberg News/Landov/
Reuters/CORBIS/Samsung Electronics/Handout/Reuters/Corbis

From commodities to cutting-edge:
Samsung products after the company's brand makeover.
Led by CEO Jong-Yong Yun, Samsung has transformed
enormous brand risk into a springboard for unrivaled growth.

the next layer of change, hoping to add the attribute of "product origi-
nality" to the company's brand image. It's the missing element Samsung
needs to evolve its brand to the next level. When we asked a group of
typical consumer electronics customers in mid-2006 about their perceptions of Samsung, we heard comments like these:

"When picking my next TV or phone, I would probably include
Samsung in my choice set."

"I don't know a lot about Samsung, but I think they're pretty
good."

"Seems as though they're coming out with some nice new design
features."

"From their ads, I have the impression that Samsung is trying to
go more upscale."

This is a big improvement from the kinds of comments we might
have heard a decade earlier, when attributes such as "basic," "downscale," "no-frills," and "cheap" would have dominated the conversation.
But what's missing is the kind of enthusiasm, admiration, and even passion that consumers once would have expressed for electronics brands
such as Sony and which they now apply to Apple's iPod. No one uses the
word *love* in the same sentence as the name Samsung.

To change this, the company needs to develop a breakthrough product comparable to Sony's Walkman or Apple's iPod. The company's
leaders recognize this. "Those sort of innovative products come once in a
generation," says a Samsung executive. "We've had lots of semi-iconic
products, but we still have to develop an iconic one." This effort requires
a major investment in technological research to complement the vast increases in design spending already described. Over the next five years,
Samsung plans to double its R&D investment; it has added 800 PhDs to
its research roster (boosting the total to 1,900) and increased the number
of R&D centers to seventeen, employing 32,000 employees. Today,
nearly 30 percent of Samsung's people are involved in research, development, design, and related activities.

Recognizing the challenge of adding yet another layer to Samsung's
revitalized brand image, Jong-Yong Yun is not taking the company's recent success as a cause for self-satisfaction. Here's how one of Yun's research managers puts it: "Vice chairman Yun stresses that if you relax, if
you become complacent, a crisis will find you." Yun himself sums up his
company's current status this way: "We stand at the crossroads to becoming a world leader or a major failure." And he is ready to do whatever is
necessary to push Samsung in the right direction. "I'm the chaos-maker,"
he says. "We must not lose the sense of crisis that helped us change.
When everything goes smoothly is the time when things go wrong."

When we look at other companies that have recently succeeded at
strengthening or revitalizing a brand, we see the same pattern as at Samsung. The focus is not merely on brand positioning or on signal investments such as advertising or marketing. Rather, the focus is on a

carefully structured combination of the right investments designed to reshape the product portfolio and the business design to support the brand. Throughout the process, the risk of brand reshaping is reduced through strategic layering of new attributes that do not destroy but rather modify, enhance, or complement the old.

For a large-scale example of brand risk reversal, consider the past decade at IBM. When Lou Gerstner came to IBM in 1994, if he had written out the brand risk story for IBM, it might have sounded something like this:

> *Until the early 1990s, IBM had perhaps the single most powerful brand in the B2B world. Buying IBM was a career-protecting move. Now, in the mid-1990s, the opposite is true. As a result of changes in the industry and aggressive moves by Microsoft, Oracle, Dell, EMC, and Cisco, IBM seems out of date and out of touch. Customer surveys show that buying IBM is no longer a career-protecting move. It is becoming a career-threatening move.*

The erosion of the IBM brand was manifested in many different parts of its business, including the simplest hardware the company sold. In 1996, a personal computer received a $200 lower price when it was branded IBM than when exactly the same object (same processor, same memory, same features) was branded Compaq.

To turn this brand erosion around, Lou Gerstner had to make countless changes in the company. Three of the most important focused on the Golden Triangle of business design, product portfolio, and brand signal. The business design change was profound. Gerstner saw a "collapse of the middle" occurring in the information technology market, and changed the IBM business design to a "barbell" design, selling technology components at one end and high-value-added services at the other. The key product change was transforming IBM from a company where services were a stepchild of hardware to a business where services were the main event. And IBM changed its brand signal investment from emphasizing hardware to emphasizing solutions. The "Solutions for a Small Planet" campaign altered the meaning of the IBM brand for its key customers.

These three shifts in investment stabilized and reversed the erosion glide path of the brand. In combination, they have enabled IBM to adroitly transform the meaning of its brand from "hardware makers with a tradition of conservative quality" to "information services providers with unmatched depth and breadth of expertise." In keeping with the layering strategy, *both* of these images are positive, though they are rather different. The common element: IBM has always been, and remains, "a reliable solver of information problems for business." What has changed is the layering of elements on top of this bedrock identity.

The simple fact that your brand may have a strongly favorable image today does not exempt you from considering whether it is necessary to change that image for sustained success in the future—as companies such as Southwest and Dell, for instance, may need to do in the near future.

SAMSUNG'S DE-RISKING MOVES

Here's a summary of the key steps Samsung has taken to reduce its brand risk. How many are relevant to the brand risk challenges your company faces?

- Commit to a new, high-quality product lineup—even at the cost of literally destroying older, cheaper goods.
- Improve brand image by layering new attributes that are compatible with the brand's existing positive traits.
- Invest billions of dollars in accelerated R&D efforts.
- Drastically improve speed to market, making Samsung an industry leader in innovation.
- Shift the balance of power from engineers to designers.
- Pull products from downscale retailers that don't fit the new brand image.
- Increase spending on advertising, marketing, and promotion to support the other two points of the Golden Triangle.
- Commit to developing an iconic product to take the brand to the next level.

BRAND INVESTMENT
AT ALL THREE POINTS OF THE TRIANGLE

The crucial importance of alignment among the brand signal, the product, and the business design means that defeating brand risk involves much more than traditional marketing or advertising spending.

All three points of the triangle affect one another; each depends on the others. Think of a football team facing a third-down-and-long-yardage situation late in a close game with playoff implications. As the quarterback steps back and scans the coverage for an open receiver, on whom does the success of the play depend? On the man with the football in his hand, scrambling to stay on his feet and find a gap in the coverage? On the offensive line, desperately trying to hold off the on-rushing defensive blitz and buy time for their quarterback and his receivers? Or on the receivers themselves, heading downfield and hoping to outrace the cornerbacks to the spiraling, descending ball? Is one of these most important? Or is the vital element the interplay among all three?

Obviously, all three are important, and all three affect one another—in terms of timing, play patterns, crisp execution. In the same way, the strength of your product can build or undermine your brand; the strength of your brand can support or weaken your business design; and the strength of your business design can enhance or erode your brand and your product.

By the same token, "investing in your brand" means much more than ad spending, merchandising costs, or marketing programs. "Brand investment" must be redefined to include *all* investments that are relevant to customers' experiences and their perceptions of your brand.

A company that invests shrewdly to create a great product and a great business design may be capable of developing a great brand name through branded customer experiences *even without significant spending on marketing and advertising.* For example, one need only consider such highly respected and valuable brands as Starbucks, Amazon, Google, and eBay.

The common driver in dozens of eroding brands is chronic *misinvestment*—failing to adjust the investment mix appropriately for the long-term protection and growth of brand equity. Some managements underestimate the amount of brand investment needed to protect (and build) their brand. Instead, they use their brands, built through large investments over decades, as convenient "piggy banks" from which value can be drawn, improving their numbers in the short term. The lack of visible bad effects in the short term then encourages more borrowing/ deferral behavior. After years of such erosion, the cost to rebuild the brands becomes enormous. Ultimately, failure to invest leads to a point of no return, where the cost to revitalize or reposition the brand outweighs the revenue upside expected. Such neglect may destroy the brand—and even the company, since for many firms brand equity may represent as much as 30 to 50 percent of the company's total market value.

Failure to invest is one of the most common investment traps that generate unnecessary levels of brand risk. But it's far from the only one (see Figure 5-8). The wrong mix of investments, the wrong investment sequence, the failure to adapt your investment strategy over time, and many other brand investment missteps can be just as damaging as failing to invest at all. These forms of misinvestment can also push brands toward the point of no return, the point at which it costs less to build a new brand than to rehabilitate the old one.

FIGURE 5-8
BRAND INVESTMENT FAILURES:
THE MANY SOURCES OF BRAND RISK

TYPE OF FAILURE	DEFINITION	COMPANY EXAMPLE
1. FAILURE TO INVEST	Assuming that your brand's value is largely self-sustaining, a mine to be exploited rather than a living thing to be fed, watered, pruned, and nurtured	**Avon** (a highly relevant brand that was outspent by new competitors)

TYPE OF FAILURE	DEFINITION	COMPANY EXAMPLE
2. WRONG INVESTMENT MIX	Investing in marketing, advertising, promotion, sponsorships, or product programs that do little to create brand value and may even damage it	**MP3 players** (invested in building the category, while iPod invested to establish a brand)
3. WRONG INVESTMENT SEQUENCE	Investing in programs with a lower expected payoff (in terms of increased customer revenue versus cost to invest) prior to or instead of programs with a greater expected payoff	**Some national and regional banks** (invested in product advertising ahead of customer service)
4. MYOPIC INVESTMENT FOCUS	Focusing only on one or a few investments while ignoring others that are essential to brand value	**Wal-Mart** (focused exclusively on retail customers, ignoring other key constituencies)
5. INVESTING IN THE WRONG TOUCHPOINTS	Investing to improve customer touchpoints of marginal relevance while neglecting touchpoints that are crucial to customer response	**Cable TV companies** (invested in technology development and adding content rather than improving customer service)
6. INVESTING IN THE WRONG POSITIONING	Investing in strategies that emphasize brand value components that do not drive customer behavior while ignoring other components that do	**Motorola** (in the late 1990s emphasized technological edge in cell phones when customers were more concerned about ease of use)

TYPE OF FAILURE	DEFINITION	COMPANY EXAMPLE
7. FAILURE TO ADAPT	Investing in brand value components that have become irrelevant to customers over time or even taken on negative rather than positive attributes in customers' eyes	**Oldsmobile and Plymouth** (failed to adapt their brands even as brand attributes took on increasingly negative meaning for most customers)
8. POORLY DESIGNED BRAND PORTFOLIO	Investing in too many brands with minimal value, brands that are focused on stagnant or shrinking markets, or brands that are rapidly becoming commoditized	**Unilever** (invested in 1,600 global brands rather than focusing on the core 400)
9. BRAND DILUTION	Investing in strategies that weaken the brand by trying to stretch its meaning to cover too broad a range of customers, markets, products, or services	**Mercedes** (heading downmarket, sacrificing quality and brand stature)
10. WRONG USE OF BRAND METRICS	Failing to measure the key leading indicators of the health of your brand; choosing to focus on measures that have little or no real significance; or ignoring, denying, or rationalizing the warning signs your brand metrics reveal	**Folgers** (relied on traditional measures such as awareness and consideration while Starbucks stole its market)

Solving (and Re-Solving) the Brand Investment Puzzle

The proper brand investment mix is not a decision that can be made once every few years. Over time, as the brand moves through the stages of its life cycle and as the market changes, the brand investment mix inevitably needs adjustment. Therefore, recognizing the current status of your brand has a direct impact on the nature of the brand investments you need to make. Smart companies realign their brand investments as dictated by the specific nature of the brand risks they are facing. Some examples include:

• A consumer bank with weak satisfaction scores on customer service had to shift its brand investment expenditures from advertising and marketing to employee training and revamped service programs.
• A packaged-goods company with a lackluster, undifferentiated product line shifted its spending from channel programs (such as slotting allowances and co-op advertising) to product development and quality upgrades.
• A clothing retailer whose stores were looking dated and unappealing shifted its brand investment from advertising to store design and refurbishing.
• A financial services firm whose genuinely excellent service had gone underrecognized in new markets had to begin making significant investments in advertising in order to update and improve its brand signal, even though this meant that profits took a temporary hit.

Changes in economic and market conditions also require changes in the investment mix. A vehicle that travels on bumpy, mountainous terrain needs realignment more frequently than a car that travels only on the highway. Today's brands don't travel on smooth roads. The brand investment mix requires much more frequent realignment. A static mix, or a mix that lags external shifts, can destroy the strength of the brand.

It's always tough to overcome spending inertia. It's particularly tough if the change cuts into accepted habits of spending and thinking. And it's a highly risky change if you make it without the right information.

DE-RISK YOUR BUSINESS

If you are uncertain about the underlying strength of your company's brand(s), here are some questions to help you get a handle on the brand risk you may be facing and the most likely solutions.

1. Do we have a real brand? What message does it deliver to the customer? What price premium does it earn? What volume premium (selling more at identical prices)?

2. Does our brand generate positive word of mouth? Does it earn our products a place in the customer's consideration set when the customer is ready to buy?

3. Why do customers choose our brand rather than competing brands or generics? What segments of customers does it appeal to most? What customers does it drive away?

4. Have we verified our beliefs about our brand by asking customers what the brand actually means to them?

5. What are the major risks that can destroy our brand's value? What's our brand risk story? If we present our risk story (in five sentences or fewer, modeled on Gerstner's risk story from this chapter) to several colleagues, do they all vigorously nod as they read it—or just as vigorously shake their heads? If so, we've already taken the right first step.

6. As we evaluate our product(s) as well as all of the major elements in the business design—customer selection, unique value proposition, profit model, scope of activities, strategic control, and organizational architecture—how well do our company's products(s) and its business design align with our brand signal? Do these elements fit logically with the signal of our brand, or are there obvious mismatches—for example, a brand that means "family fun" linked to a customer selection centered on aging baby boomers?

7. What is the total amount of dollars and management hours our firm invested in its brand last year? These dollars include advertising and marketing dollars, as well as all other dollars spent on activities that change customer perceptions of our brand: quality programs, service training, channel programs, media programs, developing new product features, and so on. Calculating the total dollars of brand investment, direct and indirect, isn't easy—the first try may be off by anywhere from 30 to 70 percent—but we need to work the numbers until they include *everything* that belongs in the brand investment pot. This becomes the index point of 100.

8. Did we spend the 100 accurately in relation to what matters to our customers? Was last year's investment mix the right mix? Why or why not? And what will be the right mix in the next twelve months? In the next twenty-four months? Why?

CHAPTER SIX

When Nobody Makes Money

Partnering with Rivals to Escape a No-Profit Zone

INDUSTRY RISK, one of the deadliest threats any business can face, is also one of the least understood. Industry risk strikes when *an entire industry* evolves into a no-profit zone. It's not about growth; industry risk can strike growing industries. It's not about obsolescence; a no-profit zone can engulf industries where innovation is robust and frequent. Industry risk is about structural factors that create an intense margin squeeze even on well-run companies. It's also about the psychology of the downward spiral—about how people react when they find themselves suddenly gasping for profits, which are the breath of life for any business.

Consider, for example, the consumer electronics business, which in recent years has become a classic no-profit zone. The structural factors causing the profit squeeze include growing retailer power, the proliferation of consumer choices, the ultra-rapid imitation of new products, and the emergence of very low-cost manufacturers from China and other regions. All of these factors combine to cause prices to fall faster than costs, compressing margins to the vanishing point.

In other no-profit-zone industries, different factors are at work. For airlines, the structural factors include very high fixed costs, commoditization of service, a highly interconnected hub-and-spoke system that is extremely vulnerable to weather disruptions, and unpredictable oil price spikes—as well as, again, the proliferation of consumer choices. As in consumer electronics, these factors work together to make it almost impossible to enjoy decent profit margins in the industry.

Once structural factors begin the downward spiral toward a no-profit zone in a particular industry, psychological factors kick in. Irrational pricing moves are met with irrational responses. At a certain point in the process, faulty logic also comes into play: "If we drive prices down and force the weakest competitors into bankruptcy, then there'll be less excess capacity in our industry and the survivors will be able to make money again."

Unfortunately, it doesn't usually work out that way. Instead, bankruptcy often *intensifies* competition, as bankrupt companies reemerge with a lower cost structure the way Northwest Airlines and US Airways did. What's more (again in defiance of economic logic), new capacity often gets added to no-profit-zone industries anyway—it has happened not only in airlines and consumer electronics but also in memory chips, carmaking, grocery retailing, and TV news.

A no-profit zone is the business equivalent of a black hole. Just as a black hole absorbs and consumes all matter and light in its vicinity, a no-profit zone absorbs and consumes capital and profits.

There is a way to reverse the risk and escape from the no-profit zone. The crucial countermeasure is *changing the compete/collaborate ratio* in the industry—that is, finding ways to cooperate with industry rivals, especially on activities that hold little potential for differentiation. Collaborating on these activities saves money for everyone in the industry, boosting profit margins and helping companies generate the "escape velocity" needed to flee the black hole. The moneys freed up can then be channeled into activities that customers care about and that create opportunities for meaningful differentiation among companies.

This is a proven formula for reversing industry risk. But it's a tough choice for most managers to make. It requires rethinking some basic assumptions about competition and collaboration.

Vigorous competition is, of course, the lifeblood of modern economies. It spurs creativity, rejuvenates markets, keeps companies agile, and guarantees consumers better products and lower prices. But as the experience of many industries reveals, competition can be bad as well as good. In dynamic economies, value is constantly migrating from outmoded business designs to those that are better calibrated to satisfy critical customer priorities. As the game changes, certain aspects of competition become outdated and irrelevant, and companies have to revisit the scope of activities they engage in. When companies fight over things that hold little value to customers or offer little potential for competitive differentiation, they are engaging in competition that's destructive rather than constructive. They are throwing away shareholders' money, wasting valuable time and energy, and reducing resources available for innovation, thereby reducing the chance for profitability tomorrow— not only their own profitability but that of their entire industry.

Much of the competition in business today has become outmoded. Indeed, the prevalence of destructive competition is one of the main reasons why a wide array of industries, from music to airlines to consumer electronics, have experienced a steady and seemingly inexorable erosion in profitability.

Why do managers persist in destructive competition? Because that's what they're trained and expected to do. The idea of setting aside the sword and working shoulder to shoulder with rivals on some part of the business is anathema to most executives.

When margins are generous, the compete/collaborate ratio is usually close to 100/0. That ratio generally begins to shift when margins have eroded and companies are scrambling to find savings anywhere they can.

But it doesn't have to be that way. A few extraordinary examples in music, aircraft, semiconductors, retailing, credit cards, and even automobiles show how effective an insurance policy the shift toward far greater collaboration can be.

THE EXTERNAL CATALYST: STEVE JOBS SPARKS COLLABORATION IN THE MUSIC BUSINESS

In the late 1990s, the pop music business was in a funk. The glory days of the previous two decades were long past. None of the post-boomer stars had equaled the sales or impact of older acts such as Elvis Presley, the Beatles, the Rolling Stones, or Bob Dylan. The (somewhat artificial) boom created by the changeover from vinyl records and tape cassettes to CDs in the late 1980s was long gone—and with it the industry's profit margins of 15 to 20 percent, which had shrunk to 5 percent.

Through it all, the price of CDs kept rising even as music fans had figured out that most CDs consisted of one or two good tunes surrounded by ten others that were much less interesting. No wonder they resented paying $18.95 for the whole package.

Yet the record company executives weren't too worried. They'd lived through demand troughs before and had always been rescued by something new—either a wave of fresh talent or an exciting new format. Surely something would come along soon to rejuvenate the industry.

Something *did* come along. Unfortunately, it was something that would make the industry's problems much, much worse.

Around 1999, a convergence of technologies—the triumph of digital music in the form of the CD, the newly ubiquitous computer CD burners, and especially the mainstreaming of the Internet—created a wave of new open-source technologies that for the first time decoupled music from the companies that owned the content. Soon millions of people were making unauthorized copies of CDs, recording and distributing unauthorized but near-professional-quality recordings of their favorite artists, and downloading music from the Internet. Suddenly there was an alternative to handing over $18.95 to the music companies.

> *Industries in distress always wind up collaborating; unfortunately, they usually take this step seven to ten years too late.*

Soon the new technologies began to have a noticeable effect on music revenues. Between 2000 and 2003, the U.S. music industry's revenues declined at a compound annual rate of 6.5 percent. And since CD prices were *still* rising, unit sales were dropping even faster.

It's a bit ironic, because the music industry had profited handsomely from previous technological breakthroughs. They'd even sold the *same* music to the *same* customers multiple times in successive formats. The new breakthrough—digitization coupled with networking via the Internet—was potentially the greatest gold mine of all, since it eliminated the expenses of manufacturing, packaging, shipping, and retailing physical copies of the music. Handled properly, this shift could save the industry from its economic doldrums. But a new distribution model that protected the record companies' intellectual property and the right of the artists to profit from their work would have to be invented.

This was the great opportunity and the great challenge. The music industry shrank from both. Seeing only the threat from digital distribution, the industry's response was both panicky and ineffective. First, it began to lobby for legislation to outlaw downloading, bring lawsuits against downloaders and the Internet companies that assisted them, and launch public relations campaigns against digital music sharing. The goal, it seemed, was to push the digital genie back into the bottle—at least until someone could figure out what to do about it.

The legal campaign had some successes. The music companies won their case against Napster, the biggest of the free-downloading networks, which was forced to close down and reorganize as a licensed, for-pay music service. But as Napster vanished, peer-to-peer (P2P) distribution sites such as Kazaa and Morpheus sprang up in its place. Because these have no central servers, they are much harder to shut down, and since the fans who use the services have total control over the content they share, it's much harder to prove that the sites are liable for any copyright infringement that occurs.

By 2001 and 2002, the industry had recognized that it would not be able to litigate or lobby downloading out of existence. So it moved on to the next logical idea—co-opting the digital movement. The record companies promised to launch paid online music services with the same limitless selection and ease of use as Napster.

Yet despite several years of warning, the music companies lacked the sense of urgency that would force them to work together to solve their problems. Such collaboration was essential. What made Napster so appealing was the fact that it gave users access to millions of music files from almost every recording artist who ever lived. Fans want the music, now, and Napster provided that. Could the record companies bring themselves to do the same?

Sadly, no. Instead, they undermined their own strategy by teaming up against one another, creating competing and therefore hopelessly fragmented distribution systems. Universal and Sony rolled out a joint venture called Pressplay, while AOL Time Warner, Bertelsmann (BMG's owner), EMI, and RealNetworks launched MusicNet. The two ventures refused to license their songs to each other, rather than collaborating to attract already skeptical customers. As a result, neither service had enough songs to attract paying customers. Those who tried the paid services soon got frustrated and returned to Kazaa or Morpheus or one of the other P2P systems.

It was left to Apple to develop a solution.

Several big pieces of the puzzle were already in place—the iPod digital music player, Apple's proprietary digital music format (AAC), the basic iTunes music software, and a brand associated with fun and creativity. Now Apple wanted to turn iTunes into a legal downloading service that would transform a pirate medium into a legitimate source of profits for artists, music companies, and Apple itself. Apple's concept: Sell songs for a flat price of 99 cents each, low enough to make iTunes an attractive alternative to buggy, virus-laden piracy sites but just enough to generate reasonable revenues for all the parties to share. Eliminate the subscription fees that music lovers hated. Build in enough flexibility so that users could enjoy their files most any way they liked—but with enough restrictions so that further uncontrolled distribution or copying would be difficult or impossible. And, of course, make the interface easy and intuitive to use in classic Apple fashion.

It was a compelling vision. But making it work meant that Steve Jobs had to convince the record labels to license their music for download— no small feat, given their history, their competitiveness, and their anti-tech sentiments.

Fortunately, Apple's built-in security features appealed to the music industry's desire for control. The AAC format includes a copy-protection scheme to thwart people from sharing the music illegally. Apple iTunes users can listen to their files on iPods or on up to five personal computers installed with iTunes software, and iTunes files can be burned to a blank CD up to seven times. But if the user tries to upload an iTunes file (to a P2P system such as Kazaa, for example), it converts into gobbledygook.

One by one, the major labels bought into Jobs's collaborative vision, and Jobs worked to win over leading musicians as well. "So many artists were on the fence about the digital world," says Island Def Jam Music Group's Lyor Cohen. "It really showed his determination to make this happen."

The iTunes Music Store was unveiled in April 2003 with four of the biggest record labels on board. It sold 1 million songs the first week. In its first eight months, the iTunes Music Store sold 25 million songs, netting an additional $22 million in revenue for the music industry. In 2005, the iTunes Music Store sold an estimated 550 million songs, generating another $490 million in revenues for the music industry—3.5 percent of the industry's estimated total revenue (and a considerably higher proportion of its profit)—and claimed 70 percent of the online music business. By 2008, Forrester Research forecasts, downloaded music will account for 23 percent of the music industry's revenues.

If iTunes continues to grow, Apple may have bailed out the music business, vanquishing (at least for a time) the specter of industry risk that has been draining the business of profits and hope. How did Jobs and his team do it?

As usual with any story of remarkable business success, it's all about the business design—in particular, the strategic control and profit model that Apple created around iTunes.

Start with the profit model. For each 99-cent download, music executives estimate that Apple pays 65 cents in record company royalties and 25 cents in credit card fees and distribution costs. This leaves about 10 cents as Apple's profit margin—not a big one. But then, Apple also has tens of millions of high-margin iPods to sell. The low price point for iTunes downloads creates a brilliant inversion of the classic razor-blade business design. Rather than giving away one razor to sell hundreds of blades (as King Gillette once did), Apple practically gives away hundreds or thousands of songs to sell one iPod.

As for strategic control, iTunes provides music in its proprietary AAC file format, which thwarts illegal music sharing. iPods do support WAV and MP3 files, which means you can digitize music you already own, store it with iTunes, and listen to it on your iPod. But you can't store music or play music downloaded from competing download services, such as Windows Media Store or RealNetworks, which creates standard-dependence among iTunes consumers.

The technical control that Apple built into the iTunes/iPod product line, combined with its smart marketing and distribution efforts, made it the de facto standard for digital music. That, in turn, helped build its customer base, its content library, and its range of partners. In effect, Apple catalyzed the music companies to start collaborating. And all have benefited. Because most of Apple's online music revenues go back to the record companies, the iTunes store has significantly boosted overall industry profits.

The industry may yet spoil the brilliant collaborative model that an outsider created. No sooner did Apple establish a clear, attractive, and profitable model than Sony, BMG Music Entertainment, and Warner Music Group pushed for variable pricing, charging more for current hit tunes, which would likely alienate customers. Jobs is defending the 99-cent standard and working hard to sustain the industry-wide collaboration that has gone so far to reverse the industry's margin decline.

It's possible that Hollywood, which faces an analogous industry risk, may do a better job in tackling the challenge of digital distribution. Several big movie production firms have already begun working together to develop shared copy-blocking techniques that may enable them to retain control over their products while still reaching the vast potential audience for electronic entertainment downloads.

And which high-tech manufacturer is positioning itself to be a major player in this new collaborative arena? Apple, of course. In October 2005, Apple launched the newest iPod with a video screen designed to play home movies, music videos, TV shows, and short films. Episodes of hit shows such as *Lost* and *Desperate Housewives* were immediately made available for downloading, along with 2,000 licensed videos from the music companies and a selection of animated shorts from Pixar. Within a week after a selection of Disney pictures was available, users downloaded 125,000 copies. The next step is the spring 2007 release of an Apple device (code name iTV) that will allow downloaded movies to be streamed wirelessly from a computer to a television. The music model that Apple pioneered may have shown Hollywood the importance of collaborating rather than competing in the process of getting its pictures onto millions of home screens.

The music industry is not the only one to have experienced the full brunt of industry risk, and the margin erosion that it leads to. Several other industries experiencing this risk shifted their compete/collaborate ratio in ways that halted and then reversed that margin decline.

SAVE MONEY, THEN REINVEST
TO CREATE NEW VALUE

In the 1960s, airplane manufacturing in Europe appeared doomed. U.S. companies, particularly Boeing and McDonnell Douglas, had become the dominant players in the increasingly capital-intensive industry. The smaller European manufacturers, scattered across the continent and fighting fiercely with one another as well as with their international rivals, lacked the scale and the capital to compete effectively against their U.S. counterparts in building big, modern passenger jets. By the end of the 1960s, the Europeans' combined share of the global aircraft market had dwindled to just 10 percent despite the fact that 25 percent of planes were being purchased by European airlines.

Then, in 1970, four of the leading European manufacturers—France's Aérospatiale, Germany's Daimler-Benz Aerospace, Spain's Casa, and the U.K.'s British Aerospace—did something radical. They formed the joint venture Airbus, pooling their resources to design, produce, and sell jet aircraft. Not only did the venture provide operating economies and reduce financial risks, but the combination of capital and talent also led to a surge of innovation. Despite early managerial conflicts, Airbus successfully pioneered new approaches to aircraft design, including fly-by-wire control technology and the introduction of a common cockpit across the entire fleet. Between 1984 and 1994, the joint venture launched three technologically advanced, highly efficient planes that proved attractive to a large number of airlines.

The collaboration didn't just provide temporary life support for the aircraft makers; it has allowed them to thrive. Although Airbus's first customers were European airlines, the venture began penetrating the American market by 1980, and in the 1990s its clientele expanded to include such U.S. giants as United Airlines, US Airways, and Northwest Airlines. Not only had European aircraft manufacturing survived, but Airbus had become in essence the only rival to Boeing (which in 1997 had acquired McDonnell Douglas). Airbus has grown rapidly over the past two decades, to the point where it now often beats its American archrival in annual deliveries of new jets. In 2000, the European partners strengthened and extended their collaboration, consolidating Airbus's management and operations at a centralized facility in Toulouse, France. While charges of unfair government subsidies from both sides surface periodically, the important business lesson is the greater efficiency and innovation made possible by the Airbus partnership.

Not all industries could or would want to work together the way Airbus did. But changing the compete/collaborate ratio can take many different forms. A classic example is the collaboration that set the stage for a turnaround in the once-beleaguered U.S. semiconductor industry. During the 1980s, American chip manufacturers were being defeated by low-cost Japanese rivals. Between 1980 and 1986, the U.S. semiconductor industry saw its profits shrink by more than $2 billion and its payrolls contract by more than 27,000 workers. The sector's ongoing collapse caused grave concerns among U.S. policy makers, for national security as well as economic reasons. Half the chips used in the country's F-16 fighter jet, for example, were being supplied by Japanese manufacturers.

Collaboration frees up cash to invest in business areas that offer the potential to generate genuine differentiation.

In response, the U.S. Department of Defense spearheaded an effort to create a research consortium to stem the industry's losses. Fourteen semiconductor manufacturers, representing 85 percent of the industry, joined together in 1987 to form SEMATECH in order "to solve common manufacturing problems by leveraging resources and sharing risks." Each of the participants, along with the U.S. government, invested $100 million in the effort, and in return they were all granted the right to share in the resulting technologies. SEMATECH's research initiative, launched from dedicated facilities in Austin, Texas, succeeded in strengthening the entire U.S. semiconductor supply chain while spurring rapid advances in chip miniaturization and speed. The joint effort played a crucial role in the industry's resurgence during the ensuing decade.

These two stories show not only that close collaboration among competitors is possible—and legal (see sidebar, "Is Collaboration Legal?" on the next page)—but also that it can dramatically improve the profitability of industries and individual companies, particularly in businesses that are undergoing margin erosion. Collaboration allows firms to capture the benefits of superior scale, rationalized assets, and combined talent in those areas of the value chain that offer little potential for strategic differentiation. But even more important is the upside potential it creates.

IS COLLABORATION LEGAL?

"We can't team up with competitors—it will get us into antitrust trouble." That may be a convenient excuse, but it's usually not true. Companies must, of course, think through the legal ramifications of any cooperative venture. They have to avoid working together in areas that would involve the sharing of pricing information or entail other actions that might harm customers. And they can't team up in a way that gives them cartel-like power over a critical component of a market's shared infrastructure.

But the goal of antitrust laws is not to prevent cooperation. Rather, it's to block business activities that damage the public interest by reducing the efficiency of markets, slowing innovation, or obstructing productive competition. Because strategic collaboration actually enhances market efficiency, spurs innovation, and intensifies productive competition, it benefits the public and thus is unlikely to be a target of government action. (Indeed, past examples of industry collaboration often involved direct governmental encouragement and assistance.) Companies launching a collaboration initiative may need to educate policy makers and the general public about the scope and benefits of the effort, but that shouldn't be a deterrent to cooperation. The potential gains—for customers as well as companies—are too great.

Proactive Moves

The examples given here also reveal something else: Collaboration usually takes place too late. The European aircraft manufacturers and the U.S. chip makers began to collaborate only after their businesses had deteriorated severely, and in both cases governmental encouragement and financial assistance were required to get the cooperative ventures off the ground.

There have been some notable exceptions to the collaboration-as-last-resort rule. A group of twenty-five small hardware stores banded together to form a cooperative for joint purchasing and advertising back in 1948—well before they were threatened by big-box retailers such as Home Depot. The cooperative, now called True Value, has grown to encompass more than 6,200 hardware, gardening, and equipment-rental stores in fifty-four countries. The organization allows its members, mainly entrepreneur-owners, to enjoy big-company scale economies without sacrificing their independence.

On the product side, True Value provides members a wide selection of private-label merchandise under such popular brand names as True Value, Master Mechanic, Green Thumb, and Master Plumber. Goods are shipped from the cooperative's twelve regional distribution centers, ensuring fast replenishment and responsive service. On the marketing front, in addition to shared advertising campaigns and sales flyers, True Value allows members to tap into a joint customer loyalty program, True Value Rewards, that not only strengthens local customer relationships but provides in-depth market data that would be prohibitively expensive for stores to assemble on their own. The cooperative also allows members to share best practices through marketing tool kits that include detailed instructions and templates for proven promotional and public relations activities.

Big companies, too, have launched proactive collaboration initiatives. Early in the history of the credit card business, for instance, card-issuing banks realized that cooperation would provide two critical benefits. First, it would allow them to develop a national (and later international) network of merchants that would accept their cards. Second, it would dramatically reduce their transaction-processing and technology costs, allowing them to focus their investments and attention on the kind of branding and service programs that can provide real differentiation. To capture these benefits, the banks formed two member-owned agencies, which evolved into today's Visa and MasterCard organizations. There are now more than 1.5 billion Visa and MasterCard cards in circulation, accepted at more than 20 million merchant locations worldwide and used for nearly $4 trillion worth of purchases annually.

The credit card agencies have created value for all parties. Consumers have been given more credit and payment options—the agencies pioneered debit cards, among other innovations. The agencies themselves generate strong revenues through fees for basic and value-added services. And member banks have dramatically reduced their costs and risks.

Most industry collaborations start from within. Sometimes, however, a savvy outsider can act as a catalyst that spurs industry competitors to begin collaborating (as Apple did with the music industry). Sometimes the catalyst may be a supplier to the industry that can strengthen its existing business by helping its customers work together to solve common problems.

That's what Cardinal Health has done in the prescription drug business through its ArcLight Systems venture. Cardinal convinced pharmacy competitors CVS, Albertson's, Wal-Mart, Kmart, and five regional drugstore chains to form a consortium to collect and market real-time drug sales data. ArcLight delivers the data and trends online to paid subscribers, such as pharmaceutical firms, that want to track the effectiveness of marketing campaigns, the impact of new-product launches, and the introduction of generic drugs.

Too Little, Too Late

Proactive collaboration remains, however, distressingly rare, especially in situations where it can reverse trends that are casting shadows on currently healthy businesses. Consider the pharmaceutical industry, where many companies continue to enjoy enviable profit margins as they reap the rewards of drugs developed years ago. Their future margins, however, are under threat from the explosion in drug development costs. In

1975, it cost drugmakers an average of $138 million to bring a new therapy to market. By 2000, the cost had reached $802 million. But pharmaceutical firms continue to compete broadly, each pursuing separate development or licensing initiatives for similar compounds. They often refuse to share even basic clinical information, such as data on liver toxicity, clinging to the belief that it will provide them with a competitive advantage. If the drugmakers continue to ignore opportunities for strategic collaboration, they seem fated to endure the kind of margin erosion we've seen in the automotive, airline, and other sectors.

What's particularly striking is that in all these industries there have been instances of competitors collaborating in the past and reaping important benefits as a result. The Big Three carmakers, for example, launched the U.S. Consortium for Automotive Research (USCAR) in 1992 to undertake studies in such areas as safety and emissions. Most major pharmaceutical companies use sophisticated licensing partnerships to reduce costs and spread risks. Yet despite their own positive experiences with cooperation, they continue to shun broader opportunities for strategic collaboration. Their compete/collaborate ratios remain overwhelmingly biased toward competition.

Improving the Compete/Collaborate Ratio

Shifting those ratios requires, first and foremost, a change in managerial mind-set. It also requires a practical, objective process for thinking through collaboration opportunities. Every company will have to weigh different factors in plotting its collaboration strategy, depending on its industry's economics and structure and its own competitive positioning. Companies will need to focus on the parts of their industry's value chain where the greatest collaboration gains will be found, on the types of collaboration that will best achieve those gains, and on the right partners.

THE GREATEST COLLABORATION GAINS

Collaboration can unlock value in different ways in different areas of an industry's economic system. At the back end, for example, it can change the economics of innovation and discovery, allowing companies to reduce redundant investments in solving common problems, tackle larger problems by aggregating their resources, and find more creative solutions by tapping into a larger and more diverse pool of talent. In operations, it can change the economics of manufacturing by enhancing scale, spreading risk, aggregating purchases, and speeding the journey through the experience curve. At the front end of the system, companies can enhance customer satisfaction by integrating the components of a solution, or they can reduce costs by consolidating low-value sales or service activities.

Start by assessing your industry's current performance in value creation along dimensions such as customer satisfaction, profitability, asset efficiency, and volatility. Different competitors will have different scores, but you'll be able to see the general trends and spot the bottlenecks that limit industry performance. Then move to the value chain itself.

In general, firms should try to identify activities that provide little opportunity for achieving competitive differentiation and that offer strong opportunities to enhance scale economies, asset efficiency, labor productivity, or innovation. It is these activities that typically represent the best returns for collaboration.

THE RIGHT TYPES OF COLLABORATION

Collaboration can take many forms, ranging from informal cooperation to formal partnership. And the right forms of collaboration will change over time as you fulfill prior objectives and as customer preferences change.

In industries that have little experience with collaboration, it may be wise to begin with modest efforts in order to build trust, learning, and momentum. You might partner on a narrowly defined project with a small number of companies with whom you have existing relationships. Timken works with competitors such as bearing manufacturer SKF to share logistics and e-business activities. In aerospace, Northrop Grumman has teamed up with BAE Systems North America to develop an integrated microwave assembly for the F-35 Joint Strike Fighter.

Or you might want to spearhead an industry-wide exploratory committee to evaluate collaboration opportunities and develop initial plans.

For example, several mobile phone network operators in developing countries decided that the best way to promote adoption of mobile phones is to reduce the cost of the handset. So they joined together to aggregate their buying power, and Motorola has agreed to supply up to 6 million handsets for less than $40 each. Such modest efforts provide a way to create a collaboration infrastructure, develop effective practices, and build relevant skills.

THE RIGHT PARTNERS

Choosing the right collaboration partners is a balancing act. Linking up with many competitors through a consortium can bring greater scale advantages than collaborating with a smaller group, but operational conflicts and complexity also tend to increase as more partners are brought into an effort. And collaborating with companies that are similar to your own—in size, culture, and heritage—can reduce managerial and operational conflicts but will also tend to decrease diversity, making it harder to think outside the box.

In choosing partners, therefore, carefully weigh both the project's goals and the characteristics of potential collaborators, asking such questions as:

- How tightly integrated will partner organizations need to be, given the project's scope, goals, and accountability arrangements?
- How similar are the potential partners' strategies and operating environments?
- What shared knowledge base or history exists among the potential partners? If the industry is tightly knit, will existing or past relationships help or hinder efforts?
- How much common ground do the potential collaborators have? Is there enough diversity in the collaborative design? Are there other potential partners, from within or outside the industry, that could inject new perspectives?
- Would there be benefits to bringing suppliers or customers into the group?

OVERCOMING THE "MORTAL ENEMIES" OBJECTION

There is a powerful psychological barrier to collaboration: *We can't collaborate with our mortal enemies.* But a quick look at the historical record suggests that this is not always the reality.

Hewlett-Packard (HP) and Canon are rivals in the printer business, yet they've worked very effectively in collaborative arrangements, such as HP sourcing printer engines from Canon.

WPP and Paris-based Havas are fierce rivals in the advertising business, yet they have worked closely together in media purchasing.

Sony and Samsung are global rivals in the consumer electronics world, yet both have begun collaborating on several fronts:

• Jointly investing $2 billion in a factory in South Korea to produce liquid-crystal displays
• Sharing 24,000 basic patents that cover a range of components and production processes
• Participating in a consortium that is trying to establish the standard for the next generation of digital video discs and players

General Motors and Toyota worked very effectively in their NUMMI collaboration, a joint production facility in California, creating significant benefits for both companies.

More recently, the auto industry produced another example in Dundee, Michigan, where a partnership among Chrysler, Mitsubishi, and Hyundai has teamed up to build small auto engines, sharing start-up costs and achieving savings they couldn't have enjoyed if they'd built three separate, smaller facilities. Smartly, the three-company alliance took advantage of the new-plant opportunity to try other innovations: The factory uses state-of-the-art technology and a uniquely flexible UAW labor contract to keep costs down, encourage quick problem solving by versatile teams of workers, and turn out as many as 840,000 engines a year while requiring just 250 hourly workers—as compared to the 750 workers needed to produce 350,000 engines at Chrysler's Mack Avenue plant in Detroit.

Crafting an effective collaboration is never easy, especially when the participants are intensely competitive. But the record shows that profitable collaboration can be achieved in ways that bring enormous economic benefits to the partners and their customers.

When you step outside the business arena, there is probably no group on earth more intensely competitive than scientists, for whom recognition and pride of place count for so much. Think about Newton competing with Leibniz to develop calculus, Darwin rushing to publish his theory of evolution once he heard that Alfred Russel Wallace had the same idea, the race to unlock the secrets of DNA recounted by Francis Crick in his memorable book *The Double Helix*, or the more recent race among teams of researchers to be the first to sequence the human genome.

Yet this hypercompetitive group is simultaneously the most collaborative of all. There is a powerful tradition of sharing scientific information across broad consortia that include universities, government agencies, and for-profit organizations. Many major projects would otherwise have been impossible—for example, the CERN accelerator in Geneva, the world's largest particle physics center, founded in 1954 as one of the first collaborative efforts of the European Union and now supported by twenty countries. Scientists have learned to become as effective collaborators as they are competitors. They've done it in a way that balances the compete/collaborate ratio and leaves everybody much better off. Many businesses can learn to do the same.

THE COMPETITION PARADOX

In 1776, Adam Smith published his great defense of free market capitalism, *An Inquiry into the Nature and Causes of the Wealth of Nations*. By showing how competition lifts living standards throughout society, Smith successfully countered calls for increased regulation of commerce—and set the stage for the great gains of the Industrial Revolution. More than 150 years later, the economist Joseph Schumpeter added a memorable gloss to Smith's ideas when he described how competition creates a cycle of "creative destruction" that continually brings new and better products into the marketplace.

Smith, Schumpeter, and the other great capitalist philosophers provide the intellectual bedrock for our faith and trust in the benefits of vigorous competition. But over the past fifty years, we have come to distort their teachings by using them to justify a blind and sometimes fanatical devotion to competition. Some business executives and pundits have promoted a view of business as a form of warfare or sport that can be won only through fierce and unrelenting conflict. That's a simplistic and dangerous view of business. Adam Smith and his followers understood that in certain cases unbridled competition may cause great harm—mindless competition can bring not creative destruction but just destruction.

Given how easily global pressures can devastate the profitability of industries, we need to return to a more balanced view of competition and a greater appreciation of the role of collaboration in engendering and sustaining healthy economies. When companies compete too broadly—battling in areas that create little value for customers—they end up wasting enormous amounts of money and weakening the very structure of their industry. By refocusing competition on areas that really matter, strategic collaboration promotes the kinds of robust rivalry that engender better products, lower prices, and stronger industries and economies. That's the great paradox of competition: By reducing it in some areas, you strengthen it in the places that provide the most benefits to the most people.

De-Risk Your Business

Here are some questions to work through if you help run a business that is facing—or that soon may be threatened by—the specter of industry risk.

1. Which of our business activities are uncompetitive, or add little or no value? (This includes any activity for which our customers do not pay, or which they would refuse to pay for if offered the choice.)

2. Which of these activities could we collaborate with others to perform? Are the best returns possible from working together on manufacturing, sourcing, primary R&D, applications, distribution, or services/training (for example, industry-wide training programs leading to new customer creation and to increased demand generation)?

3. Within each domain, what subset of activities would be the best to collaborate on? (For example, in auto manufacturing, it might be the creation of a common plant to manufacture small engines, transmissions, or other parts of the vehicle; in sourcing, it might be setting common standards, common processes, and aggregating purchasing volume through joint buying programs.)

4. Where are there friction costs in a process (such as aggregating parts from too many disparate suppliers) that can be reduced through integration (for example, the use of pre-manufactured modules) or other mechanisms?

5. Which of our activities *could* generate unique value, but only if we collaborate with others to perform them? (iTunes is an example: Music fans will only become regular patrons of a site that lets them download songs from *all* the major distributors, not just one or two.)

6. If we collaborated on these activities, how much could we save?

7. Where could we apply those savings to better differentiate our company from the competition or to create new value for customers?

It's not enough merely to save money through collaboration. That will reduce the financial stresses created by industry risk, but it won't *reverse* the risk and transform it into upside opportunity. To achieve that, you need to invest the money you save into differentiating efforts—initiatives that will enable you to create unique product or service offerings, reach new markets, and expand the value you create for customers.

SYNTHETIC HISTORY:
THE AUTOMAKERS MOVE TO COLLABORATE

What might have been different if one of the world's largest industries had applied some of the ideas practiced by smaller industries over the past decade? A synthetic history of the automotive world might provide an answer.

It's October 1996. The September new-car launches have just been completed. The fortunes of the world's great automakers vary widely, with the leading Japanese companies generally doing well, while American firms are struggling in many parts of their product lines except trucks and SUVs. Nonetheless, it's clear that there are certain problems the entire industry shares. These include the growing need for fuel-efficient vehicles in a world where oil supplies are shrinking and dependent on unstable regimes; increased demand for cars with improved safety, security, and other features; and, especially, global industry over-capacity, which is intensifying competition, increasing customer power, and driving profit margins steadily lower. What's more, the overcapacity problem is sure to become worse in years to come, as nascent auto industries in Korea, China, and India ramp up.

These problems are not new. But at this moment, something new appears to be happening. The leaders of the biggest automakers now seem to recognize that they face a shared set of problems, and for the first time they seem to be moving toward exploring some shared solutions.

On October 24, the Associated Press carries the following terse, cryptic bulletin: "General Motors has confirmed that its CEO, John Smith, will meet today with the chief executives of Toyota, Ford, and Honda to consider matters of joint concern. 'Because the meeting is private, there will be no public comment on the specific topics discussed,' a spokesman said."

The 1996 meeting isn't the first time that rival automakers have considered collaboration. In fact, a history of some joint efforts already exists. In 1986, General Motors and Toyota collaborated in founding NUMMI. In 1992, USCAR was launched by GM, Ford, and Chrysler, a joint venture for research into technologies such as battery development. But these were modest programs, especially when compared with the scope of the industry-wide challenges now looming.

The automakers recognize the seriousness of their shared dilemma, and they sense the need to work together to tackle it. But there's an atmosphere of tension in the room. Each of the CEOs believes—not without justification—that he brings to the table something that is unique and more valuable than what any of the others can bring. It's a complex cocktail of emotions swirling around: the old American hubris, the newfound Japanese pride in their undoubted quality advantage, and hurt feelings over past snubs (as when Toyota's bid to participate in USCAR was rejected by the American companies).

The conversation soon evolves into a multibillion-dollar game of poker, with subtle jockeying for individual position behind every proposal and counterproposal. But in the back of each CEO's mind, a similar calculus is taking place: "We already collaborate a bit in our industry. But just a bit. The compete/collaborate ratio is something like 95/5. How far do we dare to move it? Should we collaborate 10 percent or even 15 percent of the time? How much will we gain? Will it compensate for the control we'll lose? And can we really trust a part of our future to our rivals sitting across the table?"

As the morning wears on, a list of possible areas for collaboration takes shape.

- *More common production facilities, along the lines of NUMMI*
- *Joint development of new propulsion systems—more fuel-efficient engines that will reduce emissions and save customers money*
- *Shared research into improving systems such as transmissions— important, expensive systems that customers never see and that create no competitive advantage for any one manufacturer*
- *Development of universal standards for safety, security, and communications—areas that consumers say they care about and where shared improvements could lift all boats*
- *Most ambitious: a shared program to develop a low-cost, small car for the emerging markets in Asia and Africa—a safe, reliable vehicle that can retail for less than $7,000*

Each of these projects has been discussed and costed out at automakers around the world, and the numbers are sobering: $1 billion to develop a fuel-efficient hybrid engine, another $3 billion to $4 billion to convert the whole fleet to hybrid; $500 million for a new transmission system; $400 to $600 million for an in-vehicle security and communication system; $500 million for safety improve-

ments. The total cost would be prohibitive for any one company—but for the industry as a whole, it is manageable.

The conversation ends with a sense of new possibilities, but the agenda is ambitious and the change in attitude required is daunting. The CEOs return to their home offices for further strategizing and discussion, and with an agreement to talk further a year later.

In December 1997, the conversation resumes. Toyota has launched its Prius, and the vehicle is off to a good start, but it's no barn burner. Ditto for Honda and its new Insight. GM's OnStar system for in-vehicle communication and security is having a hard time getting off the ground. The stock prices of the automakers are high and rising, but deep down, the CEOs all know that these prices are unsustainable.

As they reexamine the list of potential areas for collaboration, there's a new urgency in the discussion. And the studies done by their financial and engineering experts back in the various home offices have confirmed the enormous advantages to be gained through joint efforts. After two days of talks, the CEOs shake hands. In each mind is the same exciting yet somewhat frightening realization: "We may be able to do this."

In early 1998, they bite the bullet. At a joint press conference, the CEOs of the world's leading automakers announce an agreement to share several basic technologies. The statement issued by all the companies reads, in part, "We realize that without highly disciplined project management accountable to the alliance, no advantage will be created, either for our companies or for consumers." Based on this realization, they create a networked development system including several R&D labs with clear project leadership, specific investment commitments, and aggressive schedules.

Over the next eight years, the industry's compete/collaborate ratio shifts dramatically. By 2002, it has moved from 95/5 to 85/15. By 2006, it is 80/20. Yet the car companies are still competing as fiercely as ever—in their styling and branding, in interior designs, in improving the dealer experience, and in increased sales of ancillary goods and services.

This competition, however, is built on a much higher base. Hybrid engines and new, dramatically improved safety systems were introduced industry-wide in 2002. An enhanced OnStar communication and security system, jointly developed and owned, was installed in every new car sold by 2003. Shared production facilities, designed with the latest flexible manufacturting techniques, have come on line in North America, Japan, and Europe, driving costs down and saving consumers money. Yet industry profits are way up—partly as a result of cost savings, partly due to worldwide customer enthusiasm over the new, improved vehicles available, and partly due to greatly increased sales of add-on services. (The car companies are making hundreds of millions just from sales of telephone minutes for the new, universal, hands-free in-car phones.)

By October 2006 when the alliance members hold their annual meeting, they can point to savings of some $15 billion since 1998—savings that continue to grow each year. With the world's installed base of vehicles being rapidly converted to the hybrid engine, global fuel consumption has already been cut by some 5 percent annually. By 2010, the reduction will be 10 percent; by 2015, 20 percent. But an even bigger breakthrough could occur if hydrogen fuel cells can be perfected. The joint research team is working aggressively to determine whether this technology will be the next big improvement in fuel efficiency. If so, it will be developed on a vastly accelerated schedule made possible by the shared talent and resources contributed by automakers from around the world.

As for the low-cost car for the burgeoning markets in Asia and Africa, its development is still in progress, spurred by Tata Motors of India's announcement that it is developing a $4,000 car.

Looking back on the achievements of the alliance, the CEOs have reason to be pleased. But they are far from complacent. "So far, so good," they say. "But what can we do for an encore?" The conversations continue....

What would have been the difference (for companies, consumers, and economies) if this type of collaboration *had* been created in the last ten years? Or if it is created and developed in the next ten years? Or if it is created in numerous other industries?

CHAPTER SEVEN

When Your Business Stops Growing

Inventing New Forms of Demand

A N INDUSTRY SQUEEZE that turns an industry into a no-profit zone is a terrible thing. Almost equally deadly is the risk that strikes when a company's sales, profits, and stock valuation hit a plateau and then stop growing. We've seen *stagnation risk* strike several companies, where shareholder value leveled off and then declined as a result of the inability to find new sources of growth in the face of market maturity.

When this risk first occurs, it doesn't *feel* all that bad. The company still makes a profit and still pays a dividend, and market share may remain high. On the surface, things seem just about the same as ever, and most people around the business assume or hope that growth will resume in a quarter or two. But once the true end of growth hits a company (as opposed to a temporary plateau for identifiable, remediable reasons), it's often there to stay.

In the long run, the consequences of stagnation can be severe. The funds to invest in innovation begin to dry up. Talent begins to leave the company, especially the brightest and most promising managers. They've done the projections and extrapolations, and they know that opportunities will be few in their now slowly growing company. They begin to believe that their career advancement will be determined not by their performance but by the age structure of the high command, and they start going elsewhere. As a result, there's a little less energy in the organization, a little less smarts, and decisions are a little less sharp. Many of them are just dead wrong. The negative trends continue, and gain strength. R&D productivity declines, new-product introductions slow to a trickle, sales growth stops altogether. You know the end of this story: stability, stagnation, decline.

If you suspect your company may be suffering from stagnation risk, you're not alone. In the 1990s and the early 2000s, as products and markets have matured and international competition has intensified, many companies have seen average revenue growth rates decline from the 10 to 15 percent range into the 1 to 3 percent range. Stagnation risk is a looming problem that hundreds of companies will confront in the next several years.

THE SISYPHUS SYNDROME

The impact of stagnation risk is extremely widespread. If you spend a few Saturday afternoons flipping through the pages of Value Line (which covers some 2,000 equities), you'll see very few consistent stock price growth curves. You notice that most companies spend most of their time recovering from hits to their stock price. Most of those hits are the result of the strategic risks we've talked about, including stagnation risk.

The constant work of recovering lost value in the wake of such collapses is the number one obstacle to growth. One of the most powerful sources of motivation to deploy an effective strategic risk management system to your business (in addition to avoiding all the disruptions and losses that these hits generate) is to enable real growth, rather than having the rock roll back down the hill for you to push it up all over again, like the unfortunate Sisyphus in the Greek myth.

The first two jobs of a strategic risk management system are to sidestep the unnecessary blows and to mitigate the blows you can't avoid. Doing this well solves half the growth problem, since you can build on a strong base rather than spend time and treasure to rebuild to the stock price you had five years ago.

But a strategic risk management system can do much more than defend. It is also an incredibly efficient means to find some of the biggest growth opportunities your business faces. As we've seen repeatedly, your biggest risks are often your biggest growth opportunities. A finely tuned, highly sensitive strategic risk radar screen will quickly pick out incipient brand erosion, customer shift, transition risk, or industry margin collapse. It will provide a healthy, long-enough lead time to evaluate the risk and design the best response, whether it's preemption, hedge, or double-betting. Managed aggressively, these responses can generate enormous new growth for the business.

Big risks don't appear on a reliable schedule, however. They may not be there when your business needs a major infusion of new growth. Fortunately, there are two other new growth vectors that you can control: demand innovation and discovering the next big idea for your business.

LITTLE BOX/BIG BOX: DEMAND INNOVATION

The first of these, *demand innovation*, involves looking at your customers and prospects differently. It requires seeing not only their functional needs (which your current products address) but also their economic needs and other, higher-order needs, such as plannability, convenience, guarantees, risk reduction (for *them*), and so on. The little box is your product, the big box is the customer's total economics. Serving the customer's big box needs can multiply the size of your market.

Demand innovation is about focusing your economic creativity on the big box. It is about redefining your customer offerings in a way that expands the value you can offer your customers, radically broadens your market, and strengthens your relationship with them. Companies that have figured out how to practice demand innovation can resist the undertow of stagnation and achieve growth in sales and profits even when the companies around them are struggling to keep from losing ground.

Demand innovation can take many forms. It includes supporting the customer through services such as installation, maintenance, financing, and training; helping the customer save money by reducing waste, trimming costs, and minimizing inefficiencies; making the customer's life simpler and more enjoyable; helping customers reduce the risks and uncertainties they face in using your products or services; and in a B2B context, helping customers grow their own businesses by finding new customers, new sources of revenue, and new forms of profitability.

Little box/big box thinking originated in the mid-1990s in the B2B world. Companies such as Continental AG, Air Liquide, and others faced stagnation risk, and they invented new ways to grow by helping their customers improve their economics. This discipline of demand innovation has spread since then, both in the B2B and B2C world.

CONTINENTAL AG:
DEMAND INNOVATION CAPTURES MORE OF THE CAR

The German-based tire maker Continental AG confronted languishing growth and profit declines during the mid-1990s. Company leadership decided to broaden its focus from the tire to integrated car safety systems, which were becoming more complex and costly due to innovations in computerized control technology.

In the subsequent decade, Continental has evolved from a leading tire producer into a supplier of complete automotive technology systems, expanding its position in the carmakers' value chain from 2–4 percent of the total to an estimated 13–16 percent. Continental has developed these capacities through both internal development and acquisitions, buying brake and chassis systems maker Teves from ITT (1998), chassis maker Temic (2001), the wheel sensor operations of Nagano Japan Radio (2003), and about 76 percent of Phoenix, a rubber and plastics technology company (2004). Most recently (2006), Continental agreed to buy Motorola's safety-oriented car electronics business.

The combination of these capabilities has enabled Continental AG to offer a very different value proposition to its customers. Consider, for instance, the evolution of Continental's business relationship with Mercedes-Benz. Prior to 1997, Continental simply supplied tires. Over the next several years, it began selling a broader array of related electronics gear. By 2005, it had become a major supplier of key systems for the Mercedes M-class and R-class vehicle lines, including programs for electronic stability control, traction control, adaptive cruise control, braking systems, air suspension systems, engine cooling systems, oil monitoring systems, heating systems, ignitions, and starters.

Continental's response to the hybrid revolution offers another striking example. In partnership with ZF Friedrichshafen AG, Continental recently unveiled a hybrid transmission that saves precious space by integrating the electric motor, clutch, torsion damper, dual-mass flywheel, and hydraulics into the system. Now Continental is developing a hybrid module that includes an electric motor, power electronics, energy management system, brake systems, and electrical auxiliaries. As hybrids become more and more important in the automotive world, Continental's technical prowess will help it grow in parallel.

Thanks to its decade-long process of helping customers solve new types of problems, Continental has developed a unique and dynamic business design. It is now the only industry supplier to sell the combination of tire, brake, and suspension systems, safety systems, hybrid technology systems, and interiors. Through public education and joint research with regulatory authorities on safety, Continental is helping convince automakers to include its safety solutions as standard features in their SUVs and other high-end vehicles.

As a result of its decade of demand innovation, Continental has been outperforming its comparator companies. From 2000 to 2005, Continental AG grew profitably at 11.5 percent. By contrast, Michelin, Goodyear, Bridgestone, and Sumitomo Rubber have had growth rates of 4.9, 6.5, 5.4, and 3.2 percent, respectively, while Pirelli has actually shrunk by 5.8 percent annually over the same period.

AIR LIQUIDE:
EXPANDING CUSTOMER OFFERINGS FROM COMMODITIZED GOODS TO UNIQUE SERVICES

Other companies are creating new forms of demand by developing ways of reducing risk *for their customers* as well as for themselves. Consider Air Liquide, a century-old French firm that originated as a specialist in providing gases such as oxygen and nitrogen to industrial users.

By the late 1980s, Air Liquide's traditional business was highly vulnerable to commoditization. Margins had collapsed and growth was minimal. However, the company's leadership realized that the technical expertise the firm had developed over decades could be harnessed to create unique new value for its customers.

Simple, seemingly low-risk gases such as oxygen can produce serious fire hazards when concentrated; other gases, harmless by themselves, become toxic when allowed to mix. To manage these risks and comply with increasingly strict regulations, Air Liquide had developed sophisticated measurement and detection systems, quality-control technologies, process automation, pollutant treatment methods, and production planning techniques. Many of these tools and practices had direct applications for customers' hazardous materials processes and were more sophisticated than what most customers were doing on their own.

These risk management tools became Air Liquide's new source of upside business potential. In time, the company was able to move beyond being a provider of industrial gases to managing its customers' broader chemical processes. For example, Texas Instruments (TI), a major chip maker, initially used Air Liquide simply as a supplier of specialty gases. At the time, TI manufactured, conditioned, and packaged its own chemicals for use in chip production. Looking for ways to divest non-core activities, TI approached Air Liquide about taking on a role in managing its Chemical Operations department.

The reliability guarantees that Air Liquide was able to provide in taking on chemicals management gave TI managers peace of mind and greater freedom to concentrate on their core business. In 2004, TI renewed its long-term contract with Air Liquide and signed a new fifteen-year agreement making Air Liquide the total gas and chemicals manager for a new TI facility.

Another example of the new kinds of demand Air Liquide is inventing can be seen at MicroTechPark in Thalheim, Germany, a large multi-company facility that is expected to become one of the primary centers for solar cell production in Europe. In January 2006, Air Liquide agreed to become MicroTechPark's sole supplier of the technical and specialty gases required for the production of solar cells. Air Liquide will also manage the entire gas supply chain, providing all services related to gas delivery and handling. Far more than a mere product wholesaler, Air Liquide will be an integral part of business management for its customers at MicroTechPark.

Air Liquide is even engaging in joint research and development projects with its customers—for example, working as a "molecule designer" with electronic equipment manufacturers to develop chemical solutions needed for chip manufacturing. One of these joint projects, with

California-based Aviza Technology, led to the development of a highly valuable low-temperature deposition process for chemical vapor known as SATIN, which is now being marketed to other manufacturers. Now the two companies have expanded their relationship to cover development of a dozen more precursor materials and advanced processes for chip manufacturing.

By inventing and capitalizing on such opportunities, Air Liquide has expanded its potential market from industrial gas to a number of markets that are each two to three times as large. Because services have grown faster and have much higher margins than the traditional gas supply business, this shift also helps shield Air Liquide from the economic swings that buffet its competitors, allowing it to increase its average revenue per contract and write longer contracts.

As a result, Air Liquide has generated average annual growth of revenues and profits in the 10 percent range, increased recurring revenue, enhanced its ability to plan for future growth, and reduced volatility of shareholder value, all in a much tougher business environment than it faced in the 1980s and 1990s.

PROCTER & GAMBLE: MASTERING THE ANTHROPOLOGY OF DEMAND

Although demand innovation originated in the B2B world, it has since been extended to the consumer world, and even to consumer packaged goods. Some of the most interesting innovations have come from Procter & Gamble.

P&G felt the impact of stagnation risk in dramatic fashion. In 1999, investment analysts formed the view that there was little growth in the company's future. In response, the stock price fell by nearly 50 percent within a quarter (from $54 per share, adjusted for splits, at the end of 1999 to just $28 by the end of March 2000). This decline led to a management change, with A. G. Lafley replacing Durk Jager as CEO in 2000, and the search for new growth was taken on in deadly earnest.

The company had already realized that it was facing a potential growth crisis. In 1998, it had launched Organization 2005, a global initiative designed to drive innovative ideas to world markets faster, and some early results had already been achieved. Under Lafley, the push to innovate was accelerated. The company quadrupled its design staff and, for the first time, began hiring product development experts who had worked at other companies and even in other industries.

For the past several years, P&G has been going street-level in the search for innovative sources of growth—literally getting down and dirty. It has descended from the high plane of marketing and brand building, benefit messaging, and TV advertising down to the spaces where the product and the consumer wage their daily battles against dirt: the laundry room, the broom closet, the carpeted living room.

Just as Continental AG lives inside the customer's world (the auto designer's studio and the car factory floor), P&G has started to live inside its customer's world. P&G people and their advisers spend weeks with customers in their homes, watching them doing the laundry, scrubbing the floors, cleaning the countertops—studying human behavior around household chores the way anthropologists study tribal folkways in remote villages.

They are doing the consumer equivalent of Air Liquide's and Continental's search for the pain points in the customer's process. They observe what really happens, draw up how the process works today, and ask a series of simple questions: What's wrong with this picture? Where are the inefficiencies? Where's the friction? What doesn't work? Then they figure out how to change that picture. How can things work better for their customers—and how can P&G make money in the process?

Swiffer, the cleaning tool, is the prototypical example. It's a mop with a detachable cloth attachment that contains a solvent and an electrostatic charge that mops up dirt with wonderful efficacy. When the cloth fills up, you simply detach it and plug in a new one. It's quick, clean, and effective.

P&G's company mythology pinpoints the morning of February 15, 1995, as the day when the Swiffer was born—not in a corporate R&D lab or a marketing workshop, but in the kitchen of an elderly Boston woman who was being interviewed by a P&G consultant about how she cleaned her floors. Legend has it that in the middle of the interview, as the woman was pointing out the attractive features of her favorite vacuum cleaner, she spotted a few spilled coffee grounds on the floor. Without missing a beat, she set the vacuum cleaner aside, fetched a broom and dustpan from a nearby closet, and used them to sweep up the grounds.

That thirty-second encounter haunted the consultant, a design expert from a firm called Continuum, Inc., that had been hired by P&G to research human behavior around floor cleaning. The woman's actions revealed so much more than her words. She loved her vacuum cleaner—but when a small, spur-of-the-moment floor cleaning job appeared, she abandoned the machine for a simpler, faster, easier alternative. She found it in the old-fashioned, messy, broom-and-dustpan combo.

Without even realizing it, this woman had a problem. And so did millions of other men and women, for whom lugging around a heavy vacuum cleaner, untangling a cord, and plugging and unplugging it was just too much trouble when small spills needed cleaning. Surely P&G, with all its cleaning expertise, could offer something better.

Recognizing the problem was one breakthrough, and a huge one. Solving it was another. The Swiffer's design was the result of many tests, experiments, and modifications. After repeated trial and error, each iteration came closer to the target of consumer delight. The ultimate result was a handy cleaning wand that uses an electrostatic charge to attract dust and tiny particles of dirt—just the kind of job consumers hate dragging out the vacuum cleaner for. And the consumer *was* delighted. Swiffer was easier, more convenient, less messy—all you could ask for, and then some. The product was launched in 1999, just as P&G stock was skidding. By 2004, Swiffer had reached $500 million in sales.

Most important, Swiffer represents a major shift in the P&G business design, from a "buy-one-product" game to a "razor-and-blades" game. The Swiffer wand is the razor, and the cloths that pick up the dirt and must be replaced periodically are the blades—a delightfully different profit model from the standard consumer packaged-goods game.

Today, the Swiffer brand is still growing rapidly. There have been seven major brand extensions, the latest of which is the Swiffer Carpet-Flick, a new kind of sweeper designed to quickly and easily pick up little messes from the 75 percent of American floors that are carpeted. As with the original Swiffer, it was a brainchild of field research—in this case, the finding that three times out of four, people pulling out the vacuum were using it to clear a small batch of grass or leaves or clippings from a corner of their rug. Swiffer is now a $1 billion product—the initial result of P&G's movement inside the bubble of the consumer's reality.

Swiffer was just a start. P&G is developing an entire repertoire of new growth moves that start with the problems discovered inside the customer's reality and work back from there to create a new offer and a new business design to provide that answer profitably.

Another move in the growing repertoire was asking, "Are there things that professionals do for consumers that consumers could do for themselves?" Crest Whitestrips were one result—a product line designed to supplement or even replace professional teeth-whitening services traditionally provided by dentists in an expensive, inconvenient office procedure. The Whitestrips system, launched in May 2001 and now available in six styles, retails for an average of $29.95—much less expensive than a dentist visit, but a hefty chunk of revenue for a company whose traditional price points had been well under $10. And two versions—Whitestrips Professional and Whitestrips Supreme—are available only through dentists' offices, helping to defuse the sense of competition that might otherwise lead professionals to discourage their clients from trying the P&G product.

These moves were made in the context of a broader growth strategy, one that created an intense focus on three elements:

• Big brands
• Big geographies
• Big retailer customers

The combination of these moves began to change the analysts' point of view. P&G's stock started coming back, reaching $54 per share by the middle of 2004. It was an excellent comeback. From an investor's perspective, however, all of this movement was just recovering lost ground. By 2004, P&G had worked back to where it had been in 1999—a Sisyphus-like labor indeed.

Today, P&G is continuing to follow this new growth trajectory. The company has launched some of the world's most ambitious research projects in consumer anthropology. There was the July 2001 program in which video crews were sent to eighty homes around the world to record families carrying out their ordinary routines over a period of four days. The result: a searchable video database that P&G experts now use to analyze the differing customs and habits of consumers from sub-Saharan Africa to India to Germany to the American Midwest.

Since then, the resources devoted to consumer anthropology by P&G continue to grow. The 4,000 consumer studies conducted by the company in 2001 have grown to over 10,000 in 2006, at a cost of over $200 million. And the growth results are impressive. Over the 2003–2005 period, the company's revenues grew at a compound annual rate of 12 percent, up from 4 percent just five years earlier. Perhaps even more impressive, the percentage of new products meeting their sales targets has risen to over 70 percent in 2006—more than double the rate in 2000.

P&G's moves (live in the customer's world, put professional services in the hands of the consumer) are part of a broader array of new growth moves. Demand innovation, born in the B2B world, has crossed over into the B2C world with a rich repertoire of available moves, from producing integrated solutions to resegmenting the market to create new times, places, and purposes for purchases. (See Figure 7-1 for a collection of such moves.)

Moves such as these enable a company to fundamentally redefine its growth frontiers and to push back the risk of stagnation for a few more years.

FIGURE 7-1
DEMAND INNOVATION—
A REPERTOIRE OF GROWTH MOVES

MOVE	DEFINITION	COMPANY EXAMPLE
INTEGRATED SOLUTIONS	Expand the product definition to include other relevant offerings and thereby reduce customers' cost or purchase complexity	**Lunchables Lunch Combinations** (packages a sandwich or other main dish with a drink and a treat)
SHIFT FROM PRODUCT TO SYSTEMS OFFERS	Transform the product into the centerpiece of a pre-integrated problem-solving system that offers greater customer value	**Bose Home Theater** (a pre-engineered sound system that makes it easy for customers to create an instant home theater with their own TV)

MOVE	DEFINITION	COMPANY EXAMPLE
SHIFT BUYER DEFINITION	Use skills, knowledge, or relationships gained in serving consumers to focus on opportunities with other businesses	**Fidelity** (uses its investment marketing savvy gained from consumer interactions to serve a new market of corporate 401(k) plan administrators and other professional investment managers)
REENGINEER THE CONSUMER PROCESS	Redesign the process for selecting, purchasing, using, recycling, and repurchasing the product to make it more convenient, enjoyable, or affordable	**Netflix** (lets movie fans pick from thousands of DVDs online and receive and return them through simple postage-paid mailings)
SHIFT FROM PROFESSIONAL TO CONSUMER DO-IT-YOURSELF	Allow consumers to save time, money, and energy by helping them perform services that previously required professional advice or help	**Crest Whitestrips** (allows consumers to whiten their teeth safely and conveniently at home rather than visiting a dentist for professional services)
RESEGMENT FOR NEW PURCHASE OCCASIONS	Redefine the conventional time, place, and purpose of purchases to meet unmet needs	**Enterprise Rent-a-Car** (moves car rental from airport counters to downtown locations for occasional errands, out-of-town trips, or vehicle replacements during service)
LIFESTYLE BRAND EXTENSION	Make the brand into the basis of a consumer lifestyle on which a host of activities and purchases can be centered	**Harley-Davidson** (whose Harley Owners Group—HOG—makes motorcycle ownership the centerpiece of a lifestyle celebrating the freedom of the open road)

MOVE	DEFINITION	COMPANY EXAMPLE
SUPPORTING OR LICENSED SERVICES	Supplement product offerings with services that make the product more useful, productive, convenient, or fun	**GM OnStar** (provides owners of GM and other vehicles with online safety and service features that make driving safer and more enjoyable)
MOVE DOWNSTREAM	Expand the customer base by providing services to customers' customers	**John Deere Landscapes** (provides services and financing to customers who patronize companies that use John Deere equipment)
REVERSE THE PYRAMID	Target low- to middle-market customers with a tailored yet low-cost offering	**Old Navy** (offers lower-priced clothing for a broader market than Gap or Banana Republic while taking advantage of infrastructure synergies with those higher-end brands)
SUPPORT AND SERVICE THE INSTALLED BASE	Use installed hardware for profitable follow-on sales of consumables	**Swiffer** (Procter & Gamble floor cleaning tool, whose electrostatic pads must be replaced periodically)
CHANNEL BUSINESS PARTNER	Provide customer support goods or services to make business easier or more lucrative for companies that distribute your products	**Clarke American** (provides a growing array of administrative and marketing services to banks whose customers purchase checks printed by Clarke American)

The repertoire in Figure 7-1 is just suggestive. Many companies have used it as a starting point, made some of the growth moves listed, and then developed others unique to their own business situation. How far could your company push this repertoire if it wanted to?

The Next Big Idea

The second major vector in addition to demand innovation is creating or discovering just one big idea for your business. Sometimes one big idea can build a decade of new growth. Little box/big box thinking can be expanded to include the "bigger box" of an idea that opens up a large new market adjacent to your current space with years' worth of growth potential.

IKEA: FROM HOME FURNISHINGS TO THE HOME ITSELF

Founded in Sweden in 1943, IKEA was a little store selling items such as pens, wallets, table runners, even nylon stockings. In 1947, furniture was added to the product mix. Since that time, the company has had no problem with growth. It has expanded to 231 stores in thirty-three countries, employs 90,000 workers, and had revenues in 2005 of over $17.7 billion, an increase of 15 percent over the previous year (on top of the previous year's 24 percent jump). What's more, there are plenty of locations around the globe available to sell consumers stylish, well-designed, ultra-low-cost furniture. IKEA has not yet come to most of those places. It hasn't even scratched the surface.

But if you do the simple arithmetic of a locational business, you can calculate when you'll hit the growth wall. For some companies, such as IKEA, that time is fifteen years in the future; for others, such as Southwest Airlines, it's five to seven years away. The time to confront stagnation risk is not when you hit the wall but a few years before that point. IKEA is far ahead of schedule.

In 1997, IKEA built its first BoKlok home in Sweden. (The name translates to "Live Smart.") It was a prefabricated house produced through a partnership with a construction firm called Skanska. It was simple, affordable, and had good design. Customers loved it. Since then, IKEA has expanded its home-building activity to various parts of Scandinavia, selling modest-sized but airy and attractive open-plan homes for the equivalent of $45,000. Now it's making a major push into the United Kingdom, where BoKlok houses sell at a starting price of around £70,000. This means they are within reach of first-time home

Live Smart @ Home

*A BoKlok duplex in the U.K. brings IKEA's unique business model
into the enormous new-house marketplace.*

buyers earning between £12,500 and £30,000. IKEA sweetens the deal
by throwing in £500 worth of gift certificates to help buyers furnish their
new home.

Consumer acceptance is high—some 2,500 BoKlok prefabs have
been sold. When a new development of sixty BoKloks opened outside
Oslo, the units sold out in forty-five minutes. And IKEA homes that are
five to six years old show that, as construction goes, they're doing extremely well. They hold up as well as conventionally built homes do.
Customer satisfaction is high, and the word-of-mouth engine is beginning to do its work.

Not everyone is a customer for IKEA furniture; not everyone will be
a customer for an IKEA home. But, just for perspective, the U.S. home
furniture market is $30 billion. The home construction industry is $1 *tril-
lion*. That's a lot of room for future growth.

DOCOMO: THE PHONE AS UNIVERSAL GATEKEEPER

NTT DoCoMo is a fourteen-year-old Japanese company that has enjoyed
a phenomenal run of success as the world's pioneer of mobile telephone

services. Prodded and tugged by its American-educated (and American-brash) senior vice president Takeshi Natsuno, DoCoMo (a subsidiary of NTT, the national Japanese telephone company) launched its famous i-mode service in 1999. i-mode expanded the uses of cell phones to include Internet access, stock quotes, video gaming, text messaging, and a host of other offerings calculated to appeal to Japan's tech-savvy, gadget-loving "thumb generation." The business design was simple: Outside companies provided content, collected fees from users via their monthly telephone bills, and paid DoCoMo a 9 percent access fee.

i-mode was a huge, instant hit. Tens of millions of people signed up for the service, DoCoMo's sales, profits, and market cap soared, and tech experts proclaimed i-mode the wave of the future in wireless technology. But today, DoCoMo's growth has slowed. The company is still huge, with a market cap over $80 billion and 49 million Japanese customers, representing more than half the market. Newer businesses such as downloadable ringtones are continuing to expand. But with the market reaching saturation, rival firms driving down prices, and an anticipated invasion of Europe seemingly stalled (with DoCoMo commanding just 4 million out of 500 million potential customer accounts), in 2005 the firm suffered a revenue decline for the first time in its history.

To reverse the trend, Natsuno is betting on a big idea—a next-generation mobile phone that acts as the equivalent of a credit card, money, personal ID, keys, and camera as well as digital communications device. If Natsuno has his way, Japanese customers will soon use their phones to operate appliances, buy movie and subway tickets, pay for gas and groceries, use vending machines, even unlock their front doors. "All that stuff in a woman's purse or a man's wallet should go into the phone," he declares.

Pieces of the puzzle are already in place. The first version of the new phone, launched in July 2004, acts as a debit card and can store up to about $450 in cash. Early in 2006, it became possible to board commuter trains in Tokyo by waving the phone near a sensor in the turnstile. In April 2006, DoCoMo bought a 34 percent stake in a leading Japanese credit card company in hopes of offering full-fledged, phone-based credit card service by 2007.

Natsuno's idea is no slam dunk. Japanese consumers aren't as credit-happy as Americans, and they tend to pay off their debts in full every month, which reduces the potential revenue stream from interest charges and fees. But the risk of doing nothing may be greater. "We have to enlarge our battlefield," Natsuno says. And Kiyoyuki Tsujimura, the managing director of DoCoMo's products and services division, adds, "If we don't change, we won't survive."

Their dream: that millions of Japanese consumers will like the idea of being able to walk out of their front doors every morning carrying only their cell phones. By 2008, we'll know whether that dream is likely to come true.

NIKE: MAKING FITNESS COOL

As of 2006, Nike is far from having a growth problem. It has enormous runway internationally. China is already a big source of business but is just getting started on its growth trajectory; India is even lower on the high-growth arc. The dollar distance is suggestive: U.S. per capita spending on athletic shoes is $56, but the comparable figure in India is 16 cents. Although developing economies won't soon achieve the U.S. saturation rate for branded athletic shoes, there's plenty of room for growth before that goal ever comes in sight.

Nike also has plenty of room to grow in the United States as it transitions from one brand (Nike) to a portfolio of brands (Nike, Starters, Converse, Cole-Haan, Bauer, Hurley). Ten years from now, Nike will be a portfolio company like Unilever, Nestlé, Johnson & Johnson, or P&G, and it will be two to three times larger than today.

With Nike's growth wall a decade in the future, *now* is the perfect time for the company to come up with its next big idea (or two).

One potentially big idea that is already coming to market is based on the fact that Nike's biggest untapped source of growth remains the core athletic shoe market. Half the market for athletic shoes is at price points below $49—new territory as far as Nike is concerned, until now. With its Starters brand, Nike is developing an extensive program with Wal-Mart to offer athletic shoes priced below $40. If it takes off as expected, another decade of growth is in the offing.

The company is also looking for more farsighted big growth ideas. That's the job of John R. Hoke III, Nike's chief designer. Hoke stalks inspiration in unorthodox ways. He'll take his team to the Milan furniture show, the Detroit auto show, or the San Diego Zoo—to look at feet. They've come up with several ideas that have the potential to drive many years of growth for Nike.

Hoke is also passionate about the idea—for him, the *imperative*—of sustainable design. He's pushing his designers to create a new shoe design that uses less energy, produces less waste, and employs less (or no) glue, plastics, or adhesives—all of which create air and water pollution, endanger workers' health, and lead to disposal problems down the road. Hoke recognizes how difficult this will be, but he doesn't care: "We are going to challenge ourselves to think a little bit differently about the way we create products." Thinking differently means using geometry instead of chemistry, natural materials instead of synthetics. Instead of glue, for example, Hoke's "sustainable"shoe will use snap-fit systems reinforced with cotton stitching; instead of foam lining, it will contain fillers made of renewable bamboo fiber.

A sustainable shoe that really works may be months or years away. It confronts Nike with a new and highly challenging three-dimensional puzzle, not unlike the hybrid engine puzzle that the engineers at Toyota ultimately solved. But if and when the glueless, renewable shoe is made reality, it will provide not only sustainability but also more than a decade's worth of growth to its creator.

And there is yet another potentially big idea that Nike—and perhaps *only* Nike—is in a position to make into reality. It's an idea built around the intersection of untapped corporate capabilities, unmet social needs, and an as-yet underdeveloped marketplace. Let's see how it might take shape over the next five years by looking at a bit of synthetic history—this time looking *forward*, not back, into a future of demand innovation that Nike just might choose to create.

When it was launched in late 2007, Nike's "Kids Just Do It" sports and fitness program for young people was hailed as the marketing breakthrough of the year. But the full scope of its impact wouldn't be apparent for several years. Today, from the perspective of 2012, we can see how Kids Just Do It has fueled unprecedented growth for Nike among the under-twelve age group—as well as playing a positive role in the ongoing quest to promote youth fitness. But that's getting ahead of our story . . .

Kids Just Do It had its roots in a number of preexisting Nike programs. By

2006, the company had already been significantly involved in promoting youth sports as a way of reaching into new markets. For example, the company had made inroads into the Chinese market for athletic gear in part through its sponsorship of hundreds of youth basketball leagues. By working with communities and schools to sign up participants and to arrange for availability of basketball courts, it had created local partnerships throughout the country and become known as a supporter of positive activities for young people.

Nike had also been developing unique technological expertise in the area of sports and fitness through its partnership with Apple—the company's electronic counterpart as a creator of products that exude "cool." The two companies worked together to create an athletic shoe connected to an iPod with the capability of monitoring an individual's activity level—minutes of exercise, miles run, and the like—and delivering periodic updates to the athlete via readouts on the iPod screen.

Kids Just Do It (KJDI) combined and built on these ideas to take youth fitness promotion to a higher level. Nike began sponsoring youth leagues in soccer, basketball, cross-country running, and other sports at the elementary, junior high school, and high school levels around the United States—initially in selected counties, ultimately wherever the demand existed and predetermined participation rates were achieved.

Modeled on Nike's college-level sports programs, these sponsorships provided a cost-effective way for the company to create connections with thousands of local coaches and teachers, and, through them, with millions of young athletes. The vast majority of kids and parents were willing to pick up their end of the bargain, too, buying customized Nike shoes specially designed for particular sports and equipped with Apple-designed electronic sensors and iPod hookups. "Hey, I'd be buying sneakers and an iPod anyway," most of them said. "Why not get my gear from Nike?"

But the true excitement of the program only became apparent after kids started using the new equipment. Naturally, the special Nike iPods provided the personalized soundtrack for their practice sessions and workouts. But they also did a lot more. Kids could download and play exclusive podcasts of Nike star athletes offering unique sports and fitness tips or just talking about their favorite career moments—LeBron James on basketball, Ronaldinho on soccer, Christin Wurth-Thomas on track. The iPods also monitored student athletes' performances, uploaded the data to a company database, and highlighted some of the finest sports accomplishments on a dedicated Nike Web site. Kids could log on to their local page and read about themselves: "Kelly Asher of Irvington High School achieves personal best time in the 1,000-meter sprint for the third straight month." Countless printouts found their way into family scrapbooks and the sports pages of local and school newspapers.

Best of all, when student athletes really pushed themselves to reach extraordinary goals, the rewards included recognition from members of Nike's unmatched roster of world-renowned athletic role models. When sixteen-year-old Carlos Reyes in Petaluma completed his first marathon run for charity—wearing his KJDI running gear, of course—his mailbox, a week later, contained a Nike cap and T-shirt autographed by LeBron James. (James was the star Carlos had selected as his personal idol on the KJDI Web site.) Imagine the awed looks Carlos got from his classmates in school the next day—and the rush of new sign-ups for the KJDI program.

Suddenly, it seemed, getting and staying fit was becoming cool—not just among a few jocks but among a wide and growing swath of American youth. Teachers, coaches, and public health officials in one city after another offered public endorsements of KJDI. Parents could be heard remarking, "Thank God for this program—it's the first time in years my kid is more interested in getting out on the field or the court than in sitting in front of the TV." And as KJDI grew— driving record sales growth at both Nike and iPod—national youth obesity statistics began to shrink for the first time in decades.

Will this piece of synthetic history really come true? We'll see. But it's the kind of future that the risk shapers at Nike could be thinking about today.

AT THIS POINT, you might be wondering, "How do I go about getting this big idea?" There is no surefire mental manufacturing process to force the big idea to appear. But there are a few questions that can help.

• Where's the big bottleneck in the system—your system, or your customer's system? Where do you or your customers get stuck and frustrated repeatedly? A simple way to unclog that bottleneck could be your next big idea, and potentially your next billion-dollar business.
• Where's the big waste—either in your company's operations or in

the life of your customers? How are you or your customers spending money, time, and energy unnecessarily, creating needless pollution or waste, or accumulating things you really don't want?
• What's the big asset you have that you haven't fully put to work yet? It could be a set of talents that your employees have, an information or knowledge base that you haven't exploited, a reputational asset you haven't capitalized upon, or a form of strategic control you haven't leveraged.

And here is a suggestion that may help, drawn not from the world of business but from that of literature. The poet and critic T. S. Eliot once remarked that while the mediocre writer waits for inspiration to strike before putting pen to paper, the great writer is constantly writing about everything under the sun, so when inspiration *does* strike, he is ready to respond. In the same way, the company that is constantly generating, testing, and discarding new business ideas will be in a better position to find, recognize, and capitalize on the big new idea when it comes along than its more slow-moving competitors.

Spending the time to search for the next big idea is the best way to transform the depressing prospect of a no-growth business environment into the rejuvenating experience of a business world ripe with fresh opportunities. And there's usually no obstacle to start practicing it today.

DE-RISK YOUR BUSINESS

Are the early warning signs of slowing growth beginning to haunt your company? Here are a series of questions that can help you recognize the problem and get a handle on it.

1. Is stagnation really a risk for our company? If it is, what is the true probability that stagnation will hit, what is the likely timetable, and what is the potential impact, especially on our top talent?

2. Do we have a risk management system designed to help our business side-step major hits or reduce their impact?

3. Which of the major risks we've discovered represent good raw material for new growth opportunity?

4. What are our major opportunities for demand innovation? Are there enough people in our organization who understand and care about it for us to succeed?

5. How much time did we invest last year to search for the next big idea?

CHAPTER EIGHT

Treasure Island

Reversing Risks to Grow

MANAGERS AT TOYOTA like to say that "problems are treasures." If that's true, then big risks are enormous treasures.

Think back to all the major company examples we've discussed. Each one faced a negative force coming at great speed. Each one reversed that force to avoid damage and to create a growth breakthrough. The outcomes represent the payoff to an effective risk management process. These final pages are designed to provide you with a methodical process for creating profitable growth from your own risk challenges.

FIGURE 8-1
RISK REVERSALS

COMPANY	RISK TYPE	GROWTH BREAKTHROUGH
Toyota	Project risk	A decade or more of growth for the hybrid fleet
Apple	Project risk	Five years of powerful growth and counting; major open doors to video, Hollywood alliance, set-top box, phones
Coach	Customer risk	From 1996, a decade of double-digit growth
Tsutaya	Customer risk	Will grow from 1,300 to 3,000 stores; another decade of growth and open doors to multiple partnerships
Microsoft	Transition risk	A new wave of growth from 1996 to 2002

COMPANY	RISK TYPE	GROWTH BREAKTHROUGH
Target	Unique competitor risk	A decade of revenue and profit growth and still counting
Samsung	Brand risk	A decade of growth from 1997
Airbus	Industry risk	Three decades of growth and innovation
Continental AG	Stagnation risk	Sharp increase in growth after 1997
P&G	Stagnation risk	Sharp increase in growth after 2000

WRITING YOUR RISK STORY

Begin by taking a close look at your business in terms of its current risk story. It's a challenging task, the equivalent of several screenings of your company's worst horror show, containing scenes with all the most frightening scenarios you can imagine.

Of course, risk isn't only about a potential Armaggedon. Don't think about the seven varieties of strategic risk in black-and-white terms. Each exists on a spectrum, from the most extreme to the least extreme—just as the risk of an earthquake may range from a devastating quake measured at 8.0 on the Richter scale (which can destroy entire communities and cause hundreds of deaths, as happened in San Francisco in 1906) to a mild shock with a Richter measurement of 5.0 or less (which might merely shatter windows and crack walls in buildings near the epicenter of the quake).

For example, the risk of industry margin squeeze may be extreme, in which case an entire industry may be transformed into a no-profit zone, as occurred in the airline industry during the past twenty years. Or it may be milder, as when an industry suffers eroding profit margins due to increased R&D costs (as in pharmaceutical development) or rising capital costs (as in semiconductors). You can think about the risks you face all along this spectrum, with the severity of the risks requiring different levels of response and preparation. (See the illustrations in Figure 8-2 for more detail on the risk spectrum.)

FIGURE 8-2
THE STRATEGIC RISK SPECTRUM

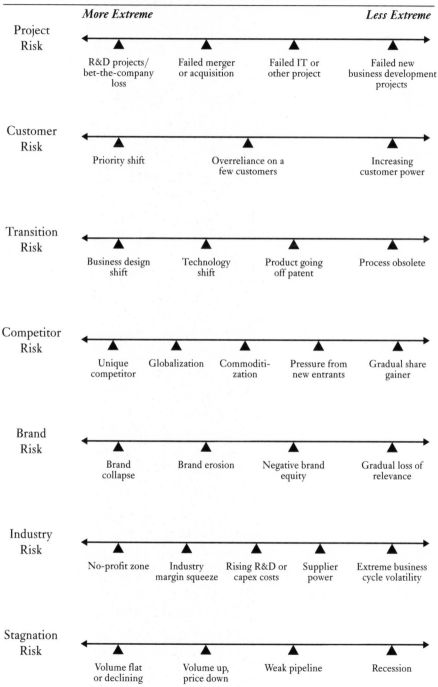

More Extreme   *Less Extreme*

Project Risk
- R&D projects/ bet-the-company loss
- Failed merger or acquisition
- Failed IT or other project
- Failed new business development projects

Customer Risk
- Priority shift
- Overreliance on a few customers
- Increasing customer power

Transition Risk
- Business design shift
- Technology shift
- Product going off patent
- Process obsolete

Competitor Risk
- Unique competitor
- Globalization
- Commoditization
- Pressure from new entrants
- Gradual share gainer

Brand Risk
- Brand collapse
- Brand erosion
- Negative brand equity
- Gradual loss of relevance

Industry Risk
- No-profit zone
- Industry margin squeeze
- Rising R&D or capex costs
- Supplier power
- Extreme business cycle volatility

Stagnation Risk
- Volume flat or declining
- Volume up, price down
- Weak pipeline
- Recession

Figure 8-2 is just suggestive, a tool to prompt thinking about your own situation. Your own business will certainly face additional categories that aren't captured here; add your own specific risks to the table.

Thinking about strategic risk is a mind-set, not a laundry list of threats to manage. Your environment is constantly evolving, and there will always be a need for regular reorientation of your company's risk profile to match the dynamism of your market. Try thinking about other categories of risk that may have an impact on your company in the near future. For example, companies have faced regulatory and geo-political risks that have the potential to disrupt their business. Microsoft's battle with antitrust authorities continues even today in the European Union. Arla Foods is a Scandinavian company whose $480 million worth of Middle East sales collapsed due to its association with Denmark, where a newspaper published controversial cartoons of the prophet Muhammad.

To start writing your business's risk story, identify the major risks facing your business—just the ones you can think of in the next two minutes. Perhaps you'll come up with a list of ten or so. The best way to do this is to shift gears and become an outsider to your own business. What risks would you see if you were an investor, customer, or competitor? Very often, outsiders can see our risks more clearly than we can.

You may feel reluctant to do this exercise because it seems to be all downside. But think about Bill Belichick and how he prepares his New England Patriots football team for every game through a similar exercise in downside visualization. Somehow, at the end of the process, those downsides tend to get converted to big wins.

Consider also the City of New York under the leadership of Mayor Rudolph Giuliani. In the late 1990s, Giuliani organized and led a series of decidedly unpleasant advance exercises designed to identify and plan for the worst downside disasters the city could imagine. Here's how Giuliani explains his approach in his memoir, *Leadership*:

Throughout my time as mayor, we conducted tabletop exercises designed to rehearse our response to a wide variety of contingencies. We'd blueprint what each person in each agency would do if the city faced, say, a chemical attack or a biomedical attack. We went through how we'd act in the event of a plane crash or a terrorist attack on a political gathering. We didn't just choreograph our response on paper, either, but did trial runs in the streets, to test how long the plans took in practice. We even simulated an airplane crash in Queens and a sarin gas attack in Manhattan.

During these disaster preparedness exercises, photos would be taken that strikingly resembled newspaper pictures of real emergencies. The photos were enlarged and displayed in a room at the city's Office of Emergency Management (OEM) that came to be known as the "Hall of Horribles."

Of course, there's no way a city government can completely prepare for every possible emergency. The only option is to prepare for every risk you *can* imagine—and create systems for ringing alarm bells whenever anything out of the ordinary occurs. Giuliani recalls:

> We implemented a procedure called the Syndromic Surveillance System to check with the hospitals on a daily basis to note any elevated levels of symptoms: careful data analysis could predict when certain statistical patterns showed something was about to erupt. Even if we didn't know exactly what it was, we could begin preparing ourselves with extra personnel near the expected hot spot.

Think about Belichick and New York City's exercises and the value of being prepared for the worst. Then write out your own lists. It's like creating your own personal Hall of Horribles—a scary, sobering experience, one that often reveals how much we've relied on a magic blend of inertia and luck to get us through. We no longer need to bet our business on those two.

THE PROBLEM OF PERSPECTIVE

If you were giving a speech before a roomful of people and had a blemish on your forehead, the only person who wouldn't see the blemish is you—even though you are the person closest to it.

Sometimes we're in the worst possible position to see what can hurt us the most. What's obvious to other people is invisible to us—not because of any character flaw or intellectual weakness but just because of where we happen to be located.

Journalist Michael Lewis of *Moneyball* fame spent a week trailing Bill Parcells, the legendary coach of the Dallas Cowboys (and formerly of the New York Giants, New England Patriots, and New York Jets) and recorded his observations in a story titled "What Keeps Bill Parcells Awake at Night." One of Lewis's most astute insights was this one:

> Pacing up and down the sidelines, the head coach has the worst view in the house—except for everyone else on the sidelines. The sidelines are an obstacle course of thick cables, Cowboys cheerleaders, flatbed trucks with TV cameras, pushy cameramen and wide people with even wider sound dishes. So the only way to tell if a play is good or bad for the Cowboys is by the crowd's reaction and the replay on the Jumbo-Tron, which the players themselves watch when they're curious about what has happened. The closer you are to the action, the more desperately your eyes search for the televised image. All in all, the sidelines illustrate that physical proximity to a complicated event doesn't necessarily help you understand it.

So how do you get perspective on your business story? After all, you don't have the benefit of instant replay on the JumboTron. But you can have the equivalent of another head coach's best friend: the coach in the TV booth, wired for sound, who provides in-game scouting reports from high above the playing field.

Find and cultivate a couple of good friends from business arenas other than your own—or, if possible, a whole network of them. If you work in manufacturing, get to know some managers from service or media or marketing firms. If you're in high tech, befriend a banker, a discount store manager, an art director from an ad agency, and someone who runs a hotel chain.

Make these people your informal advisory board. Ask them to spend a few minutes every week scanning the news about your industry—just enough to know the basic vocabulary and some of the key challenges you face. And when you've developed your company's risk story, invite them to lunch and spend a couple of hours of picking their brains. Ask questions like: What am I missing here? What big risks are you worrying about in your own industry that I'm ignoring—perhaps at my peril? Does learning about my business make you want to enter it? If not, why not? What are the pitfalls I've never thought about? Where might my next unexpected competitor come from?

This may seem like a lot to ask, even of a good friend. But you might be surprised how much smart businesspeople actually enjoy taking a close look at an industry that is totally different from their own. They'll probably have fun and learn a thing or two in the process. And of course you could volunteer to do the same for them when they create their own risk story.

DEVELOPING A STRATEGIC RISK MANAGEMENT SYSTEM

Having crafted your company's true risk story, there's a process that you can follow, preferably with a team of trusted colleagues and a few thoughtful outsiders (customers, for example, or suppliers, or anyone with an informed but different point of view), to begin developing a strategic risk management program for your company, division, or department. The process follows six steps:

1. Identify and assess your risks.

2. Quantify your risks.

3. Develop risk mitigation action plans.

4. Identify the potential upside.

5. Map and prioritize your risks.

6. Adjust your capital decisions.

As you work your way through the six steps in this process, you can track your work on the Strategic Risk Framework chart (Figure 8-3).

FIGURE 8-3
THE STRATEGIC RISK FRAMEWORK CHART

Risk	How big?	How likely?	Prevent	Mitigate	Maximize upside	Action plan — Percent completion
				What can I do? Action plan to		0 20 40 60 80 100
1.						
2.						
3.						
4.						
5.						
6.						
7.						
8.						
9.						
10.						

1. Identify and assess your risks. Start by carrying out, in a more thorough, tough-minded, formal fashion, the "risk brainstorming" exercise we described at the start of this chapter. (You can brainstorm risks just as you brainstorm big ideas—after all, they are often the flip sides of each other.) Work your way through each of the main categories of strategic risk, and list the specific risks in each category that your company may face.

Naturally, the risks you face will vary from those that seem extremely likely to those that seem very far-fetched. An example of the former might be a risk that has been widely predicted and may in fact already be happening— for instance, a customer shift that has begun affecting younger users of your products, causing the average age of your customer base to increase noticeably and threatening the long-term survival of your brand. (As novelist

William Gibson once said: "The future has already happened, it's just un-evenly distributed.") An example of the latter might be a risk that has oc-curred in other industries but for which there is no real cloud on the horizon yet, and which therefore seems only theoretically possible.

2. Quantify your risks. This step proceeds in two parts. First, for each risk on your list, estimate the potential cost to your company if the risk were to strike with full force. Come up with a dollar amount, roughly calculated on the basis of your organization's annual revenues and profits and the percent-age of those revenues and profits that might be lost in case of a risk event.

For example, suppose you are working on a risk management plan for a company division with annual sales of $800 million. Next year, you plan to launch a new product (now in the final phases of testing) that is expected to gen-erate 10 percent of that division's revenues in its first year. Thus, the potential cost of a new-product failure risk in this case (if the market were to completely reject the new product, for example, or if some government agency were to step in to forbid its sale on health or safety grounds) would be $80 million.

Next, calculate the likelihood of the risk event. This is tricky. As we've seen, the natural human tendency is to *underestimate* the likelihood of risk events. It therefore pays to err on the high side when estimating the likelihood of a risk event. Your estimates are probably already more accurate today than they would have been before you started thinking hard about strategic risks; they will be better still the more time you spend studying your company's history and track record in areas such as new product development, expan-sion plans, and the like.

3. Develop risk mitigation action plans. This will be the most complex and valuable step. You and your team will examine each of the risks you've identified and come up with a strategic move, an action plan, or a management system to eliminate or at least reduce the potential damage from each one.

Obviously, the countermeasures described in each chapter can be the key starting point for your development of these plans. However, it will take con-siderable time, research, analysis, and discussion to turn these plans into con-crete programs for practical action. This process will probably involve cross-functional teams with knowledge of the business areas affected and the ability to connect with others who can provide detailed information with which to evaluate and strengthen the specific plans proposed.

THE UPSIDE

Having developed your countermeasure plans, you'll want to periodically ask yourself: For each of our top ten risks, how far along are we toward having effective countermeasure action plans in place?

This question should stimulate a set of conversations based on a chart something like the one in Figure 8-4. More important will be a new sense of awareness and urgency about the nature of strategic risk—and a general feeling of uneasiness over the size of the gaps you've tolerated between true preparedness and your current state.

FIGURE 8-4

SAMPLE RISK PROFILE WORKSHEET (MANUFACTURING AND SERVICES FIRM)

RISK	ODDS	IMPACT	COUNTER-MEASURE	PLAN COMPLETION
1. Brand collapse	5%	80%	• Emergency response plan/system	100%
2. Customer shift	20%	20%	• New service offering	50%
3. Recession	60%	20%	• Cost reduction plan • "Help customers cut costs" plan	80%
4. Tech shift	10%	80%	• Double-bet preparation	30%
5. Our most important project fails	70%	10%	• Three business design alternatives to raise the odds of success	90%
6. Brand erosion	40%	40%	• License-in new products • Radical improvement in service levels	90%
7. Project portfolio fails to deliver	50%	35%	• Prune portfolio/focus resources on "big six"	35%
8. Top-decile talent leaves	20%	10% short term 30% long term	• Change comp plan, training plan • Increase growth-oriented initiatives, investment	80% 30%

216

RISK	ODDS	IMPACT	COUNTER-MEASURE	PLAN COMPLETION
9. Major product goes off patent	100%	20%	• Product extensions	50%
			• Major licensing deal	50%
10. Industry margin erosion	30%	20%	• Pool manufacturing resources	10%
			• Pool "pre-product" R&D with two major rivals	10%

4. Identify the potential upside. Here is where creative thinking can play the lead role. For every risk, ask yourself how this potential negative force could be turned into a positive. If your company is in danger of losing all or some of its customer base, is there a way of refocusing your product development, marketing and promotion, or customer information management programs in a way that not only retains those customers but also increases their buying and draws new customers as well? If your company faces significant risks of new product failure, is there a way to redesign your R&D, testing, marketing, and business design efforts not only to reduce those risks but also to improve the potential breakthrough sales value of your new product pipeline?

5. Map and prioritize your risks. Based on the information developed so far, create a Risk Exposure Map like the one shown in Figure 8-5. Specific risks are located on this map based on the two quantitative factors we discussed in step two—the potential size and estimated likelihood of a risk event. Events located toward the top of this map are bigger and potentially more costly; events located toward the right-hand side of the map are more likely to occur. Thus, risks in the upper right-hand quadrant deserve your most immediate and focused attention. You can also designate which risks have a mitigation plan in place. The result is a "risk dashboard" that lets you see at a glance where your company's greatest risks lie and how far advanced your efforts are to mitigate them.

FIGURE 8-5
THE RISK EXPOSURE MAP

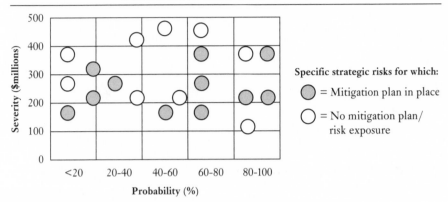

6. **Adjust your capital decisions.** The last step in formulating your risk management plan involves restructuring your current investment decisions. As we saw when discussing project risk, brand risk, and transition risk, investment decisions are some of your most fundamental tools for managing the major risks your company faces. You're not serious about strategic risk management unless your assessment of the risks affects your major financial allocations. And, of course, the decisions you make at this stage must be shaped by all the information you've gathered to this point, including the size and likelihood of the specific risk, the estimated cost to the company that this represents, the value of any potential upside, and the nature of the proposed countermeasure plans.

FOSTERING RISK MANAGEMENT
MIND-SET AND SKILLS

Developing a well-designed program for identifying, measuring, monitoring, minimizing, and reversing the strategic risks your company faces is just the beginning. It's also important to inculcate the risk management and reversal mind-set among managers at every level of your organization. It is extremely important, and it is startlingly difficult to do.

THE IMPORTANCE

Front-line managers play a crucial role in any risk management program. They are closest to the realities of the marketplace, fielding customer complaints, tracking competitive initiatives, and dealing with suppliers, distributors, and other players throughout the value chain on a daily basis. As your company's eyes and ears, they are the ones most likely to be the first to recognize tomorrow's threats in time to respond, as well as the ones most likely to see the opportunities bundled with the risks. And of course, middle-level leaders will be charged with implementing the risk management moves developed by the company. If they don't understand or support the initiatives, nothing meaningful will happen.

A recent paper published by Babson Executive Education describes the frustration that can arise when middle managers are reluctant to buy into a company's risk management strategy. The company in question is Harrah's, the casino firm that has become the paradigm of knowledge-intensive risk management:

> Harrah's has developed a centralized real-time yield management system for all of its hotels that needed to be sold to property managers.... When a customer calls for a reservation, the system's algorithms weigh a number of variables and data . . . to calculate a price to offer to the customer. The system almost always produces higher revenues for individual properties when it is employed. *Yet property managers usually have to be convinced the system is more effective than traditional approaches to yield management and local decision making.* [Emphasis added]

THE DIFFICULTY

The fact is that middle-level managers have an effective veto power over whatever risk management system is created. If they don't buy it, it won't happen. In some cases, they may prevent it from being implemented by refusing to follow the system (as some Harrah's managers did). In other cases, they may block its effectiveness by failing to participate in the discovery, gathering, combining, sharing, and analysis of information needed to keep the risk countermeasures up to date and accurate. Either way, the best intentions of senior management will not get executed.

Unfortunately, the culture and communications systems of most companies actively *discourage* middle managers from contributing to risk assessment, mitigation, and response in many ways:

• Companies tend to punish those who deliver bad news, which is often viewed as "negative," "pessimistic," "defeatist," or "discouraging." As a result, unfavorable developments from the outside world end up taking longer to reach top management's attention, or they take top leadership by surprise despite the fact that managers at lower levels were aware of the looming problems for months.

• Overvaluing confidentiality and secrecy, many companies try to restrict the flow of information that's deemed sensitive, even internally. In combination with the traditional silo-like structure of many corporations, this tendency produces cadres of managers who are well informed only about their corners of the business and therefore are unable to connect the dots in a way that might generate a larger, more informative, and more actionable picture of how the company's world is changing.

• Silo structures impede broad-based risk management in other ways. Most companies incentivize managers based largely or even entirely on departmental or division performance. And job promotions, of course, are driven mainly by the perceived success of a manager's own group. This is logical and to a degree unavoidable, but the sense of interdepartmental competition it sets up inevitably reduces the willingness of managers to share information and ideas. The result isn't *always* data hoarding, but the energy that managers apply to cross-fertilization of knowledge is, at least, drastically diminished.

THREE DISCIPLINES

There are three disciplines that can help management teams get consistently better at managing their portfolio of risks: knowing the true odds, seeing the earliest warning signals, and constantly comparing the risk profile of their business design against the risk profiles of others.

I. KNOWING THE TRUE ODDS

The first discipline is developing a talent and an institutional skill for *odds assessment*. This involves developing realistic techniques for measuring the true chances of success for any new venture. As researchers Daniel Kahneman and Dan Lovallo show, cognitive biases and organizational pressures lead managers to routinely overestimate both the odds for success and the potential payoff from any new business initiative. As a partial solution to this problem, the authors recommend developing what they call the "outside view": a forecast based on an objective analysis of comparable initiatives drawn from the histories of several companies, not just from internal comparisons or intuitive assessments.

Author Bill James (who helped found the field of baseball statistical analysis known as sabermetrics) recommends that every aspiring big-league manager invest a few months in playing a tabletop baseball game, where the outcomes of particular strategies are determined by the tossing of dice or the spinning of a wheel. At the least, James notes, this will provide a gut-level sense of the relative plausibility of various strategies— the realistic likelihood that a hit-and-run play with the number seven hitter at bat and the tying run on first will ultimately produce the crucial score versus the odds for success of a sacrifice bunt in the same situation. It's an easy way for a baseball strategist to develop Kahneman's "outside view" without having to sit on the bench through a dozen real seasons.

If business is your game rather than baseball, there's no tabletop version available. Instead, start by looking at your own company's history of success and failure in your own industry. (Create your own sabermetrics.) For example, you could start with this question: What is the true failure rate experienced by you or your company when launching major new initiatives—new products, company expansions, mergers or acquisitions— over the past fifteen years? Let's say it's 70 percent. (Although that sounds high, check the record. At many companies, the real failure rate is closer to 90 percent.) Now, adjust it by *type* of initiatives. For brand extensions, the failure rate might be 50 percent. For completely new products, it might be 90 percent.

Building your company's internal sample is a great start; doing so can be incredibly revealing. But the sample size is probably too small to be as useful as you need it to be. Look outside. Examine the experiences of other companies in your industry and in other industries. In food, in pharmaceuticals, in movies, the failure rates for new product launches range from 60 to 90 percent.

The pharmaceutical industry gives an example of stratifying, showing how new product failure rates change as various phases of the development process are successfully hurdled:

FIGURE 8-6

FAILURE RATES IN PHARMACEUTICALS BY DEVELOPMENT PHASE

	FAILURE RATES
From screened compounds to preclinical	95% don't make it
From preclinical compounds to clinical	98% don't make it
From clinical compounds to FDA approval	80% don't make it

Of course, just as project risk is only one kind of strategic risk, product failure rates aren't the only kind of statistical analysis that can help you determine the true risks your company faces. We've seen the odds for industry transitions in Chapter 3 and brand erosion in Chapter 5. Your priority areas may be different, but developing the true odds for the main types of events and decisions in your business can give your company an enormous competitive advantage.

2. SEEING THE EARLIEST WARNING SIGNALS

Does your company face unique competitor risk? Most companies think they don't. If you're not sure, it may be because you haven't been looking at the right numbers, or battle maps, or both. In most cases, the advent of a unique competitor is accompanied by clear advance signs that most of its rivals could have seen and taken warning from. As we saw in Chapter 4, competitive retailers and airlines could clearly have foreseen the impending arrival of a unique competitor in their markets simply by tracking the gradual expansion of that unique competitor's activity over a wider and wider swath of the American landscape.

Perhaps you don't feel concerned about unique competitor risk but instead worry about brand risk. If so, the process we outlined in Chapter 5 for performing a brand equity analysis will provide early warning signals about weaknesses in your brand. It can help you identify the changes in your brand investment program that can avert erosion before it strikes. Scoring your brand equity against key characteristics valued by your customers can be very revealing, especially when you compare your performance against that of the most effective competitor. For example, Figure 8-7 shows how one financial firm's brand performed against that of a key competitor in eight areas of importance to customers:

FIGURE 8-7
COMPARATIVE SCORES

IMPORTANCE TO CUSTOMER	EQUITY ELEMENT	CUSTOMER RATES ME	CUSTOMER RATES MY BEST COMPETITOR	THE BRAND RISK DIFFERENTIAL	
5	Trust and peace of mind	3	4.5	−1.5	*This is how brand risk begins...*
5	Local strength	3.5	5.0	−1.5	
4	Professional relationship	3.2	4.2	−1.0	
4	Performance	3.5	4.3	−.8	
3	Exclusive service	3.7	3.9	−.2	
2	Projected customer personality	3.9	3.2	+.7	
2	Driven	4.3	4.0	+.3	
1	Modern with innovative services	4.3	3.9	+.4	

Unfortunately, the areas in which the client company scored lowest were those with the greatest impact on customer satisfaction, while the areas in which the firm scored highest were those with the least customer impact. The resulting table is an archetypal image of an early warning signal of brand risk.

What if your chief concern is customer risk—the inevitable drift in customer preferences and needs that, in time, takes its toll on virtually every business? Then consider the alarm bells that a simple, methodical statistical analysis could have rung for anyone connected with major automotive products whose market share erosion played out progressively over time. The chart in Figure 8-8 tells the tale for what was once a dominant product in the industry.

FIGURE 8-8
MARKET SHARE BY STATE

MARKET SHARE	1999	2003
4% +	4 states	1 state
3.0–3.9%	9 states	5 states
2.0–2.9%	17 states	9 states
0–1.9%	20 states	35 states

This chart is a subset of data that were trackable over twenty years. The greatest market share losses first occurred in the coastal states; then they started moving inland. The rate of movement was precisely measurable and provided more than ample warning of a systematic, widespread customer shift.

The future will not always send you a perfect signal. The signal will often be faint, and it will be incomplete—that's how they come. Your ear has to be fine-tuned, and your eyes have to fill in the details that will be missing.

In a way, risk signals from the future are a bit like the Carraccis' (sixteenth-century Bolognese family of painters) "loaded little portraits"—incomplete, but just enough to see the picture:

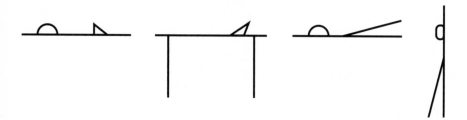

As they were described a century later: "The first sketch is a mason seen from the other side of the wall; he protrudes over it with the top of his head and his trowel. The second is a pulpit, where a Capuchin monk, having delivered the first part of his sermon, is leaning down to catch his breath for the second. The third is a knight, who jousts from the other side of the lists with a lance; and the fourth is a blind beggar leaning on the other side of the corner, who we discover from our side only by his cup and his cane."

So too, in anticipating major risks, we won't always get the fully formed picture. But we will get enough to at least raise our suspicions and motivate us to take a closer look. Quite often, it's not even foresight but a close reading of the company's own history that matters most. As one senior manager of a manufacturing company put it: "Most future risks are the result of time bombs that we ourselves had planted in the past."

The truth is that most strategic risk management is not very esoteric. The problem is not that the signals are weak, but that our receptors are closed. If you can train yourself, through simple observation, to get a firm grasp on what is *totally predictable*, you will probably end up way ahead of most of your competitors.

3. CONSTANTLY COMPARING RISK PROFILES

We've looked at two disciplines important for any team that wants to improve its risk management capabilities. The first is *knowing the true odds of success* in any business situation. The second is *seeing the earliest warning signals of risk* so that you can give yourself the greatest lead time to prepare.

There's one more discipline, just as important as the first two, that can help you recognize the risks you face and formulate plans for controlling them. It is understanding your own risk profile by comparing it with that of other companies in your industry.

Consider the example in Figure 8-9. It's a more detailed version of the table we discussed in the Introduction.

FIGURE 8-9

COMPARATIVE RISK PROFILE: FORD VS. TOYOTA

	FORD	TOYOTA
FIXED COSTS	High	Low
INVENTORY RISK	High	Low
PORTFOLIO CONCENTRATION	High	Low
SETUP TIME/CYCLE TIME	High	Low
PLATFORM FLEXIBILITY	Low	High
PROJECT: RAISE-THE-ODDS APPROACH	Weak	Strong
TRANSITION RISK	Five years behind	Double-bet/ five years ahead
BRAND MOMENTUM	Downward spiral	Upward spiral

The risk level of the business design also affects the financial characteristics of the business.

	FORD	TOYOTA
ROA (2005)	.8%	4.8%
5-YEAR REVENUE CAGR (2000–2005)	.8%	11.1%
S&P EQUITY RATINGS	B−	Not rated
S&P DEBT RATINGS	B	AAA
BETA	1.85	.58

Another example of a business design risk comparison can be drawn from the apparel industry.

FIGURE 8-10

COMPARATIVE RISK PROFILE: GAP VS. ZARA

	GAP	ZARA
PRODUCTION FLEXIBILITY (% OF PLANNED VOLUME)	~20%	~45%
CUSTOMER INFORMATION	Periodic	Continuous
INVENTORY TURNS (2005)	5.6	6.7
PRODUCT LEAD TIME (MINOR MODIFICATION)	8 weeks+	1 week
PRODUCT LEAD TIME (NEW PRODUCT)	30 weeks	3 weeks
FASHION RISK	High	Low
EARLY WARNING SYSTEM	Low coverage	High coverage
BRAND MOMENTUM	Stagnant	Upward spiral
ROA (2005)	12.6%	16.6%
5-YEAR REVENUE CAGR (2000–2005)	3.2%	30.0%
S&P EQUITY RATINGS	BBB-	Not rated
S&P DEBT RATINGS	BBB+	Not available
BETA	1.39	0.49

As we've seen throughout, companies that shape risk not only reverse risks to grow; they've also learned to de-risk their business designs in a way that creates higher returns and lower risks than their competitors.

If you've carried out the other exercises described in this chapter, you are probably in a good position to create such a risk profile for your company and its chief competitors. Profile the key risk characteristics of your business design (fixed costs, cycle time, customer information, etc.) and compare them to the competing company you most worry about—or perhaps *should* be worried about—using Figure 8-11. The comparison will be illuminating, and it will generate specific ideas for improving the risk profile of your business design, moving it toward a position of higher returns *and* lower risks (as Toyota, Coach, Samsung, and others have done).

FIGURE 8-11

COMPARATIVE RISK PROFILE: MY KEY COMPETITOR VS. MY COMPANY

	MY KEY COMPETITOR	MY COMPANY
FIXED COSTS		
INVENTORY RISK		
PORTFOLIO CONCENTRATION		
CYCLE TIME		
EARLY WARNING SYSTEMS		
CONTINUOUS CUSTOMER INFORMATION		
BRAND MOMENTUM		
OTHER		
ROA		
5-YEAR REVENUE CAGR		
S&P EQUITY RATINGS		
S&P DEBT RATINGS		
BETA		

In the end, there are three key variables that impact your business: volume fluctuation, cost fluctuation, and price fluctuation. Strategic risk, in all its forms, manifests itself through these three variables.

To be prepared to deal with these variables, you need a business design that is flexible enough to float up and down with the fluctuations. You can achieve this through several specific strategies:

- Reduce your fixed costs (unless you are using high fixed costs as a barrier to entry or a strategic control point).
- Design your production facilities to be as flexible and easy to change as possible.
- Develop a powerful network of suppliers to whom you outsource as many functions as appropriate.
- Analyze every cycle time and shorten it, whether it's manufacturing setup times, supply delivery schedules, product development programs, or decision-making processes.
- Have multiple sources for every important input.

Interestingly enough, there's evidence that the Patriots' Bill Belichick has applied this kind of systemic thinking about risk and "unexpected" bad events to football. In pro sports, most of the key variables have to do with personnel—the quality of draft picks, the risk of losing talented players to free agency, and, above all, injuries. Belichick manages the Patriots so as to maximize the team's flexibility and minimize its vulnerability to these kinds of fluctuations. He signs players who are capable of playing several positions, works them out at all these positions, and even trains players on both offense and defense. He is frugal with compensation so that the fortunes of the team are not dependent on the performance of a handful of extremely high-paid stars. He pays more attention than most to the depth of his roster (as when he signed veteran quarterback Vinny Testaverde to a relatively inexpensive contract so as to ensure skill continuity at a key position in the event of an injury to team leader Tom Brady). And in training camp, he develops and teaches an unusually complex assortment of plays, especially on defense, so as to create maximum flexibility, to throw lots of confusing defensive "looks" at opposing teams, and to be prepared for virtually any style of offense.

No-Surprises Management

The CEO of an Asian technology company commissioned the creation of an enterprise-wide risk management system. Having led the organization through a successful zero-defects quality campaign, he wanted to upshift its thinking by creating a "no surprises" style of management. "Of course I know you can't avoid *all* surprises," he admitted. "But over the last twenty years, I've found that ninety percent are absolutely unnecessary. Those are the ones I want to get rid of—starting now." (And he added, "The others, we'll get to later.")

The results of the CEO's "no surprises" campaign were gratifying. In the short term, the company developed a risk management system for dealing with a series of technological, regulatory, and competitive changes that were coming within the next two years. The company's managers found they were able to anticipate most of the changes and prepare for them through double-betting, shifting brand investment, improving the development and deployment of proprietary information, and other techniques described in this book.

But there were other long-term benefits that the CEO never anticipated:

- Everybody in the organization began spending more time thinking about the future.
- They got noticeably better at grasping the elusive nature of probability and began estimating the odds of specific future events more accurately.
- They started spotting problems six to twelve months earlier than before, which enabled them to fix them when it was still cheap to do so. ("They fixed problems for a penny that would have cost a dime next month or a dollar next year. So the system paid for itself a lot faster than we ever imagined.")
- Most important, people changed what they spent their time on. They devoted fewer hours to responding to crises, more to innovation and growth.

These second-level impacts enable significant improvements in company performance. You never realize the true cost of risks until you start eliminating them, one by one by one.

THE UPSIDE OF RISK

Basketball star Bill Russell was a great rebounder, seizing control of the ball after an opposing player missed a shot. While rebounding is considered a defensive skill, Russell always insisted that "rebounding is the start of the offense." By the time Russell grabbed the ball, he was already thinking about the teammate to whom he would pass and, ultimately, the shot he was setting up. He was constantly turning a defensive move into an offensive opportunity.

Similarly, strategic risk management allows you to move from defense to offense. People typically focus on the perils of risk, and the managerial response is to seek ways to minimize exposure to it. In fact, the greatest opportunities often are concealed within the defensive countermeasures we've discussed.

Unmanaged risk is the greatest source of waste in your business and in our economy as a whole. Major projects fail; customer shifts make our offers irrelevant; billion-dollar brands erode, then collapse; entire industries stop making money; technology shifts or unique competitors kill dozens of companies in one stroke; companies stagnate needlessly. When these risk events happen, thousands of jobs get lost, brilliant organizations are disassembled, expertise gets lost, and assets are destroyed. Yet all of these risks can be understood, identified, anticipated, mitigated, or reversed, thereby averting hundreds of billions of dollars in unnecessary losses.

Is it easy? No. But in the past decade, pioneering companies such as those we've profiled have demonstrated the power of a range of tools for controlling and transforming risk. In the years to come, you'll have more and more opportunity to shape the risks you and your business face by mastering and applying the disciplines explained in these pages.

We live in a world where risk is ever-present and, by many measures, steadily increasing. There's little doubt that your company is likely to face a moment of maximum danger—a Little Round Top crisis—sometime in the not-too-distant future. If you're lucky, you'll be blessed with the resolute, insightful leadership of a Joshua Chamberlain, who saw the upside potential hidden in a seemingly hopeless situation and seized the chance to act upon it.

You have the opportunity *now* to prepare yourself and your company for tomorrow's crises. Taking a page from Bill Belichick's book, you can examine the environment, the nature of the game you're playing, and the moves that your opponents are likely to throw at you. Study the tapes tirelessly, work to identify the chief sources of looming risk, and develop innovative ways to throw the opposition off stride. Like Belichick's Patriots, you may find yourself walking away with some games that the oddsmakers say you have no business winning.

Finally, keep in mind the experience of Frank Lloyd Wright and his Imperial Hotel in Tokyo. The design decisions he made to protect the building against earthquake risk—the flexible floating foundation, the hollow lightweight bricks, the copper roof, and the rest—were innovative and brilliant. But more than this, we can admire the personal and intellectual integrity he brought to the process *before* making a single design choice.

Imagine being one of the greatest architects in history, an artist in steel and stone, who has been handed one of the most challenging assignments of his career. And now imagine realizing what the geological history of the Japanese islands means for the project: You are going to build one of the most beautiful buildings you have ever conceived, pouring your hard-earned knowledge and artistry into its design—all the while knowing that, sooner or later, it will be destroyed by a major earthquake. How would that realization make you feel? How would you respond?

To Wright's abounding credit, he responded with realism, foresight, and determination. Facing the risks head-on, he rethought the craft of architecture and transformed the danger into an opportunity for creativity and innovation.

Everyone in business today faces a challenge analogous to the one

Wright faced. We're all building businesses in earthquake zones, where upheavals are inevitable. We can follow Wright's example and design against the risks we face. If we do, the structures we create will have a chance to last and create enduring value for our customers, employees, investors, and communities.

Reversing Strategic Risk

The Upside Half-Day Workshop

Aɴʏ ᴍᴀɴᴀɢᴇᴍᴇɴᴛ ᴛᴇᴀᴍ (corporate, divisional, business, geography, or function) can develop its own strategic risk and upside profile. All it takes is a room, a morning, three flip charts, and a dozen managers with a huge appetite for value creation and the patience to work through every relevant question.

The following is a recommended workshop agenda. Total time required: 4½ hours.

OUR RISK STORY

• What is our strategic risk management process today? How do we analyze and tackle strategic risks? (5 minutes)
• What are the three to seven major risks that could damage all or part of our business design? (10 minutes)
• What are the odds that these risks will manifest in the next three years? If they happen, what will be the impact on our company's value? (10 minutes)

PROJECTS

• How much cash, time, and opportunity cost have we lost on projects that failed in the last three years? (10 minutes)
• What are the true odds of success for our projects in each major category? (10 minutes)

> • Research and development
> • Information technology

- Mergers and acquisitions
- New business development
- Other

• How many projects do we have active in each category today? Which ones should be discontinued? Which ones should we overinvest in to improve the odds of success? (20 minutes)
• What can we do to ensure that we always design the business as obsessively as we design the project? Consider all the key elements of business design. (10 minutes)

- Customer selection
- Unique value proposition
- Profit model
- Strategic control
- Scope

CUSTOMER

• Do we generate proprietary customer information? How much? How well do we put it to use? (5 minutes)
• Do we typically get our information closer to point T_2 or to point T_3? (5 minutes)

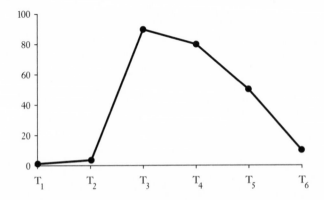

• Where do we fall on the spectrum between the conventional business model and the knowledge intensity model? (See Figure 2-2.) (5 minutes)

TRANSITION

• Have there been any major technology or business model transitions in our industry in the last ten to twenty years? How well did we manage the transition? (5 minutes)
• Will there be a major transition in the next several years? What are our odds of success for surviving it? How can we improve them? (15 minutes)

UNIQUE COMPETITOR

• Is there, or will there be, a unique competitor in our business? (5 minutes)
• What's the degree of overlap between our business model and that of our unique competitor today? How can it be reduced? (10 minutes)
• Could *we* become the unique competitor in our business? (5 minutes)

BRAND

• What's our brand value? Is it stable, increasing, or declining? Why? (10 minutes)
• On a scale of 1 to 10, with 10 being the highest score, how do we rate our product, our brand, and our business design? (10 minutes)
• Do our product, our brand, and our business design reinforce one another or conflict with one another? (5 minutes)

INDUSTRY

• What is our industry's margin history? What will it be over the next five to seven years? Why? (5 minutes)
• What is the compete/collaborate ratio in our industry? What should it be? What are some of the best areas for working together? (10 minutes)

STAGNATION

• What's been our year-over-year revenue growth rate for the last fifteen years? What will it be over the next five years? (5 minutes)
• What's our little box/big box picture? What's our next big idea? (15 minutes)

OUR RISK MANAGEMENT SYSTEM

• What other types of major strategic risks do we face? (5 minutes)
• What can/should we do about them? (15 minutes)
• Given our conversation:

  • What data do we need? (5 minutes)
  • How, if at all, should we change our processes? (15 minutes)

• What early warning systems:

  • Do we already have in place? (5 minutes)
  • Do we need to create? (5 minutes)

• Other than brainstorming our strategic risks, do we have a good risk search engine? How sophisticated/accurate/answer-oriented is it? If we don't have one, what can we do to create one? (10 minutes)
• How does the risk level of our business design compare to that of other companies? (10 minutes)

  • Our best competitor?
  • The best company in a similar industry?

• What de-risking moves could we use to design a more shock-resistant and resilient business model? (10 minutes)

  • Earlier warning signals
  • Lower inventory levels
  • Lower fixed costs

- Partnering with rivals
- Reduced cycle times
- Production flexibility
- Continuous customer information
- Higher-level customer relations
- Product/offer diversification
- Reduced competitive overlap
- Constant (versus periodic) investment mix adjustment
- Multiple options
- Complexity reduction
- Contingency plan repertoire
- Profitability transparency (where exactly do we make money?)
- Geographic mix / balance
- Performance-based compensation

NOTES

Introduction: From Risk to Opportunity

SOURCES AND REFERENCES

The story of Joshua Chamberlain at Little Round Top has been told many times, perhaps most memorably in Michael Shaara's classic novel *The Killer Angels* (New York: Modern Library, 2004). Good nonfiction accounts include:

Stand Firm Ye Boys from Maine: The 20th Maine and the Gettysburg Campaign, by Thomas A. Desjardin. Gettysburg, Pa.: Thomas Publications, 1995.

Gettysburg: The Second Day, by Harry W. Pfanz. Chapel Hill: University of North Carolina Press, 1987.

The data on utilities earnings comes from "A Comparables Approach to Measuring Cashflow-at-Risk for Non-Financial Firms," by Jeremy C. Stein, Stephen E. Usher, Daniel LaGattuta, and Jeff Youngen. *Journal of Applied Corporate Finance* 13, no. 4 (Winter 2001).

Warren Buffett's "rules" about preservation of capital are drawn from *The Essays of Warren Buffett: Lessons for Corporate America,* by Warren E. Buffett and Lawrence A. Cunningham (Boston: The Cunningham Group, 2001).

Sources of information on Bill Belichick's approach to football coaching include:

The Education of a Coach, by David Halberstam. New York: Hyperion, 2005.

"Belichick Is Always Interested in Learning," by Judy Battista. *New York Times,* November 7, 2005, page D1.

Information on Frank Lloyd Wright's design for the Imperial Hotel in Tokyo was drawn from *Frank Lloyd Wright: The Masterworks*, edited by Bruce Brooks Pfeiffer and David Larkin (New York: Rizzoli International, 2000).

CHANGING THE ODDS: THE DICK LIGHT STORY

The notion that it's possible to radically improve the odds of success in any kind of situation extends into our personal lives. Think, for example, about the average person's educational career. How many are truly successful? How many students get the *most* out of their college years, in terms not just of credentials but also of knowledge, skills, wisdom, and maturity? And can anything be done to improve the success rate?

Richard J. Light, a professor at Harvard's Graduate School of Education, set out to answer these questions. More important, he wanted to find ways of improving the odds for success of the average college student. His chief tool: the Harvard Assessment Project, in which teams of trained student interviewers interviewed about 6 percent of Harvard undergraduates, or 380 students. They asked questions developed by a large panel of faculty and other interested people and then used these questions as the basis for in-depth two-hour interviews.

The ultimate result was a specific set of moves for raising the odds of success for any college education:

• Don't put off courses you're truly interested in taking. The standard approach is getting required courses out of the way during freshman year and postponing the studies you find most fascinating. Don't.

• Every semester, choose one professor you'd like to learn something from and *talk* to him or her.

• Choose courses that provide *early* feedback on your performance rather than ones in which the entire grade is based on a final exam or a single paper.

• Take *small* classes (defined as those containing fifteen students or fewer). Light reports: "The correlation between the number of small classes any student takes and his or her self-reported personal satisfaction with the overall academic experience is about .52. That indicates a very strong relationship."

• When you take a science course, join a study group. ("Specifically, those students who study outside of class in small groups of four to six, even just once a week, benefit enormously.")

• Develop a list of activities you want to participate in during your freshman year—then cut it in *half.*

• Befriend a fellow student who is the *opposite* of you in interests, background, religion, philosophy, or values.

We all know people for whom college was largely a waste of time and money. For others, college is a golden period of intellectual excitement, expanding friendships, and growing maturity. Light's research demonstrates that the difference isn't a matter of luck or personal qualities that are practically impossible to change, but rather is due to specific behaviors that can be readily altered to improve the odds of success.

What's more, Light's system raises not only the odds of success (let's say, from 40 percent to something closer to 70 percent) but also the limit of what success itself might mean, opening up new heights of opportunity most students otherwise could only dream about.

Multiply those tuition bills by the number of students who could benefit and we're looking at a risk-reduction system that is literally worth billions of dollars.

More information on Light's system can be found in *Making the Most of College: Students Speak Their Minds*, by Richard J. Light. (Cambridge, Mass.: Harvard University Press, 2001).

Chapter 1: Changing the Odds
SOURCES AND REFERENCES

For an insightful analysis of how and why business leaders consistently misjudge the odds of success, see "Delusions of Success: How Optimism Undermines Executives' Decisions," by Dan Lovallo and Daniel Kahneman. *Harvard Business Review,* July 2003, page 56.

The probabilities of project success were drawn from the following sources:

Hollywood movie
Oliver Wyman analysis based on data from MPAA 2003 Statistics, MGM 2003 Operating Results, and http://www.factbook.net/wbglobal_rev.htm.

Venture capital
"Why Good Projects Fail Anyway," by Nadim F. Matta and Ronald N. Ashkenas. *Harvard Business Review,* September 2003.

Corporate M&A
Investment Dealers' Digest, November 24, 2003.

"The Acquisition Process Map: Blueprint for a Successful Deal," by Paul Mallette. *Southern Business Review,* Spring 2003.

Information Technology
Does IT Matter? by Nicholas G. Carr. Boston: Harvard Business School Press, 2004.

Food
"Most Pioneers Got Killed, but Some Got Rich," by John L. Stanton. *Food Processing,* July 2003.

Pharmaceuticals
Pharmaceutical Industry Profile. Pharmaceutical Research and Manufacturers of America, 2004

James Surowiecki's notion concerning the advantages of group-based decision-making is elaborated in his book *The Wisdom of Crowds* (New York: Anchor Books, 2004).

Information on the development of the Toyota Prius was drawn from customer interviews, the author's interview with company executive Takeshi Uchiyamada (September 26, 2006), and published sources that included the following:

The Toyota Way: 14 Management Principles From the World's Greatest Manufacturer, by Jeffrey K. Liker. New York: McGraw-Hill, 2003.

"Building Ba to Enhance Knowledge Creation and Innovation at Large Firms," by Ikujiro Nonaka, Ryoko Toyama, and Otto Scharmer. June 2001. Online at http://www.dialogonleadership.org/Nonaka_et_al.html.

"Prius Got Top Support," by James B. Treece. *Automotive News,* February 23, 1998, page 30.

"Hybrids' Rising Sun," by Peter Fairley. *MIT Technology Review*, April 1, 2004.

"The Birth of the Prius," by Alex Taylor III. *Fortune*, February 24, 2006.

"Takehisa Yaegashi: Proud Papa of the Prius," by Chester Dawson. *Business Week,* June 20, 2005.

"Cost Cuts Are Key to Success of the Prius," by James Mackintosh. *Financial Times,* June 16, 2005, page 28.

"Why Hybrids 'Are Here to Stay,'" by Chester Dawson. *Business Week Online*, June 20, 2005. Online at http://www.businessweek.com/print/magazine.content/05_25/b3938029.htmlchan=gl.

"What Makes a Hybrid Hot," by David Welch. *Business Week*, November 14, 2005, page 41.

As this book goes to press (February 2007), the world in which Toyota and the Prius compete is changing again. Gas prices have declined from their highs of mid-2006, reducing the perceived benefit from owning a fuel-thrifty hybrid. U.S. federal tax credits that helped encourage hybrid sales have run up against a mandated limit of 60,000 vehicles. And the EPA has just announced that fuel-economy ratings for 2008 model cars will be calculated using a new, more accurate method that tracks such factors as high-speed highway driving, more-rapid acceleration, and the use of air-conditioning. These changes will lower the ratings for all cars, but are expected to have the greatest psychological impact on consumers considering the Prius and other cars famed for their gas-saving qualities.

In combination, these factors are putting a damper on hybrids' sales growth—the first serious bump in the road for Prius. Having recently added new manufacturing capacity, Toyota is having to adjust to the downshift in demand—for example, by offering sales incentives on hybrid cars for the first time.

The lesson? Strategic risk management is a never-ending story, with a new challenge always waiting around the corner. The fact that so many factors in the business environment are beyond anyone's power to predict—let alone control—puts an even greater premium on working the factors you *can* control, making it easeier to adapt successfully to whatever tomorrow brings. Toyota still enjoys the strongest position in hybrid vehicles among all manufacturers, and the fuel-economy ratings for Prius and the rest of the hybrid fleet will still outshine those of practically every other car, even as the "Wow!" factor of eye-popping mileage numbers decreases. We will see whether Toyota's skill at risk reduction will help it weather the current changes better than rival car-makers.

Background information on the Apple iPod and iTunes story (discussed here and in Chapter 6) was drawn from customer interviews and from sources including the following:

"Songs in the Key of Steve," by Devin Leonard. *Fortune,* May 12, 2003.

"From Discs to Downloads." *The TechStrategy Report,* Forrester Research, August 2003.

"Show Time!" by Peter Burrows. *Business Week,* February 2, 2004.

"iTunes Sounds the Alarm," by Adam Woods. *Financial Times,* April 6, 2004, page 2.

"How Big Can Apple Get?" by Brent Schlender. *Fortune,* February 21, 2005.

"Apple, Digital Music's Angel, Earns Record Industry's Scorn," by Jeff Leeds. *New York Times,* August 27, 2005.

"How Apple Does It," by Lev Grossman. *Time,* October 24, 2005, page 66.

"Video Comes to the iPod," by Nick Wingfield and Ethan Smith. *Wall Street Journal,* October 13, 2005.

For more details on the Pathfinder project, see *Sojourner: An Insider's View of the Mars Pathfinder Mission,* by Andrew Mishkin (New York: Berkley Trade, 2004).

CHANGING THE ODDS FOR A PORTFOLIO: MGM AND MERCK

The challenge of portfolio management is a daunting one, filled with obstacles:

• The weed-choked garden of projects, each competing for attention, resources, bottleneck resources, talent, money, time.

• Varying levels of passion that your people bring to projects, not always as a result of rational business factors but simply due to personal interests and values (the "cool" factor).

• Bottlenecks that tend to clog any system, preventing resources from getting to the crucial projects in time.

• The balance between prudent corporate oversight (to prevent runaway enthusiasms from draining resources in a futile attempt to nurture a quixotic initiative) and excessive micromanaging (that squelches new but only partially formed ideas before they get a chance to develop).

The Pathfinder project illustrates a number of techniques that can be used to de-risk projects despite severe financial constraints. But there are other techniques that apply specifically to the task of the project portfolio manager, pioneered by such great risk shapers as MGM's Irving Thalberg and Merck's Roy Vagelos.

Back in the 1930s, Irving Thalberg was the "boy genius" who ran MGM during the glory years of the studio system, when creative personalities (from producers, directors, and writers to actors, musicians, and designers) were controlled by tough exclusive contracts and organized into ever-changing teams charged with churning out hundreds of movies a year for a ravenous public.

Thalberg knew how to make the system work better than any other executive. As explained in *The Genius of the System,* Thomas Schatz's brilliant history of Hollywood in the studio era (New York: Owl Books, 1996), Thalberg pioneered techniques such as excess options and parallel engineering, applying them to the moviemaking process: "Thalberg thought nothing of putting half a dozen of his best writers on a project at different times—or even at the same time working separately—to keep the approach fresh and to vary the interpretations of the material."

Thalberg also spent freely but shrewdly on movie elements he knew would raise the odds of box-office success:

> From the high-gloss look and all-star casts of its pictures to the army of well-paid writers and dependence on presold properties [i.e., movies based on best-selling novels and hit Broadway plays], there was a logic of excess, a calculated extravagance at Metro. In fact, by the early 1930s, Thalberg's system was in many ways less efficient and less systematic than any other studio's.

But Thalberg was convinced his strategy would pay off in the long run—quite literally, in terms of long-running releases—so long as he controlled the entire process.... He shepherded each story property as it went through script development and into final preparation before shooting, then monitored production itself through written reports and the screening of dailies, then oversaw the postproduction process of editing, previews, retakes, and reediting until the picture was ready to be scored and sent to New York. Thus, without ever stepping onto the set, Thalberg was intimately involved in every MGM production.

Notice the similarity to the Toyota and Apple systems. Like those later project masters, Thalberg employed methods that seemed wasteful, even extravagant. But his goal was to apply maximum attention, intensity, and resources at the key pressure points where the odds of success could be raised by 3 or 5 or 7 percent at a clip. Where Toyota threw two-thirds of its prototyping capacity at the Prius challenge and Jobs made his best designers pull one all-nighter after another until the look and feel of the iPod was just right, Thalberg obsessed over details of script development, casting, design, and editing, leaving no element of an MGM picture to chance. In all three cases, overinvestment led to victory. Different businesses, different problems, same underlying approach.

Thalberg's odds-raising methods were spot-on. Under his leadership, MGM turned out an unprecedented string of artistic and financial successes in almost every movie genre, from musicals such as *Broadway Melody* and *The Merry Widow* to dramas like *The Champ, Anna Christie, Grand Hotel,* and *The Barretts of Wimpole Street,* as well as the Marx Brothers' most popular comedies, *A Night at the Opera* and *A Day at the Races.* When Thalberg died suddenly at age thirty-seven in 1936, he had just led MGM through the most successful year in its history, boasting five of the ten movies nominated for Best Picture Oscars and profits greater than the rest of the Big Eight studios combined. Never again would any single studio so dominate Hollywood.

Merck's Roy Vagelos was another pioneer odds-raiser. In 1979, with Merck facing a series of patent expirations for its most lucrative products in the mid-1980s, Vagelos realized that the company's traditional system for managing research and development was never going to replace the losses that would hit in the mid-1980s as generics flooded the market in competition with Merck's most profitable drugs. At the time, seventy to eighty R&D projects were in the works throughout Merck. The odds of success for any one of these projects were very low.

Vagelos had a choice. He could fight a rear-guard defensive action, trying to fend off the generics with lawsuits, price reductions, and product tinkerings, or he could tackle the pipeline problem head-on.

Soliciting guidance from the firm's twenty top research managers, Vagelos came up with a plan for reshaping the project portfolio. He sharply focused the company on half a dozen projects identified as having truly high market potential. Resources and attention were channeled to these key projects. As a result, Merck produced more blockbuster drugs during the following decade than the next three competing pharmaceutical companies combined.

Today, in the post-Vagelos era, Merck's pipeline has diminished significantly, taking Merck back to where it was in 1979. The next few years will show whether Merck's current managers can rebuild the controlled risk-taking record of the 1980s.

The odds for product success will always be long. And having to cope with a portfolio of projects just increases the challenge. But managers can improve the equation by (1) systematizing their portfolio management process, (2) identifying and focusing on a few most-promising projects rather than spreading resources too thin, (3) locating and attacking the key pressure points where the odds for success can be improved, and (4) accelerating individual projects as necessary to maximize the chances for success when resources are scarce. Easy? No. But vitally important—and possible to achieve, not just once but consistently, as the careers of risk shapers such as Thalberg and Vagelos demonstrate.

CHAPTER 2: WHY DO CUSTOMERS SURPRISE US?

SOURCES AND REFERENCES

Information on Coach's use of customer information to reduce risk was drawn from customer interviews, the author's interviews with company executives Lew Frankfort, Andrea Resnick, and Kathleen Newman (New York, June 19, 2006), and published sources including:

"Style and Substance: A Yen for Coach," by Ginny Parker. *Wall Street Journal,* March 11, 2005, page B1.

"Keeping Their Firms on Top—The Best of 2004." *Investor's Business Daily,* January 3, 2005, page A4.

"Case by Case," by Ellen Byron. *Wall Street Journal,* November 17, 2004, page A1.

"Coach Has Japan in the Bag," by Yuri Kageyama. Associated Press, September 30, 2004.

"How Coach Pulled into Luxury's Fast Lane," by Lauren Foster. *Financial Times,* June 30, 2004, page 12.

"Coach's Driver Picks Up the Pace," by Robert Berner. *Business Week,* March 29, 2004, page 98.

"Consumer Research Is His Bag," by Marilyn Much. *Investor's Business Daily,* December 16, 2002, page 3.

"How Stodgy Turned Stylish," by Erin White. *Wall Street Journal,* May 3, 2002, page B1.

"Coach's Split Personality," by Diane Brady. *Business Week,* November 7, 2005, page 60.

Information on Tsutaya's customer information systems was drawn from customer interviews, the author's interview with company executives Muneaki Masuda, Ken Kiyoshi, and Dennis S. Miyata, and published sources that include the following:

"How Do You Say 'Cool' in Japanese? Tsutaya," by Irene M. Kunii. *Business Week,* May 13, 2002.

"Interview: Video Rental Chain Seeks 'Lifestyle' Business," by Akio Tamesada. *Nikkei Weekly,* August 16, 2004.

"Convenience Done Cheap Is the King of Cool," by Tomiko Saeki. *Japan Inc.,* May 1, 2003, page 13.

"Customers Are Disappearing," by Eric Almquist. *Across the Board,* July/August 2002, page 61.

"Broadband Era Tunes In Synergy." *Nikkei Weekly,* July 11, 2005.

"Case Study: Tsutaya, a Tokyo Video Store, Goes Mobile." *Ziff Davis CIO Insight,* February 2002.

"Voices from Entrepreneurs: Creating the Effect Is More Important than the Result," by Muneaki Masuda. *Career Quest—Axiom* Web site, 2000. Online at http://www.careerquest.jp/e/voice/masuda_e.html.

CHAPTER 3: THE FORK IN THE ROAD
SOURCES AND REFERENCES

Sources of information on Microsoft's double-bet include:

"Inside Microsoft," by Kathy Rebello. *Business Week,* July 15, 1996.

How the Web Was Won, by Paul Andrews. New York: Broadway, 1999.

http://www.cornell.edu/about/wired.

Sources of information for the Netflix versus Blockbuster "synthetic history" story include:

"The Mail-Order Movie House That Clobbered Blockbuster," by Timothy J. Mullaney. *Business Week,* June 5, 2006, page 56.

"Blockbuster Set to Offer Movies by Mail," by Martin Peers and Nick Wingfield. *Wall Street Journal,* February 11, 2004.

"Netflix Bets on DVD Rental Market," by Adam L. Freeman. *Dow Jones Newswires,* April 30, 2003.

CHAPTER 4: UNBEATABLE
SOURCES AND REFERENCES

Information on Bill Russell's approach to basketball strategy was drawn from *Russell Rules: 11 Lessons on Leadership from the Twentieth Century's Greatest Winner,* by Bill Russell with Alan Hilburg and David Falkner (New York: NAL, 2001).

Information on Target Corporation's approach to retailing was drawn from customer interviews and from published sources including:

"Bob Ulrich: Chairman, CEO, Dayton Hudson and Target," by Richard Halverson. *Discount Store News,* December 4, 1995.

"Target Flush with Cash, and Cachet," by Keith McArthur. *Globe & Mail* (Toronto), August 14, 2004, page B4.

"Robert J. Ulrich, 1944–." *Business Reference: International Directory of Business Biographies.* Online at http://www.referenceforbusiness.com//biography/S-Z/Ulrich-Robert-J-1944.html.

On Target: How the World's Hottest Retailer Hit a Bull's-Eye, by Laura Rowley. Hoboken, N.J.: John Wiley & Sons, 2004.

"How Target Does It," by Julie Schlosser. *Fortune,* October 18, 2004.

"Masters of Design: Robyn Waters," by Linda Tischler. *Fast Company,* June 2004, page 73.

Information on the coaching record and methods of Mike Leach at Texas Tech was drawn from the college's Web site (online at http://www.cstv.com/printable/schools/text/sports/m-footbl/mtt/leach_mike00.html?frame=bottom) as well as from the article "Coach Leach Goes Deep, Very Deep," by Michael Lewis, *New York Times Magazine,* December 4, 2005.

CHAPTER 5: POWERFUL, PROUD, AND VULNERABLE
SOURCES AND REFERENCES

Jeremy Bullmore's statement ("Brands are fiendishly complicated . . .") was drawn from his British Brands Group lecture, "Posh Spice & Persil," December 5, 2001, online at http://www.britishbrandsgroup.org.uk/Lecture%202.pdf.

Information on Sony's brand decline was drawn from sources including:

"The Welshman, the Walkman, and the Salaryman," by Marc Gunther and Peter Lewis. *Fortune,* June 12, 2006, page 70.

"Sony's Sudden Samurai," by Brian Bremner in Tokyo, with Cliff Edwards in San Mateo, California, and Ronald Grover in Los Angeles. *Business Week,* March 21, 2005, page 28.

Information on the Ford/Firestone tire safety issue was drawn from sources including:

"Inside the Ford/Firestone Fight," by John Greenwald. *Time*, May 29, 2001.

"Tire Trouble: The Ford-Firestone Blowout," edited by Dan Ackman. *Forbes.com,* June 20, 2001. Online at http://www.forbes.com/2001/06/20/tireindex.html.

"Ford: A Crisis of Confidence." *Business Week,* September 18, 2000. Online at http://www.businessweek.com/2000/00_38/b3699191.html.

Interbrand's annual brand value rankings can be found online at http://www.ourfishbowl.com/images/surveys/BGB06Report_072706.pdf.

The quotation from James Surowiecki on the "halo" effect that great products can produce for brands comes from his article "The Decline of Brands," *Wired*, November 2004. Available online at http://www.wired.com/wired/archive/12.11/brands.html?pg=1&topic=brands&topic_set=.

Information on Samsung's brand turnaround was drawn from customer interviews as well as from sources including:

"Raising the Bar at Samsung," by Martin Fackler. *New York Times,* April 25, 2006.

"Flooring the Research Engine: Samsung Is First with WiBro Phones and Aims to Unseat Intel as No. 1 in Chips," by Moon Ihlwan. *Business Week,* November 28, 2005.

"A Perpetual Crisis Machine," by Peter Lewis. *Fortune*, September 19, 2005.

"Samsung and Sony, the Clashing Titans, Try Teamwork," by Ken Belson. *New York Times,* July 25, 2005.

"Samsung Design: The Korean Giant Makes Some of the Coolest Gadgets on Earth," by David Rocks and Moon Ihlwan. *Business Week,* December 6, 2004.

"Seoul Machine," by Frank Rose. *Wired*, May 2005. Online at http://www.wired.com/wired/archive/13.05/samsung.html.

Notes

Chapter 6: When Nobody Makes Money

For sources of information on the iTunes music industry collaboration story, see the list of sources given for the iPod story in the notes to Chapter 1.

Sources for the Airbus collaboration story include:

"Rivals in the Air." BBC News, June 23, 2000.

"New Approach: Airbus Revamp Brings Sense to Consortium, Fuels Boeing Rivalry," by Daniel Michaels. *Wall Street Journal,* April 3, 2001.

"Reshaping European Aerospace," by Arthur Reed. *Air Transport World,* May 1, 1993.

"Birth of a Giant: The Inside Story of How Europe's Toughest Bosses Turned Airbus into a Global Star: EADS," by John Rossant. *Business Week,* July 10, 2000.

"Airbus Industrie Executive Sees Collaboration or Attrition." *Aerospace Daily,* February 25, 1994.

For a contextual discussion of the technical and business logic of the chip-making industry in the late 1980s and the early 1990s, and Sematech's role in it, see "Debating George Gilder's Microcosm: TJ Rodgers vs. Robert Noyce." *Harvard Business Review,* February 1, 1990.

For a discussion of how the U.S. government influenced collaboration in the chip-making industry, see "The Sematech Story." *The Economist,* April 2, 1994.

General information on TruServ, its components, and its structure was gleaned from the company overview and histories at the official Web site: www.truserv.com

The history and evolution of credit card powerhouses MasterCard and Visa can be found at the International Directory of Company Histories, edited by Thomas Derdak, and at the companies' official Web sites. Additional reading includes:

"Visa Stirs Up the Big Banks—Again," by Arthur M. Louis. *Fortune,* October 3, 1983.

"How a New Chief Is Turning Interbank Inside Out." *Business Week,* July 14, 1980.

For additional details on Cardinal Health's ArcLight venture, see:

"Pharmacies Band Together to Share and Sell Drug Data," by Christopher T. Heun. *Information Week,* August 6, 2001.

"Pharmacy Venture Pools Efforts to Cull Prescription Marketing Information," by Mike Duff. *DSN Retailing Today,* August 20, 2001.

"Pharmacies to Market Sales-Trend Data." *Chain Store Age,* September 2001.

Information on the steep costs of pharmaceutical R&D, and some companies' efforts to collaborate through licensing arrangements—particularly Pfizer's—can be found at:

"Success and Failure in Collaborative Research Alliances," by Ripert Winckler and Katie Lay of PharmaceuticalVentures. *Pharmaceutical Discovery and Development,* 2002/2003.

"Marathon Man: Interview with Pfizer CEO William Steere," by J. P. Donlon. *Chief Executive (U.S.),* September 1998.

"Finding New Drugs Through Alliances: Pfizer's Search for Drug-like Compounds Leads to Investments in File Enrichment Programs to Boost Its Chemistry Efforts," by Tanuja Koppol. *Drug Discovery and Development,* December 1, 2003.

The United States Council for Automotive Research (USCAR) was founded in 1992 to strengthen the technology base of the U.S. auto industry through cooperative precompetitive research and development. For more information and recent news, see the organization's Web site: www.uscar.org.

Notes

Chapter 7: When Your Business Stops Growing
Sources and References

Information about Continental AG's growth strategies was drawn from sources including:

> "Driving Force: An Old-Line German Tire Maker Sees Radical Innovation as the Way to Break Out of the Pack," by Christopher Rhoads. *Wall Street Journal,* September 25, 2000.

> "Continental: A Company in Transition—or Transformation?" *Automotive Components Analyst,* April 1, 2000.

For an extended discussion of Air Liquide's demand innovation strategy, see Chapter 8 of *How to Grow When Markets Don't,* by Adrian Slywotzky and Richard Wise with Karl Weber (New York: Warner Books, 2003).

Additional information about Air Liquide's growth strategies was drawn from company annual reports, press releases, and "Air Liquide Carves Niche in Semiconductors," by Ivan Lerner. *Chemical Market Reporter* 266, no. 7, September 6, 2004.

Information about Procter & Gamble's growth strategies came from customer interviews as well as from sources including:

> "Get Creative! How to Build Innovative Companies," by Bruce Nussbaum. *Business Week,* August 1, 2005.

> "Studying Messy Habits to Sweep Up a Market," by Sarah Ellison. *Wall Street Journal,* July 14, 2005.

> "Observe. Learn. Invent. Newton Product Designers Keep an Eye on the Consumer," by David Arnold. *Boston Globe,* April 7, 2005.

> "Welcome to Procter & Gadget," by Robert Berner. *Business Week,* February 7, 2005.

Information about Ikea was drawn from customer interviews as well as from sources that included the following:

"Ikea: How the Swedish Retailer Became a Global Cult Brand," by Kerry Capell. *Business Week,* November 14, 2005, page 97.

"Ikea Are Bringing Flatpack Houses to Drumchapel," by Vivienne Nicoll. *Evening Times* (Glasgow), September 9, 2005. Online at http://www.eveningtimes.co.uk/print/news/5043277.shtml.

"Prefab Homes Get Fabulous," by Reena Jana. *Business Week,* November 1, 2005.

"Ikea's 'Boklok' Houses." *Houses of the Future* Web site, June 14, 2006. Online at http://www.housesofthefuture.com.au/hof_what06F.html.

Information about DoCoMo was drawn from sources that included:

"Takeshi Natsuno: The Incrementalist." Interview in *Japan Inc.,* June 2001, page 34.

"Dialing for Dollars," by Ginny Parker Woods. *Wall Street Journal,* August 16, 2005, page A1.

"A Remote Control for Your Life," by Charles C. Mann. *Technology Review,* July 1, 2004, page 42.

Information about Nike's growth strategies was drawn from sources including:

"Can Nike Still Do It Without Phil Knight?" by Daniel Roth. *Fortune,* April 4, 2005, page 58.

"Nike Is Entering Discount Arena with Starter Line," by Stephanie Kang. *Wall Street Journal,* August 12, 2004, page B6.

"Green Foot Forward: Nike's Hoke Is Prodding His Designers Back to Nature and Away from Plastics," by Stanley Holmes. *Business Week,* November 28, 2005, page 24.

Notes

CHAPTER 8: TREASURE ISLAND

Information on Rudolph Giuliani's approach to risk management as mayor of New York was drawn from *Leadership,* by Rudolph W. Giuliani with Ken Kurson (New York: Miramax Books, 2002). For a skeptical look at the Giuliani record, see *Grand Illusion: The Untold Story of Rudy Giuliani and 9/11,* by Wayne Barrett and Dan Collins (New York: HarperCollins, 2006).

The article about Bill Parcells is "What Keeps Bill Parcells Awake at Night," by Michael Lewis, *New York Times,* October 29, 2006.

The cited paper that discusses Harrah's is "Competing on Analytics," by Thomas H. Davenport, Don Cohen, and Al Jacobson, Babson Executive Education, May 2005.

Readers interested in an introduction to Bill James's approach to baseball strategy can consult *The New Bill James Historical Baseball Abstract,* by Bill James (New York: Free Press, 2003).

The Carraccis' "loaded little portraits" are described in Carlo Cesare Malvasia's classic text *Felsina Pittrice*, originally published in Bologna, Italy, in 1678.

The financial data for the comparison tables of Ford and Toyota were drawn from Compustat and S&P. The financial data for the comparison tables of Gap and Zara (Inditex) were drawn from Compustat, S&P, and Thomson Financial. The betas for all companies were as of February 2007, and were sourced from Reuters.

ACKNOWLEDGMENTS

The Upside derives from client work at Oliver Wyman. The experience gleaned from working closely with clients caused us to look beyond traditional growth tools and risk management tools to explore the dynamics of strategic risk. We want to thank the business managers who provided valuable points of view, on and off the record, on the challenges of getting organizations to focus on strategic risk and to see it for what it really is: an unconventional but powerful path to create new growth.

In particular, we thank several CEOs and senior executives for their wide-ranging and insightful conversations on strategic risk and growth: Lew Frankfort, CEO of Coach; Muneaki Masuda, CEO of Tsutaya; and Takeshi Uchiyamada, the chief engineer of the Toyota Prius development project. We also appreciate the perspectives and support of Andrea Resnick of Coach and Masaaki Imai of Toyota.

Understanding the root causes of risk and business change inevitably requires numerous in-depth conversations with customers—the ultimate arbiters of success and failure in the marketplace. We are grateful to the many customers who spoke with us about their perspectives (and frequently, their excitement about) the companies and products we've discussed, including Toyota's hybrids, the iPod, Coach's bags and accessories, Tsutaya's media, Samsung's consumer electronics, Target's stores, P&G's household products, and others.

Many people contributed to producing *The Upside*. Karl Weber shaped the writing and kept up the pace of the narrative through his ability to communicate complex analysis, as well as to tell a good story. John Mahaney at Crown Business provided the motivation to produce a book-length treatment of the subject, and has never flagged in his enthusiasm for the project. The senior leadership of Oliver Wyman—John Drzik and Bob Fox—provided crucial organizational support.

Various colleagues at Oliver Wyman shared their skills, ideas, and

Acknowledgments

enthusiasm. John Campbell helped write an initial article on strategic risk that was published in the *Harvard Business Review,* and provided valuable edits and suggestions on the manuscript. Valerie Sachetta was tireless in keeping track of the many revisions and iterations throughout the project. Eric Almquist shared his extensive knowledge about brand strategy and brand value. Hanna Moukanas, Peter Baumgartner, and Jan Dannenberg illuminated the competitive dynamics of several companies and industries. Nancy Lotane provided useful advice on sharpening the message. Ted Sato of Marsh Japan helped arrange interviews in Japan and hosted us there. Nancy Schwartz organized and carried out many of the customer interviews. And many thanks to the research team of Steve Won, Jason Tsai, Jonathan Bernstein, and Beth Hamory, who gathered much of the research material on companies, industries, and people discussed in the book. Their energy and insights were invaluable.

In addition, Nicholas Carr contributed significantly in developing the logic and narrative of Chapter 6.

Finally, I want to give a special note of thanks to my wife, Christine, not only for her infinite patience during an often bumpy writing process, but even more for her repeated, careful, and meticulous reading of drafts and redrafts and final drafts. Her unflinching objectivity, always gently delivered, made an enormous difference, both in the manuscript and in the entire process of getting it to completion.

Adrian J. Slywotzky
Cambridge, Massachusetts
December 2006

INDEX

ABOUT THE AUTHORS

Adrian J. Slywotzky, a director of Oliver Wyman, is the author of many groundbreaking, best-selling books such as *The Profit Zone,* of which *Business Week* noted that "rarely—if ever—have any observers so skillfully dissected these executives' strategies to create lessons that can be taught to anyone."

He has published widely, including articles in the *Wall Street Journal* and *Harvard Business Review,* and has been a featured speaker at the Davos World Economic Forum, the Microsoft CEO Summit, the Forbes CEO Forum, and the Fortune CEO Conference.

Karl Weber is a freelance writer who specializes in topics related to business and current affairs. He has collaborated with Adrian Slywotzky on several books, including *How Digital Is Your Business?* and *How to Grow When Markets Don't.* Weber also collaborated with Jonathan Tisch, CEO of Loews Hotels, on the best-selling *The Power of We: Succeeding Through Partnerships,* and he edited *The Best of I.F. Stone,* a collection of writings by the legendary independent journalist.